Using SPSS Syntax

Using SPSS Syntax

A Beginner's Guide

Jacqueline Collier

SAGE

Los Angeles | London | New Delhi
Singapore | Washington DC

SAGE Publications Ltd
1 Oliver's Yard
55 City Road
London EC1Y 1SP

SAGE Publications Inc.
2455 Teller Road
Thousand Oaks, California 91320

SAGE Publications India Pvt Ltd
B 1/I 1 Mohan Cooperative Industrial Area
Mathura Road
New Delhi 110 044

SAGE Publications Asia-Pacific Pte Ltd
33 Pekin Street #02-01
Far East Square
Singapore 048763

Library of Congress Control Number: 2009920677

British Library Cataloguing in Publication data

A catalogue record for this book is available from the British Library

ISBN 978-1-4129-2217-3
ISBN 978-1-4129-2218-0 (pbk)

Typeset by Glyph International, Bangalore, India
Printed by CPI Antony Rowe, Chippenham, Wiltshire
Printed on paper from sustainable resources

Mixed Sources
Product group from well-managed
forests and other controlled sources
www.fsc.org Cert no. SGS-COC-2953
© 1996 Forest Stewardship Council
FSC

Contents

List of Syntax Command Examples

Preface

This book is primarily aimed at people who have never used the syntax option in SPSS, or have just started to use it. SPSS syntax is the command language used by SPSS to carry out all of its commands and functions. Most users are unaware of this command language, using the more usual drop-down, menu-driven method of accessing the commands and functions of SPSS.

Many students and researchers may wonder why you need to consider the command language (syntax) in addition to the drop-down, menu-driven method of accessing the commands and functions of SPSS. The first chapter will illustrate the various ways in which syntax is a useful tool, but SPSS syntax's key points are that it can save you time, reduce errors and, perhaps best of all, will not actually require any initial knowledge of programming.

Using SPSS syntax *instead* of the drop-down, menu-driven method would require the acquisition of a considerable body of new knowledge, attainment of new skills and development of new expertise, all of which require a considerable degree of effort and time. However, this book does not encourage the use of syntax instead of drop-down menu-driven methods, rather it encourages the use of them *side-by-side*, with a gradual increase in use of syntax a possibility for the enthusiastic and those wishing to be more efficient. 'Converts' to the use of SPSS syntax are not unusual as, in common with other useful tools, syntax can become invaluable once it is mastered and indeed you can get to a point where it can be hard to imagine working without it.

The amount of effort and time required for complementary use of syntax and drop-down menu-driven method is up to the user, as using SPSS syntax to complement the drop-down menu-driven method (rather than instead of) allows you to pick and choose how much you rely on one method over the other. The numbered examples of syntax commands which are in this book can be found on the SAGE website www.sagepub.co.uk/colliersyntax. You can download the syntax and start 'having a go' and see for yourself the outcomes obtained by running the commands outlined in the book.

If the very thought of 'computer programming' leaves you in a cold sweat and wanting to shut the book right now, it can be helpful if you don't think of getting to grips with SPSS syntax as learning about computer programming - it doesn't mean that that's not what you are doing, though, it's just that it often helps not to think of it in that way.

Acknowledgments

I would like to thank SPSS for the permission to use the sample datasets and to use images of the screenshots throughout the book.

Introduction

*Examples in this chapter will use the SPSS sample dataset
demo.sav*

The chapter will provide a brief overview as to what SPSS syntax is and how to begin
using it. It will outline: how to become familiar with the syntax commands through
the use of the Log; how to create and manage the SPSS Journal and syntax files; and
how to use syntax throughout the data entry, management and analysis process.

It will also explain how the use of syntax can: allow a data audit trail; enhance
analysis options; and, once mastered, how it can save time. This chapter will set the
context for the rest of the book, promoting SPSS syntax as additional to the usual
drop-down, menu-driven method, using the two methods in a complementary way.

SPSS is one of the most commonly used statistics packages in today's higher education institutions. Most users find the drop-down, menu-driven method of accessing commands and functions easy to use and often consider it sufficient for their
needs. For those completing analysis for a one-off small dissertation, that appraisal
is almost certainly correct. However, for anyone who is likely to spend a considerable amount of time carrying out quantitative analyses or needing to repeat analyses
(perhaps for different sub-groups or for later datasets), then it is worth learning to
work with the command language responsible for carrying out the SPSS commands
and functions, SPSS syntax.

One of the common misconceptions about the use of SPSS syntax is that it
requires an 'either/or' approach – that you have to use *either* the drop-down menu
interface *or* the syntax programming language. This view is unnecessarily polarised.
The approach in this book is that the two methods of using SPSS can be used alongside each other to optimise their usefulness and be tailored to the level of expertise
of the user.

It is anticipated that the newcomer to syntax, already familiar with the
drop-down, menu-driven SPSS, will *gradually* learn about SPSS syntax, passing
through several stages of use. A suggested route is that you start by first just looking
at the commands generated automatically by SPSS in the Log or the Journal
(explained below); then start creating syntax files using the paste function; and, in

time, beginning to add to and amend the commands building from commands acquired through the paste function; and finally through creating commands based on a library of previous syntax files or even completely afresh. This suggested route of progression can be halted at any level because at any stage of use syntax can still be a useful adjunct to the user of SPSS. This first chapter will outline how each of these stages can be initiated and developed.

Good Practice

- Always have your Journal set to Append.
- Always have your Journal saved to a safe location.
- Back up your Journal periodically.
- Always have your Log set to show in the output sheets.
- Set your options so that a blank syntax sheet opens automatically whenever you open SPSS.

Explanations and Illustrations of the Log and the Journal

Whenever I begin SPSS work with someone new, I start by ensuring that two SPSS elements called the 'Journal' and the 'Log' are set up to record the actions of the researcher using SPSS. They both record the actions undertaken in SPSS – the Journal keeps a 'behind-the-scenes' record and the Log produces an immediately visible record on the output viewer. Setting these up correctly is an essential step for any user of SPSS and even if you do nothing else because of this book except set up your Journal and Log then the book has still been of value.

The Journal – What it Is, and How to Set the Journal Options Appropriately for Syntax Use

Most people do not realise that SPSS runs and stores a background record of all the commands run by the program. This background record is called the Journal. SPSS creates this record all of the time and most of its users are unaware of this silent-running part of the program. The Journal becomes a valuable record of the SPSS commands that have been executed although its usefulness can be difficult to appreciate until you need to use it.

To show you how the Journal looks, a small section from a Journal is set out in Syntax 1:1 below with a brief outline of its contents. The Journal was produced when one of the SPSS sample files was opened (demo.sav) and a frequency analysis carried out for the variable **marital**. There was no intentional input to the Journal or awareness of the record being made; the Journal just produced and stored this record automatically.

Syntax 1:1 Journal entry for opening a file and running a frequency

The SPSS sample dataset demo.sav was used.

Mon Nov 10 14:38:16 2005: Journaling started
GET FILE='C:\Program Files\SPSS\tutorial\sample files\demo.sav'.

FREQUENCIES
VARIABLES=marital
/ORDER= ANALYSIS.

The above excerpt from a Journal identifies the date and time of the work, the name of the file being worked on, and the analysis carried out. These tasks were all carried out in the more usual drop-down menu-driven method of using SPSS, but behind the scenes the Journal stored the actual computer program language responsible for the actions.

The first line **Mon Nov 10 14:38:16 2005: Journaling started** simply tells you the date and time that the Journal was begun.

The second line is an SPSS command **GET FILE** and an equals sign followed by the filename and location (enclosed in inverted commas), this command will open the file specified. Then because this is the end of the command it is completed by a full stop.

The next three lines are the command **FREQUENCIES** and the keyword **VARIABLES** followed by an equals sign and the name of the variable to be explored. Lastly there is the sub-command **/ORDER** for the frequency that was requested. Again you will see a full stop after the last sub-command; a full explanation of the **FREQUENCIES** command can be found in Syntax 8:1.

Whenever I do any SPSS work with someone I check that the Journal is set up to record their actions as they use SPSS. As the Journal can keep an ongoing record of your SPSS activity, it is important to optimise the Journal settings to reduce the risk of losing that record. The value of this may not be immediately apparent to the novice, especially as the Journal may not make much sense initially. However, even if you never use any other aspect of SPSS syntax, the Journal can prove to be a useful tool if you have a problem with your analysis that you cannot understand and are seeking more expert advice. If your advisor or supervisor is a user of syntax he or she can access the Journal to review retrospectively actions such as how any derived variables were created.

Example of Journal Usefulness

The most notable example of the Journal's usefulness I have experienced was a doctoral student nearing the end of his research who suddenly realised that he had wrongly sorted his data in Microsoft Excel prior to moving it across to SPSS. This had resulted in the wrong data being associated with the wrong individual, for at least half of the variables. The analysis to date was nonsense, the values calculated for the derived variables incorrect. The student was panic-stricken, seeing the last six months work down the drain and anticipating months to rectify the situation. His supervisor recommended that he come to see me and see if there was anything that could be done. The student was not a user of syntax.

However, at the beginning of his studies his Journal had been set to store the commands he used, as an ongoing process, and to a safe location.

Thankfully the student had a copy of the original (unsorted) Excel file of his data, which could be imported into SPSS. Through using the student's SPSS Journal it was possible to:

- identify all of the commands used to create the required derived variables, and to create a syntax file to re-make them;
- to identify all of the analysis commands required to replicate the analysis reported in the results section of his thesis, and to create a second syntax file to re-run the analysis.

This sifting of the Journal took about a week, the re-creation of the variables and the re-running of the data each took a further week. The student was able to continue with his doctoral studies with much less of a delay than he had dared to hope.

There are no disadvantages to using the Journal, nor to altering the settings to optimise the Journal's storage settings. The recording of the Journal has no observable effect on the running of the PC or program, nor is it apparent to the user how it has been set up unless the user checks the settings in person.

How to Set the Journal

You will find the Journal settings by going to the EDIT menu, selecting OPTIONS, and clicking on the FILE LOCATIONS tab. This is represented below using arrows to show each change in menu level.

EDIT → OPTIONS → FILE LOCATIONS

The Journal can be set to be saved into a specific file location and there are options either to **Append** commands at each session creating a cumulative record or to **Overwrite** and create a fresh Journal each time you open SPSS. You should set the Journal to append commands thus saving a complete and ongoing record.

1. Click on the drop-down EDIT command, and select the OPTIONS option EDIT → OPTIONS → FILE LOCATIONS (see Figure 1.1).
2. The box for 'Record syntax in Journal' should be ticked already, if it is not then tick this box now.
3. Ensure that it is set to append and not overwrite (append continually adds the new syntax activity to the Journal with each use, overwrite instead starts a fresh one each time SPSS is opened and wipes the previous one).
4. Set the file destination. Recommendations vary depending on your user situation (shared PC, own machine, networked or not).
5. Click APPLY and then OK.

You can find out where your Journal file is currently being stored either by looking in the SPSS options section, or by doing a file search for a file with the **.jnl** suffix.

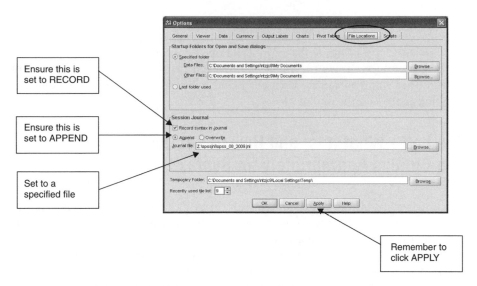

Ensure this is set to RECORD

Ensure this is set to APPEND

Set to a specified file

Remember to click APPLY

Figure 1.1   The FILE LOCATIONS tab in the OPTIONS dialogue box accessed via the EDIT drop-down menu

How best to set up the Journal depends on whether you are on a single-user PC or whether you are on a shared, multiple-user PC (e.g. in a university communal computer room). What you do need to do is identify the safest folder in which to store the Journal and set the save option to that folder. There is a default setting within SPSS, and that is for the Journal to be stored in the Windows Temp folder. There is no problem with that per se if you are on a single-user PC, but I recommend that the Journal be set to a specific folder rather than mixed up with all the temporary PC files, which may accidentally be deleted during a tidying-up or emptying of the temp files. To keep it straightforward I suggest the folder be called something really clear like SPSS Journal and stored as a primary folder on your main drive, rather than be hidden as a sub-folder within a sub-folder. If you are on a shared, multiple-user PC in a university setting you may be fortunate enough to have access to a small bit of server storage space, in which case you should create a folder on the drive to which you have access to save onto.

An issue with any shared, multiple-user PC is that you may need to remember at the beginning of each session to reset the target folder for the Journal to your specified folder. This is because shared PC systems are frequently designed to reset basic program settings to a default at the beginning of any individual's session, a necessity to prevent users having to check each time how the programs have been left by the previous user.

Syntax and Journal files are, in computing terms, small. For example, I am a heavy user of SPSS and my Journal for 14 months was 2.6 MB – and that was made up of enough syntax to fill more than 1000 pages' worth of text. For those using a shared, multiple-user PC without access to server space it may be advisable to save to a USB drive if necessary. Again you will need to remember at the beginning of each session to reset the target folder for the Journal to your specified folder.

As mentioned earlier the Journal is an automatically generated, 'behind the scenes' record. If you want to examine the commands recorded in the Journal then you explicitly have to locate the journal and open it in order to see them. What can be more useful (in terms of learning) is to have a Log of the syntax in the output viewer. That way you can see each command recorded immediately preceding the resulting analysis in the output file.

The Log – What it Is, and How to Set the Log Options Appropriately for Syntax Use

The Log is a useful way to get started with the syntax commands, enabling you to get used to how they look without having to use them, and a very useful way to start the audit trail of your data analysis.

The Log is a facility in SPSS for the commands to be documented on the output sheets. This is achieved by SPSS printing (on the output sheet) the actual command language used 'behind the scenes' to carry out the drop-down, menu-driven commands.

When you use a computer package via the more usual drop-down, menu-driven graphical interface there is rarely a need to consider that, behind the scenes, this method of use still relies upon the *computer language* operating behind the interface. It's a bit like driving a car, in that we do not usually need to consider the detailed workings of the internal combustion engine, electronics and so forth. To start a car the requirements can simply be to understand what you need to do to make the car perform (e.g. the key in the ignition), rather than understanding how the engine starting is actually achieved (umm … sorry, but despite driving for more than 20 years I do not actually know what happens to make the car start so cannot illustrate this bit; see what I mean?).

How to Set the Log

The Log can be easily set to be displayed in the output sheets.

1. Click on the drop-down EDIT command, and select OPTIONS. The GENERAL tab is usually the view that you will have as the OPTIONS dialogue box opens so you will need to click on the VIEWER tab, see Figure 1.2 (EDIT → OPTIONS → VIEWER).
2. Tick the box in the bottom left labelled 'Display commands in the Log'.
3. Click APPLY and then OK.

The default in SPSS is for the Log not to be set to show in the output files. Thus if you do not actively set the Log and if you were to open the SPSS sample dataset demo.sav and carry out a frequency analysis of the **marital** variable, the output would look as in Figure 1.3.

If, conversely, the Log had been set to show in the output sheet (by ticking 'Display commands in the Log' in the edit options described above and shown in Figure 1.2) then the output would look as in Figure 1.4. Here you can see the actual commands that were generated (behind the scenes) when the frequency option was selected and run from the drop-down menu.

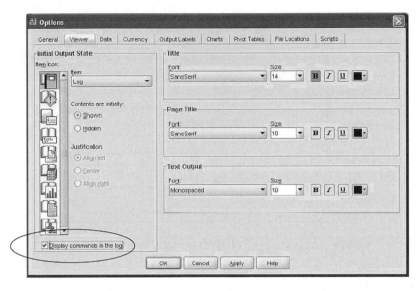

Figure 1.2   **The VIEWER tab in the OPTIONS dialogue box accessed via the EDIT drop-down menu**

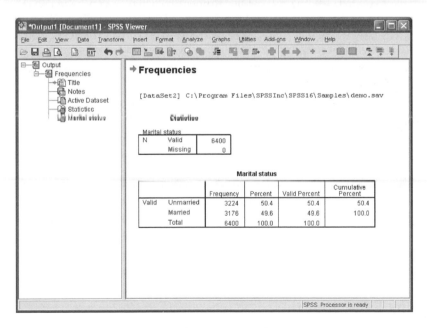

Figure 1.3   **Analysis of frequencies with no Log set to record on the output viewer**

The results of the analysis are preceded by a Log of the command that performed the analysis. The inclusion of the commands is useful to see in the output for several reasons:

1.   If you return to your analysis after weeks or months you can see how you have created new variables, carried out the analysis, which cases you have selected and so forth.

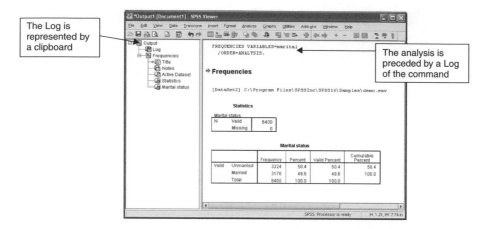

Figure 1.4 **Analysis of frequencies with Log set to record on the output viewer**

2. You can print off your output and show it to someone else (e.g. your supervisor) to go through your results. He or she can instantly see the commands that you have executed, helping him or her to identify whether you have created your derived variables correctly and carried out the correct analysis – this can be particularly useful when you are using the SPLIT FILE or SELECT CASES commands, or when complex multivariate analyses have been used.

3. Viewing the Log in the output files allows you to gradually get used to seeing how the syntax looks.

Example of Log Usefulness

One of the Log's most beneficial uses is when you wish to discuss an output file with another user – especially your supervisor. The Log clearly allows the other person to see what you have done, from creation of derived variable to details of analysis. It is especially useful for exploring the analysis and rapidly being able to identify reasons for 'inexplicable' results or changes in the numbers of cases included in an analysis. For example, use of the Log allows easy identification of whether the SELECT command may have been left on, or the file may have been SPLIT and that action then forgotten. This identification is sometimes quite difficult to do without use of the Log.

Syntax Files

So far we have not really altered the way that you use SPSS, only altered the record-keeping associated with your use of it. However, to gain greater benefit from SPSS we need to explore use of a new SPSS file type, a syntax file. Syntax files start as 'blank sheets' on which SPSS commands are then entered. Such sheets are known as syntax editors. When saved they become syntax files and have an .sps suffix.

The syntax editor can be opened in several ways: (1) via the drop-down menu, (2) by changing the default settings to always open a new syntax file each time you

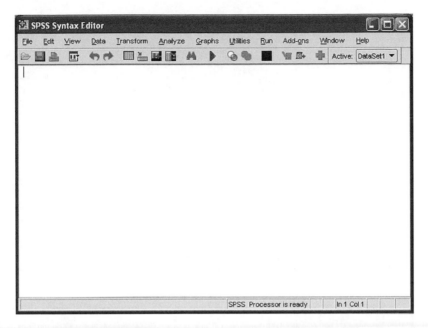

Figure 1.5   **A blank syntax editor**

open SPSS. or (3) through use of the PASTE button in most of the dialogue boxes obtained through the ANALYZE, TRANSFORM or DATA menus.

Methods for Opening the Syntax Editor

Method 1 – Directly open a new syntax editor via the drop-down menu FILE → NEW → SYNTAX.

Method 2 – change the default settings so that SPSS routinely opens a blank syntax editor whenever it is opened. You only need to do this once and the settings are stored for future occasions that you use SPSS.

1. Click on the drop-down EDIT command, and select the OPTIONS option (EDIT → OPTIONS → GENERAL). The GENERAL tab is usually the view that you will have as the OPTIONS dialogue box opens (see Figure 1.7).
2. Tick the box on the left labelled 'Open syntax window at start-up'.
3. Click APPLY and then OK.

Method 3 – Use the PASTE button available through many dialogue boxes which are accessed via the drop-down menus. If a syntax editor is already open then the command will be pasted onto that one and a new one will not be opened. However, if there is no syntax editor already open, clicking on the PASTE button will open a syntax editor and automatically paste the command onto the blank editor. Syntax editors that are opened via the paste function differ from those opened through the first two methods outlined above, in that they will not be blank; instead they will open with your initial command already recorded.

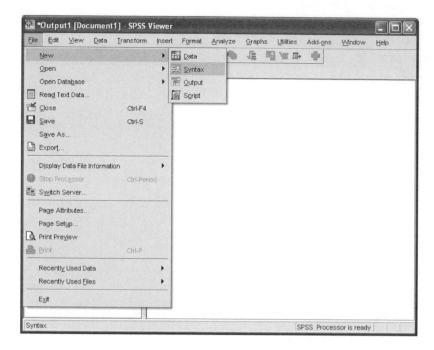

Figure 1.6   **Drop-down, menu-driven method of opening a new syntax editor**

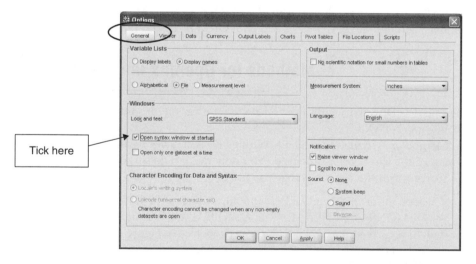

Figure 1.7   **Setting up the option of opening a new syntax whenever SPSS is opened**

In the example below we will again use the SPSS sample dataset demo.sav and carry out a frequency analysis of the **marital** variable. The frequency function is accessed via the drop-down menu ANALYZE → DESCRIPTIVES → FREQUENCIES. Once in the Frequency dialogue box, select the variable required for the analysis, move into the variable box and, instead of pressing the OK button as usual, press the PASTE button (see Figure 1.8). Note that, just like the OK button, the PASTE button remains 'greyed out' until you are in a position to complete the command and execute it, for example until variables have been moved into the correct boxes within the dialogue box.

Once the PASTE button is clicked, the syntax file will open with the command written on it (see Figure 1.9). For more information on syntax for the frequencies command you can refer to Syntax 8:1 in Chapter 8.

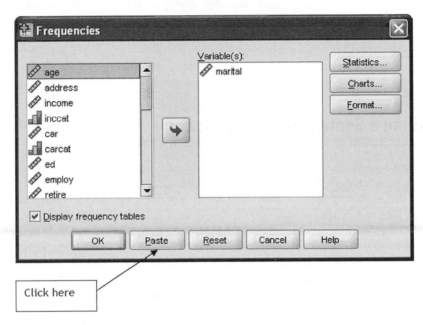

Figure 1.8   **Frequencies dialogue box**

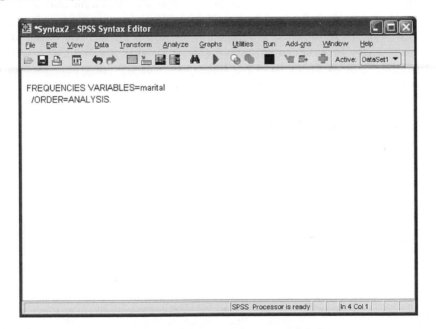

Figure 1.9   **Syntax editor created from the dialogue box in Figure 1.8**

Confusion Alert

It is important to note that pasting the command into a syntax file will not run the command, and the output sheet will remain blank. This is a small point but one that can easily confuse new users of syntax, as they press the PASTE button and yet no analysis/transformation etc. takes place. People sometimes wonder what has gone wrong, but it is simply that there is just one more step to take, that of *running* the command. If you have just pasted the command onto the sheet and want to run it immediately, all you need to do is check that your cursor is positioned in that command line and then press CTRL+R. Alternatively you can (1) use the drop-down RUN menu, or (2) press the small RUN button (▶) towards the centre of the toolbar (see Figure 1.9).

Writing a Syntax File Using the Log

The next step in the use of syntax is the writing of syntax files with a series of commands, which together carry out an analysis plan or a section thereof.

In the early stages there are two ways in which a beginner can start to write syntax files and neither requires you to know any computer language, nor to know how to compile any SPSS syntax commands. For both of these methods you carry out the analysis as usual but either you (1) work through the analysis but rather than press the OK button you instead press PASTE to put the command on the syntax editor, then go to the syntax editor and press RUN; or you (2) press the OK button to run the analysis and then copy from the Log in the output file and paste into a syntax editor.

Both methods are useful and may be as far as the early user wishes to go for some time. Creating such a syntax file can be beneficial as it creates a file that stores the commands for an analysis plan, or part thereof. This in turn is often useful either simply as a record of the analysis carried out, or for use if you wish to repeat the analysis, perhaps because you have more data or because you want to repeat the analysis on a sub-set of the data. For this reason this type of syntax file will be referred to as a 'repeat analysis syntax file'.

Example of Log Usefulness

The Log's usefulness in assisting with the creation of a repeat analysis syntax file can be seen if you consider a scenario where you have carried out analysis on the data as a whole and then, perhaps unexpectedly, require a repeat of that analysis (e.g. if a batch of questionnaires is returned late). If the Journal is set up correctly you can use that to find the commands required. However, the Journal may possibly have other commands in there, from work on other datasets and projects. In the output sheets that you have saved and reviewed, it should be relatively easy to identify which of the analyses you wish to repeat. Also, the output sheets are more 'viewer-friendly', and a supervisor or colleague can look through the results on the data output sheet, identifying the data to be re-analysed. You then take the Log associated with that analysis, and use this to create a syntax file. Creation of syntax files is covered in more detail in the next section, but fundamentally the process to create a 'repeat analysis' syntax file can simply involve copying the Log associated with the required analysis and then pasting into a syntax editor.

Creating a Repeat Analysis Syntax File

One of the easiest ways that you can create a repeat analysis syntax file is by copying and pasting the Log from an output file.

1. Open the output file (see Figure 1.10).
2. Open a new syntax editor (FILE → NEW → SYNTAX).
3. Select each of the Log sections in turn and copy and paste them into the syntax editor (see Figure 1.11).
4. Save the syntax file.

The three Logs seen in the output (see Figure 1.10) are copied and pasted into the syntax editor (see Figure 1.11). All you need to do now is to save the syntax file, preferably with a meaningful name and in an appropriate place. I suggest that the syntax commands be saved in groups, such as 'project A_deriving variables', 'project X_descriptive syntax', 'project Y_regression analyses' and so forth. These files keep a record of the specific analysis process involved.

A similar syntax file would have been created if you had worked through the analysis pressing PASTE and then RUN each time rather than the OK button. Note that the Log can sometimes have extra commands in it that are auto-generated, for example the **GET** element of a syntax file can be found in the first Log of an output file. A syntax file created using the PASTE method for individual commands would not have this command as it is an auto-generated one, created when the datafile was opened and recorded onto the output automatically.

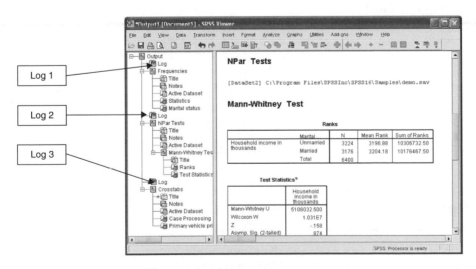

Figure 1.10   **An output file from analysis of demo.sav**

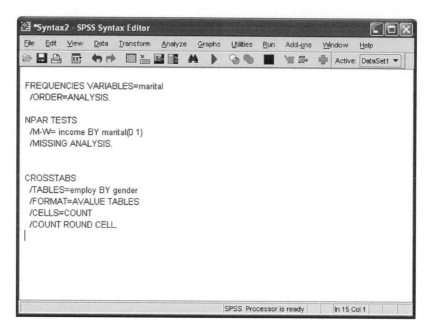

Figure 1.11   **Syntax file created by copying and pasting the Logs in Figure 1.10**

SPSS continues to write commands consecutively within a Log until some other form of output is generated, for example, tables, graphs or analyses. If you copy and paste a Log into a syntax file and then find that it contains extra commands that you do not want to include, you can simply delete the unwanted text. Just bear in mind that even small changes to text within the syntax files can have unexpected effects.

Confusion Alert

SPSS syntax, in line with other computer languages, is very particular, and relies on correct spellings, placing of spaces, full stops and keywords. During the learning processes required for SPSS syntax most of my students have, at some point, come to me for advice about some syntax that just will not work. Often they have been trying to rectify the syntax for some time, only to leave my office after just one or two minutes muttering under their breath about full stops or other small but crucial characters that they had missed or misplaced and failed to notice. SPSS is not being overly fussy though; after all, if you misdial a phone number by one digit you should not expect to be put through to the correct number.

Summary

SPSS syntax is the name given to the computer programming language that is the basis of all SPSS functions. Use of SPSS syntax can be employed to complement the drop-down, menu-driven method; it does not have to be an either/or choice.

A behind the scenes record of the commands used in SPSS sessions is called the Journal and this can run without the user being aware of it. SPSS can be set up to show an ongoing report (Log) in the output viewer. The Log records the commands being used via the drop-down, menu-driven method. An introduction to syntax can be gained by reading these Logs displayed on the output sheets. A repeat analysis syntax file can be created by using the paste function from commands recorded in either the Journal or the Logs recorded in an output file.

Use of syntax, passively through the Journal or Log, or actively through creating syntax files, allows an audit trail to be set up to identify:

- Which file was opened to carry out the work on. This is not difficult if you only have one datafile for your data, but some people have been known to have old and new versions of details – or even datafiles that have some but not all participants, or some but not all variables. This is generally not to be recommended as this can lead to errors. However, at least the Journal and Log will enable you to check back should queries arise.
- How variables are created.
- What variables are in the analysis.
- What analysis has been carried out.
- Whether certain cases have been selected prior to running analyses.

Useful Tips

- Save your Journal periodically, with a new name indicating the time period covered, and begin a new one.
- Get started by reading the Log associated with each of the analysis or variable creation activities carried using the drop-down menus – see if you can work out what it says and how it has resulted in the action you see.
- Name your syntax sheets with meaningful names.
- Save syntax sheets alongside the project data to which they relate.
- Read the Log associated with any error reports – see if you can work out what it says and how it has resulted from the actions preceding it, and in the action you have seen. Understanding error messages is addressed in Chapter 13.

SPSS Conventions

Note the following conventions which are used in this text and are designed to produce syntax files that reflect the style recorded in the SPSS-generated Log and Journal. Maintaining SPSS conventions assists ease of reading and navigating through a syntax file as experience increases.

S.1. The 'case' of the text is not usually important in SPSS syntax. However, good use of upper- and lowercase text can make reading through the syntax much easier. I recommend that you follow the same format as the Log and Journal, with the commands and sub-commands in uppercase and variable names, labels, etc., in lowercase.

    a. Case does not matter for variable names. In syntax the name of the variable 'AGE' is the same as 'Age' and 'age'.

    b. When referring to text in string cases then case is important (see Chapter 5 on string variables). SPSS will treat 'Male' as different to 'male' and different to 'MALE'.

S.2. Each command must start on a new line. For ease of reading, in this book I have placed commands on the extreme left with no spaces and any following sub-command lines are indented.

S.3. Sub-commands should start with a forward slash /. Note – it is possible for the forward slash to be omitted when a subcommand follows on immediately after the command.

S.4. Each command is completed by a full stop (the command terminator). This needs to be at the end of the last line of the command (or the sub-commands if present). SPSS will also count a blank line as a command terminator if there is no full stop.

S.5. Before a command may be executed the word EXECUTE is sometimes required, again followed by a full stop. It is mainly the commands that alter the datafile in some way that require this EXECUTE command to be run.

S.6. Variable names must be unique within any dataset: there cannot be more than one variable with the same name. Up to SPSS version 14 the variable name could be a maximum of eight characters long. From version 14 onwards this was raised to a maximum of 64 characters long. Variable names must not begin with a number, a space, a hyphen, forward slash, backward slash, exclamation mark and so on. Underscores are permitted anywhere. Full stops are permitted only in the middle of a variable name, not at the beginning or the end. Numbers are permitted providing they are not the very first character of the name.

S.7.   In this book I have added comments to syntax files. You can start a comment with the COMMENT command or with an asterisk. See Syntax 2:7 for further details.

2

Syntax for Data Entry

It is expected that readers of this book are able to enter data into SPSS using direct data entry into SPSS via the datasheet view or by importing data from compatible file formats such as Excel. This chapter will outline the advantages and disadvantages of the different ways of entering data, including the use of syntax for direct data entry. It will also outline the basic steps involved in the different processes.

Good Practice

- Allocate a unique identifier per case.
- Where possible, ensure you can track your electronic data back to the original data source (e.g. paper copy, Excel file).
- Select the most appropriate method of data entry, for example it may not be advisable to use direct syntax data entry unless you have only very small, simple datasets.
- When you have individual items then enter data in its rawest form (not in already manipulated forms such as totals and averages).

Whatever program you build a datafile in, and whichever method you use to do that, there are some basic rules that you should try to adhere to. There needs to be a unique identifier for each case; this may just be a consecutive numbering system (1, 2, 3, 4, 5, 6, 7, 8, 9, ...), or it could be more meaningful and contain implicit information. Whatever method you choose to use for the unique ID, ensure it is also on the original data entry sheet or file. That way you can go back at any later date if you have concerns about data integrity.

When entering data, it is advisable to enter it in the most raw form possible. For example, imagine you carry out a survey and have asked for date of birth; you also have the date of completion of a survey. You could just calculate the age and enter that into SPSS instead of the two separate variables. However, it is much better to enter the two variables, not the age. A quick syntax command will do the age calculation for you, will do it consistently for all cases, and will be auditable. In addition to these benefits you still have the extra information in the raw data – this may allow some exploratory analysis later. For example, following your original analysis you may later read about a new study that suggests that the month of birth may be of importance in your area of research, say winter babies suspected to be at more at risk of depression in adult life (or whatever your outcome is). As the raw data is already in your dataset, you could easily explore this hypothesis in your data without having to return to the original data source, link it to the ID numbers in your SPSS dataset and enter the month of birth as a new variable.

Example of Usefulness of Entering the Most Raw Form of Data Available

When I did my PhD I used the Perceived Stress Scale PSS14 (Cohen et al., 1983). I entered each item's individual response, not just the total score. As I was entering the data I was suspicious that responses to one of the data items did not seem to be 'fitting' with the responses to the other items (the question asked about how often you thought about things that you needed to do). I was able to test this using the raw data, looking at the strength of the association between the response for the individual question and the total score for the rest of the questions. My suspicions were confirmed and the individual item scores had proved to be very useful. However, before I could publish a methodological paper pointing this out, I realised that it had already been identified and a new version of the PSS was being recommended by the authors which omitted that particular question and three others, the PSS10 (Cohen and Williamson, 1988). This meant that I needed to calculate a new PSS10 total to use for my analysis. As I had entered the individual item scores in the dataset this was relatively straightforward and using syntax meant that the PSS10 total could easily replace the PSS14 total in all the analysis also.

Different Methods of Data Entry in SPSS

Syntax can be used to enter raw data. Syntax purists (and those who require absolute auditable links showing each data entry point to be associated with the data analysis) can use syntax commands to enter the data. However, for most people there is little value in entering data using this method. Indeed, for the vast majority of data users data entry may be less problematic via the usual datasheet view of SPSS.

Importing data from other programs such as Excel is also an option. The pros and cons of each method of data entry are outlined below.

Raw Data Entry Using Syntax

Raw data entry using SPSS syntax is a demanding task, involves lots of work and attention to detail, and has huge scope for messing up your data. It is not usually necessary to use this method at all.

Table 2.1   **Raw data entry in syntax**

Pros	Cons
Each data entry point is recorded and can be inextricably linked to the analysis.	Datafile needs to be set up with each variable's name, data type and length.
The data points entered can of course be altered in the datasheet view at a later date without record, but you simply have to re-run the complete syntax for the original data to be restored.	Data needs to be entered using the variable length as the framework. Data is entered in a long line with spaces or zeros required between variables and where the data is 'shorter' than the variable. For inexperienced data enterers there is scope for error here.
	It may be more time consuming to enter data this way.
	It may be less easy to get a feel for the data as it is entered compared to data entry on the datasheet view where the data is seen much more in context.

Table 2.2   **Data entry direct to SPSS datasheet**

Pros	Cons
Details of the variable in which data is being entered are clearly on view.	The data points entered can be altered at a later date without any record of this.
If variable labels are in the dataset then drop-down data options are available for nominal data.	If data is (unwisely/incorrectly) transformed in the original SPSS variable then the original data is lost.
The length of the variable is set automatically to accommodate the data entered.	To address both issues above, it is sensible to create a master copy after data entry but before any analysis, transformations, etc.

Table 2.3   **Importing data from a compatible program such as Excel**

Pros	Cons
Data can be acquired quickly from other sources. For example, many data entry companies use csv files or local audit may use Excel.	SPSS may assign a different variable format to the one intended for some variables.
The source of the data is recorded in the Log and in the Journal.	Older versions of programs such as Excel may allow some operations (such as sorting some but not all of the variables) that render the data completely inaccurate.
The length and type of the variable is automatically set to accommodate the data entered.	Variable names in other programs may not be compatible with SPSS conventions in earlier versions of SPSS. However, new names are allocated v1, v2, etc., and the old name is stored as the variable label.
The original data is available for review in case of query or need to start afresh due to errors.	

Syntax 2:1 Raw data entry in syntax using DATA LIST

DATA LIST
/ ID 1–3 age 5–8 score 10–12 location 13–32 (A).
BEGIN DATA
001 17.4 399 city
002 0008 088 town
003 0039 489 rural
004   325 city
END DATA.

The first line is the command **DATA LIST** to create a new datafile.

The second line is a sub-command line (identified by the initial forward slash) and finishes with a full stop to indicate the end of the **DATA** command.

/ ID 1–3 age 5–8 score 10–12 location 13–32 (A).

This sets up the variables ready for the data to be entered.

In SPSS, data is assumed to be numeric unless indicated otherwise. To enter text, there is an (A) after the variable 'location' which permits a text variable to be entered (think of A for alphabetic). After each variable name (e.g. **ID**, **age**, **score**, **location**) there are numbers. These numbers indicate the number of 'character spaces' allocated for that variable's data. ID has been given the first three spaces (1–3), age allocated four (5–8), score allocated three (10–12) and location allocated twenty (13 to 32).

The 'checkers' among you may have noticed that characters 4, 9 and 13 have not been allocated. This is because these character spaces are occupied by the spaces that have been left between each piece of data on the line.

The next line is a new command **BEGIN DATA** and indicates that the data will follow. There are then four lines of data, one line per case. The data is followed by **END DATA.** to indicate that data has finished and this also finishes with a full stop to indicate the end of a command.

Use of syntax to enter raw data can be learnt for when there are few variables and simple and consistent data formats. The layout of the data entered is of great consequence and attention to detail is vital.

Data entry using DATA LIST is very demanding and exact. You *must* use up the character spaces allocated. If age has four spaces to allow for one decimal place (two digits, one decimal point and the first decimal place) but all you have is an age of 39 years, you must put 39.0 or you must put two spaces (or two zeros) in front of the 39. When data is missing (as in age for ID004 in Syntax 2:1 above) you need to put spaces to 'fill the character spaces' to indicate there is missing data. You could not put zeros as they would result in an age of zero which is incorrect. Alternatively you can enter a four-character value allocated to represent missing data, for example –999.

There is a further (slightly different) method available for entering raw data using syntax, using the command DATA LIST LIST (note the duplicate LIST). This does not rely on you counting each and every character space on each line as you enter your data. Instead a space is recognised as the end of one variable and indicates that the next character is the data for the next variable. In exchange, you are required to enter at least one piece of data for each variable for every case, even when data is missing. If a variable is omitted SPSS does not know that and unfortunately whatever data is entered next will be put into the unfilled variable – a fundamental error that renders the datafile flawed and worse than useless. Thus, using this second method, it is imperative that you enter a 'missing value' for variables where the data is missing.

You need to identify the name of each variable, the type of data for each variable and also the maximum length of data to be entered for each variable. However, you will not need to fill the maximum length as a space automatically indicates the next variable. I suggest you have a default missing value (say –99) that you routinely enter for missing data. Remember, the default missing value should not be a number that is actually feasible within the variable data or you can mix up genuine data values and missing data values. It is good practice for missing values to be properly labelled and given missing value status (see Chapter 3, in particular Syntax 3:4 and Syntax 3:5).

Syntax 2:2 Raw data entry in syntax using DATA LIST LIST

DATA LIST LIST
    / ID (F3) age (F2.1) score (F3) location (A20).
BEGIN DATA
1   17.4 399 city
2   8 88 town
3   39 489 rural
4   -99 325 city
END DATA.

The first line is the command **DATA LIST LIST** to create a new datafile.
The second line is a sub-command line (identified by the initial forward slash) and finishes with a full stop to indicate the end of the **DATA** command.
/ ID (F3) age (F2.1) score (F3) location (A20).
This sets up the variables ready for the data to be entered.
In the sub-command line, note that after each variable name (e.g. **ID**, **age**, **score**, **location**) there is a letter and a number indicating the type and size of the data entry for that variable.
The F part of (F3) instructs that the variable is numeric, and the 3 part indicates the variable will be a maximum of three characters long. F2.1 indicates that the variable is numeric, and the 2 part indicates the variable will be a maximum of two characters long, including an option for one decimal place. The A part of (A20) instructs that the variable is alphabetical, not numerical, and the 20 part indicates the variable will be a maximum of 20 characters long.
The next line is a new command **BEGIN DATA** and indicates that the data will follow. There are then four lines of data, one line per case. The data is followed by **END DATA.** to indicate that data has finished and this also finishes with a full stop to indicate the end of a command.

ERROR ALERT
If you try to run this command without the second additional LIST in the initial command line it will not work correctly.
  If you ran the following syntax you would get incorrect data entry:

DATA LIST ←———————————————————— | Note the absence of the second LIST |
  / ID (F3) age (F2.1) score (F3) location (A20).
BEGIN DATA
1 17.4 399 city
2 8 88 town
3 39 489 rural
4 -99 325 city
END DATA.

LIST var=all.

With the following incorrect output.

```
ID age score location

 . 7.0       99 city
 .  .8   .  own
 .  .9  489   rural
 . 9.9   32 5 city
```

as opposed to the correct input obtained from

DATA LIST LIST ←———————————————————— | Note the second LIST |
  / ID (F3) age (F2.1) score (F3) location (A20).
BEGIN DATA
1 17.4 399 city
2 8 88 town
3 39 489 rural
4 -99 325 city
END DATA.

LIST var=all.

```
ID age score location

1   17  399  city
2 8.0   88  town
3   39  489  rural
4 -99  325  city
```

Syntax can be used for more complicated datafile construction also, but this beginner's guide is not the place to cover this. If you want to know how to use syntax for more complicated datafile construction then a recommended read is Chapter 3 in the textbook *SPSS® Programming and Data Management* (Levesque, 2003).

Data Entry Direct to SPSS Datasheet

Entering data directly into SPSS datasheet view requires no use of syntax and this method of data entry is commonly used and understood. A recommended read is Chapter 2 in *SPSS Explained* by Hinton et al. (2004). You could use syntax to save the file but, to be honest, it is just as easy to use the drop-down menu method.

Importing Data from Compatible Programs such as Excel

Importing from an external source can be carried out just as easily with syntax or with the drop-down menu-driven method. The advantage of using syntax is that you have a record of the file from which the data was obtained. However, if you use the drop-down menu-driven and have your Journal and the Log set up correctly (see Chapter 1, pages 2–8) then the source of the data will be recorded anyway.

If the variable names in the imported file are not compatible with SPSS variable name formats then SPSS will alter them to meet conventions. If the variable names are not compatible, for example 1st score, 2/score, etc., then the incompatibilities (start with a number or have illegal characters such as forward slash '/') are removed and the variable names are adapted @1stscore, 2score, etc., with the original names being imported in as the variable labels. SPSS may give the names V1, V2, V3, etc., instead of an adapted one. You can change these to names that you prefer to work with: just use the RENAME VARIABLES command found later in Chapter 3, Syntax 3:1.

The syntax command to import data from another source can easily be obtained by going all the way through the drop-down, menu-driven method FILE → OPEN → DATA and once you have selected your file etc. then just clicking the PASTE button instead of clicking OK.

Syntax 2:3 Importing from a non-SPSS datafile by pasting a GET DATA command

The syntax below is pasted from SPSS when a file was opened using the drop-down, menu-driven method and is not author-amended or author-created at all.

```
GET DATA
  /TYPE=XLS
  /FILE='C:\data.xls'
  /SHEET=name 'Sheet1'
  /CELLRANGE=full
  /READNAMES=on
  /ASSUMEDSTRWIDTH=32767.
DATASET NAME DataSet1 WINDOW=FRONT.
```

This may look like a complicated bit of computer programming. However, let's unpick it line by line and hopefully this will help to make sense of syntax:

The first line is a command and specifies that you are getting data **GET DATA** and it is followed by six sub-commands.

The first sub-command **/TYPE=XLS** specifies that the data will be in Excel format.

The second sub-command **/FILE='C:\data.xls'** specifies the location and name of the file.

The third sub-command **/SHEET=name 'Sheet1'** specifies which sheet to take the data from as the file type is Excel.

The fourth sub-command **/CELLRANGE=full** specifies the range from which to take the data. In this example the syntax indicates that all the rows and columns with data should be included.

The fifth sub-command **/READNAMES=on** specifies that the first line of Excel data contains the variable names.

The sixth sub-command **/ASSUMEDSTRWIDTH=32767** is a default command which permits any string (text) variable to be a maximum of 32,767 characters long, the assumed string width. Note that this can be set to any number smaller than that, such as 12 or 25 depending on the maximum expected text length.

There is then a full stop to indicate the end of the command.

The last command is to accommodate SPSS's ability to have open more than one dataset at a time and it controls which open data source is active at any point in the session. In this example no other dataset is open **DATASET NAME DataSet1 WINDOW=FRONT.**, so this is given the value '1' and your newly opened dataset is 'dataset1'. Newly opened datasets are the active dataset **'WINDOW=FRONT'**. Note this command does not save the dataset.

Now that we have unpicked Syntax 2:3 it may be possible to consider amending it a little to suit your purposes better. For example, the syntax below is based on the syntax above, but this time has been author-amended a little. Again, take it line by line and try to understand what each line is doing. Full details are just below.

Syntax 2:4 Amending the GET DATA command

The syntax below is amended from Syntax 2:3.

```
GET DATA
  /TYPE=XLS
  /FILE='C:\data.xls'
  /SHEET=name 'Sheet1'
  /CELLRANGE= range 'A1:G35'
  /READNAMES=off
  /ASSUMEDSTRWIDTH=20.

SAVE OUTFILE='C:\data.sav'
  /COMPRESSED.
```

Most of the syntax is left unchanged from Syntax 2:3. Unchanged are: the command specifying that you are getting data; the first sub-command specifying the data format; the second sub-command specifying the location and name of the file; the third sub-command specifying which sheet to take the data from.

The following lines have been author-amended.

The fourth sub-command **/CELLRANGE=range 'A1:G35'** specifies the range from which to take the data. This allows only the specified data rows and columns to be imported.

The fifth sub-command **/READNAMES=off** has been set to off, meaning that the header row does not contain variable names but data instead.

The sixth sub-command **/ASSUMEDSTRWIDTH=20** has been set so that string (text) variables can be a maximum of 20 characters long. As before there is then a full stop to indicate the end of the command.

One additional command has been added (copied and pasted from SPSS when the file was saved using the drop-down, menu-driven method). This step saves the file as an SPSS datafile to the location of your choice **SAVE OUTFILE='C:\data.sav'/COMPRESSED.** There is a full stop to indicate the end of the command.

Two commands were used in these examples that are really helpful ones to know and use. First, the LIST command that can be seen in the ERROR ALERT section of Syntax 2:2 which I used to print the data into the output viewer and, second, the SAVE OUTFILE command that can be seen in Syntax 2:4 which I used to save the file. Below are these two additional commands to extend your use of syntax plus a command to enable you to annotate your files.

Once data is in your datafile you can check the data that has been entered by running the LIST command, which simply lists the data for any specified variables.

Syntax 2:5 Printing data in the output file using the LIST command

This syntax will work with the dataset created in Syntax 2:2.

LIST VARIABLES = id age score location.

The single command line **LIST VARIABLES=id age score location** begins with the command **LIST**, is then followed by the keyword **VARIABLES** and then an equals sign and the list of variables that you want listing. There is then a full stop to indicate the end of the command.

Alternatively you can indicate that you want to list the data for all of the variables in a dataset by use of the word **ALL** and you can also shorten the keyword **VARIABLES** to **VAR.**

LIST VAR=ALL.

At the end of Syntax 2:4 the file has been saved simply to the C drive. Other locations may be more complicated, and the drop-down, menu-driven method may be the simplest way to save into sub-folders etc. However, you may want to create a complete syntax file recording all that you have done. In this case probably the easiest thing to do is to save the file with the drop-down, menu method and then take the generated command as printed on the Log and simply copy and paste it into the syntax file.

Syntax 2:6 Saving a dataset using the SAVE OUTFILE command

SAVE OUTFILE='C:\Documents and Settings\User\My Documents\
survey.sav'
  /COMPRESSED.

This command saves the file as an SPSS datafile to the location of your choice.

SAVE OUTFILE='C:\Documents and Settings\User\My Documents\
survey.sav'.

There is a full stop to indicate the end of the command.
  The sub-command /COMPRESSED. is a default command and compresses the data so that it takes up less disk space. As a default sub-command, even if it was omitted, it would be assumed to be there and the file would still be compressed. Just for information, uncompressed files are bigger, but are quicker for SPSS to process.

You can easily annotate your syntax files. There are two methods that you can use to do this in your syntax file. Any line beginning with the command COMMENT is treated as precisely that, just a comment – right up to first full stop. If this command

---

Syntax 2:7 Annotating syntax files via the COMMENT command and via an asterisk beginning a command line

---

COMMENT This syntax lists the data that is found in all the variables in the datafile.

LIST var=all.

*This works as a comment also as an asterisk is as good as the word
COMMENT.

The first command COMMENT This syntax lists the data that is found in all the variables in the datafile. will be printed on the output viewer.
  The second command line will then be run (see Syntax 2:5).
The last command line *This works as a comment also as an asterisk is as good as the word COMMENT. will also be printed on the Output viewer.

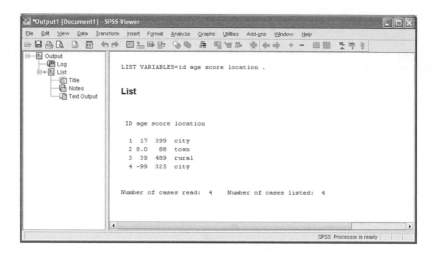

Figure 2.1   **Screenshot of the output generated from Syntax 2:7**

is run before or after other syntax the comment element will just print in the Journal and the Log (providing the Log is set up as recommended on page 6). An alternative to this is to use an asterisk * to start a comment line rather than the word COMMENT. Both ways are effective and both are acceptable.

The COMMENT command is very useful to enhance the syntax files, explaining how commands were written, or what they will do. Alternatively, comments can be written into the syntax in order to enhance the usability of the output, printing out alongside analysis etc. to explain details or the rationale for those reading it through. See Figure 2.1 to see how the comments in Syntax 2:7 would look if run on the dataset created by Syntax 2:2.

Summary

It is possible to use SPSS syntax as little or as much as you please in data entry. Use of syntax for full raw data entry is complex and requires extreme attention to detail. Syntax can be used to import data from other sources, to record data sources and save the datafile. Direct data entry is not really where the beginner is likely to find SPSS syntax to be particularly beneficial as syntax is cumbersome and rather exacting for data entry; its strengths are in supporting and recording other methods such as direct data entry into the datasheet, or retrieving data from other sources.

Useful Tips

- Direct entry using syntax is probably an overly complicated way to create your data-file unless you have a very small, simple dataset.
- Direct entry is useful only if you have an absolute need to have an auditable trail of your analysis inextricably linked to the data entered.
- When pasting syntax from the drop-down menus, commands start at the far left of the page, sub-commands start with a couple of spaces and then a forward slash '/'.
- Remember, you need a full stop at the end of commands.
- You do *not* put a full stop at the end of sub-commands.
- Annotate your syntax files using the COMMENT command.
- Whatever program you store data in (e.g. Excel, Microsoft Access) try to use SPSS compatible variable names in all of your datafiles.

Resources

Resource 1 – Sample Datasets

There are examples of syntax commands throughout the book with accompanying explanations, options and outcomes. Most of these syntax commands can all be used with the sample datasets that come in the SPSS 'samples' folder. The sample datasets can be found on the SPSS CD or, if the program is already loaded onto your PC, they can usually be found in the SPSS folder located in the program files folder. If you are accessing SPSS via a networked application the best way is usually to click on the FILE drop-down menu, click OPEN, select DATA and usually you are presented with the samples folder and the sample files. If you need to do a search for the folder, then in versions 13.0, 14.0 and 15.0 the folder is called 'sample_files' and from 16.0 onwards the folder is called 'Samples'.

Resource 2 – Syntax Files

The numbered examples of syntax commands which are in this book can be found on the SAGE website www.sagepub.co.uk/colliersyntax. There is a syntax file for each chapter and most of there commands can be run with the sample datasets.

Resource 3 – *Command Syntax Reference* Guide

The *Command Syntax Reference* guide is available in searchable Portable Document Format (pdf) format and you can usually access this via the SPSS HELP drop-down menu, see Figure R.1.

The *Command Syntax Reference* guide has commands listed down the left-hand frame (see Figure R.2) and you can scroll down and click directly on the command you want. Alternatively, you can use the Find box to the right on the top toolbar and search for the term you want.

The *Command Syntax Reference* guide is very comprehensive – with more than 2000 pages, over 100 of which form the index alone. The *Command Syntax Reference* guide is also available in paperback (SPSS, 2007a).

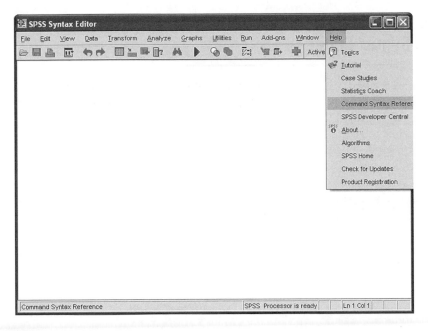

Figure R1

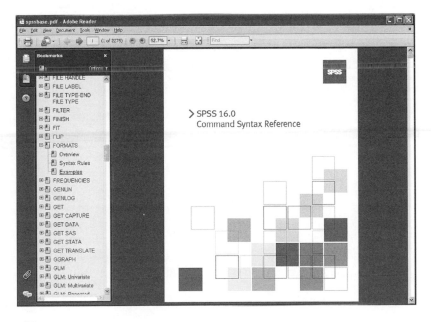

Figure R2

Resource 4 – Use of the F1 Key When in the Syntax Editor

When in the syntax editor you can get help about specific commands that are in the syntax. Just place your cursor in the command line that you want help with and press the F1 key. Help that is specific to the current command will appear. The screenshot in Figure R3 was generated by pressing the F1 key while the cursor was on the FREQUENCIES command line.

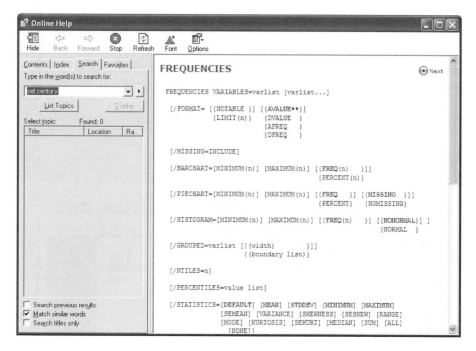

Figure R3

3

Increasing the Usability of the Datafile

Examples in this chapter will use the SPSS sample datasets
survey_sample.sav
testmarket.sav
coffee.sav

This chapter will explain the syntax commands that enable the user to: rename variables; label the variables; create the value labels; and ascribe missing values.

Good Practice

- Always clearly label the values ascribed in nominal variables.
- Always allocate informative and clear variable labels, indicating the meaning of high and low scores where necessary.
- Try to allocate variable names that are both systematic and indicative of the variable content (e.g. q23_boredom, q24_happiness, q25_worry, ...).
- Formally identify missing values, and label them.
- Only allocate missing values that cannot feasibly be found in the real data for that variable.

The information that is required for each variable should be clear by the end of this chapter. It often helps if you actively design your datafile with your supervisor or co-researchers in mind, trying to imagine what information they would need in order to use your datafile easily. Picture a datafile with all of the numerical and text data in the variable columns but no other information available. For example, students could be working with a questionnaire next to them so that they can see the 20 questions on the survey, plus the 4 pieces of participant information. The students may know that the variables in their SPSS datafile named v1, v2, v3, v4, v5, ..., v20 correspond to the 20 survey questions, and that the next four variables (v21–v24) relate to the participant information. The students then calculate the total for the question-naire and pop that at the end of the datafile (v25). They then make a new dichoto-mous variable using the age of the participants to identify those that are of pensionable age and those that are not (v26). Having such a datafile with no variable information may sound extreme but such datafiles may be created by students doing a small research project for a dissertation. It is feasible for the students to complete their analysis with no further information, no labels, etc. However, the supervisor would find the output files impossible to understand without the student being present.

Whichever method is used to enter data, the datafile should have enough information to make the data usable by others. That is, there should be sufficient information in the datafile for your supervisor or co-researchers to be able to access the data meaningfully. Without clear variable information other users of the dataset can struggle to understand derived variables or to monitor the data quality. It is also less easy to have a data audit trail. Additionally, data may invite later exploration and a well labelled dataset means that if you need to return to the data after a long break then data will still 'make sense' to you.

So, good practice requires us to keep our data in a state that would enable some-one to check our data management and analysis, to audit what we have done with the data, and for us to be able to defend to others the findings. To do all of these things, certain key information ought to be contained within the data:

- The **variable names** should allow quick identification within the dataset. Everyone has a different way of doing this. This is OK. Choosing the correct way of naming your variables could save loads of work once you start using syntax for data transformations and analyses. Try to name variables systematically.
- The **variable labels** should contain sufficient information to allow others to identify accurately what the variable contains. For numeric data which is not self-explanatory further information can be added in the variable label (e.g. a high score reflects greater stress).
- The values within a variable need to be identifiable and understandable. For nominal data that has been coded numerically, there needs to be a clear label attached to each value within the code. This is added in the **value labels** of the datafile. These values can also be written on a blank copy of the data collection form if appropriate.

Most people work with variable names, labels and value labels via the Variable View, but you can also work with variable labels and value labels via the drop-down, menu-driven method. Access is via DATA → DEFINE VARIABLE PROPERTIES. Using syntax allows you to carry out anything that you can do with these two methods, and you have a record of your activity. It can also be more efficient using syntax once you become experienced.

Variable Names

Variable names must be unique within any dataset; that is, there can only be one variable with the name quest_1, even if there are responses to more than one ques-tionnaire each with a question 1. Up to SPSS version 14 the variable name could be a maximum of eight characters long. From version 14 onwards this was raised to a maximum of 64 characters long.

Variable names must not begin with a number, space, hyphen, forward slash, backward slash, exclamation mark, and so on. Underscores are permitted anywhere. Full stops are permitted only in the middle of a variable name, not at the beginning or the end. Numbers are permitted providing they are not the very first character of the name.

Variable names are best if they are consistent in their style and (where possible and appropriate) follow 'a pattern'. This allows easier recall and grouping of variables when writing syntax.

Giving New Names to Variables

When data has been imported from another source, or has been entered by someone else, you may want to give some or all of the variables different names. You can change these in the Variable View, but typing directly into the Variable View provides no record of the changes. Furthermore, if you imported a second set of data from the same source with the same names that require changing, you would need to go through the changes again. Using syntax provides a record, and also if the process needs repeating at a later date, it is simply a case of opening the syntax file and running the command.

Syntax 3:1 Changing the names of existing variables using RENAME VARIABLES

The SPSS sample dataset survey_sample.sav was used.

GET FILE='C:\Program Files\SPSSInc\SPSS16\Samples\survey_sample.sav'.

RENAME VARIABLES
  news1 = news_paper
  news2 = news_mag
  news3 = news_tv
  news4 = news_radio
  news5 = news_web.

The **GET FILE** command opens the datafile if not already open.

The command is **RENAME VARIABLES**. This is then followed by the old variable name, followed by an equals sign and then the new variable name. As many variables as you wish can be renamed in one command. After all variables have been listed, the command must be finished with a full stop.

The above syntax renames five variables: **news1** will become **news_paper**, **news2** will become **news_mag** and so on. Two alternative ways of laying out the command are set out below and both follow accepted SPSS conventions.

RENAME VARIABLES (news1 = news_paper) (news2 = news_mag) (news3 = news_tv) (news4 = news_radio) (news5 = news_web).

or

RENAME VARIABLES (news1 news2 news3 news4 news5 = news_paper news_ mag news_tv news_radio news_web).

It is a matter of personal preference which layout you decide to use. I favour the first 'list-wise' view as in Syntax 3:1 because I find it much simpler to read and navigate my way through, especially when I am looking for my syntax errors.

ERROR ALERT for Syntax 3:1

If you accidentally put full stops after each variable as below then only the first variable **news1** would be renamed (easily done but very frustrating if you cannot work out why the syntax is 'nearly' working).

COMMENT do not use the syntax below as there should only be one full stop which should be at the very end following **news5 = news_web.**

RENAME VARIABLES
  news1 = news_paper.
  news2 = news_mag.
  news3 = news_tv.
  news4 = news_radio.
  news5 = news_web.

The **variable name** is the text visible at the top of the column in the Data View of the datasheet. The **variable label** is a longer bit of further information visible when you place the cursor over the variable name in the Data View, and also visible in the Variable View. The label is the variable information which appears in SPSS outputs for data analysis, graphs, etc.

Labelling the Variables

In older versions of SPSS it was essential to *label* the variables, as the limitations of eight characters per variable *name* meant that it was highly unlikely that the variable names could contain sufficient information for supervisors or co-researchers to be certain of the data that the variables contained just from the variable name only. The labelling of the variables was therefore vital for accurate use of the datasets.

Even though variable names can now be much longer, my preference remains for keeping the variable names short and providing additional information via the variable labels. This permits you to see variable names easily in SPSS dialogue boxes for data analysis, transformations, graphs, etc. Short variable names also make for easier writing of syntax commands.

Once the variables have been created and named, it is advisable to provide a label for the variable. How to do this is shown in Syntax 3:2.

Syntax 3:2 Adding variable labels through the use of the VARIABLE LABELS command

The SPSS sample dataset coffee.sav was used. Note that the labels given below have been made up by me and will not reflect the true meaning of the information in those variables.

GET FILE='C:\Program Files\SPSSInc\SPSS16\Samples\coffee.sav'.

VARIABLE LABELS
    image 'what the smell conveys'
    brand 'coded brands for blind smell test'
    freq 'how often reported'.

The **GET FILE** command opens the datafile if not already open.
    The command is **VARIABLE LABELS** followed by the variable name, then an inverted comma followed by the variable label that provides the information required to understand the variable, and then closed with a further inverted comma.
    After all variables have been listed the command must be finished with a full stop.

As with the RENAME VARIABLES syntax, an alternative layout is permissible where it is not a list format but rather a stream of text, as illustrated below.

VARIABLE LABELS

   image 'what the smell conveys' brand 'coded brands for blind smell test' freq 'how often reported'.

Once more, I prefer the first 'list-wise' view as in Syntax 3:2 as I find it easier to read.

Just to note, it does not matter whether you use speech marks or inverted commas but you must be consistent and close the variable label with the same as you open it. I tend to stick to the use of inverted commas, which is in keeping with the Log and the Journal.

ERROR ALERT for Syntax 3:2

If you accidentally put full stops after each variable as below (easily done but very frustrating if you can't work out why the syntax is 'nearly' working), then only the first variable would be labelled.

COMMENT do not use the syntax below as there should only be one full stop which should be at the very end following freq 'how often reported'.

VARIABLE LABELS
    image 'what the smell conveys'.
    brand 'coded brands for blind smell test'.
    freq 'how often reported'.

The syntax below is the list of commands that you would see in the Log if you used the drop-down, menu-driven method DATA → DEFINE VARIABLE PROPERTIES to use the dialogue box to create the variable labels. Alternatively, it is also what would appear in the syntax editor if you had used the DEFINE VARIABLE PROPERTIES method and then clicked on [Paste].

* Define Variable Properties

*image.
VARIABLE LABELS image 'what the smell conveys'.
*brand.
VARIABLE LABELS brand 'Coded brands for blind smell test'.
*freq.
VARIABLE LABELS freq 'how often reported'.
EXECUTE.

The syntax above may look a little more complicated but the additional lines which start with an asterisk are just COMMENTS. The first comment identifies that the syntax was written through the DEFINE VARIABLE PROPERTIES dialogue box. Each of the following comments just identifies which variable is being defined. The command **VARIABLE LABELS** is repeated for each individual variable (which is fine) and each command is completed with a full stop; there is only one **EXECUTE.** command to 'action' all the preceding commands.

Labelling the Values of Data in the Datafile

Some data entered into a file are able to be understood fully from the variable name and label (e.g. **Birth_wt 'Birth weight in kilograms'**). Other data is not so clear and often the data values need to be labelled also.

In categorical data entry (as opposed to free text) data falls into one of several identified categories and each of these categories can be ascribed a numerical value that serves to identify the category. If categories can be placed into a meaningful order (e.g. very small, small, medium, big, very big) then the values should also be ordered (e.g. 1, 2, 3, 4, 5). If they have no meaningful order (e.g. UK, Canada, Australia, USA) the numbers could be any value at all (e.g. 21, 34, 67, 17). However, it is sensible (both for later syntax reasons and to make it easier on the imagination and memory) to be consecutive in the allocation of numbers and begin at a sensible starting point (e.g. 1, 2, 3, 4).

In categorical data entry the value labels contain the information that explains what the numbers represent. You could just enter the words in the datafile for MALE and FEMALE resulting in a text variable (known as a **string** variable in SPSS). However, this limits what you are permitted to do with the data (see Chapter 5 for more information about string variables). One example is that you cannot use a string variable as a grouping variable in some data analysis processes such as Mann–Whitney or ANOVAs; and if you entered gender as text you could not compare the ages of the males to the females using either of these methods of analysis. However, if you enter gender using a numerical coding, such as 1 and 2, then the analysis can be carried out.

I recommend that you develop consistent and understandable codes for commonly used categories such as male and female, yes and know, etc. I find 0 and 1 better for 'no' and 'yes' because I believe that there is a logic linking 'no' with none or nothing, and that people are more consistently likely to associate 'no' with zero or nought, whereas if you use 1 and 2 instead there is no dominant rationale for favouring either number to represent 'yes' or 'no'. When numeric codes are used instead of text to represent a category, then the numbers require labelling to identify clearly the category that is being represented by the number.

Overall, value labels should:

- accurately convey the original meaning behind the category allocated the numerical code;
- be clear;
- be consistent within any one dataset (and also across datasets where applicable).

A variable can have as many value labels as you need. Furthermore, the same set of value labels can be shared by more than one variable. After the command VALUE LABELS list the variables that will be sharing the same set of values for their labels, then list the first value followed by its label in inverted commas, then list the next value and its label, then the next and so forth.

Syntax 3:3 Adding value labels through the use of the command VALUE LABELS

The SPSS sample dataset testmarket.sav was used.

Note: The labels given below have been made up by me and will not reflect the true meaning of the information in those variables.

GET FILE='C:\Program Files\SPSSInc\SPSS16\Samples\testmarket.sav'.

VALUE LABELS promo
   1 'Buy one get one free'
   2 'Three for the price of two'
   3 '£2 off voucher'.

The **GET FILE** command opens the datafile if not already open.
   The command is **VALUE LABELS**. This is then followed by the variable name, then an inverted comma followed by the value label that provides the information required to understand the value, and then closed with a further inverted comma.
   After all values have been listed the command must be finished with a full stop.

It does not matter whether you use speech marks or inverted commas, but as per the VARIABLE LABELS command you must be consistent and close the variable label with the same one as you open with and then finish the completed command with a full stop.

As with the RENAME VARIABLES syntax and the VARIABLE LABELS syntax, an alternative layout is permissible where it is not a list format rather a stream of text, as illustrated below.

VALUE LABELS promo

   1 'Buy one get one free' 2 'Three for the price of two' 3 '£2 off voucher'.

You may have more than one variable which requires the same value labels. For example, in the sample dataset survey_sample.sav used in Syntax 3:1 there are four variables about educational attainment (**educ, maeduc, paeduc, speduc**). All four have the same labels for possible missing values, but these are currently less informative than you may want (97 = NAP, 98 = BK and 99 = NA). You can put value labels (new or amended) on all four variables by simply listing *all* of the variables on the VALUE LABELS command line as below. You can list as many variables as you wish as long as they all need the same value labels.

VALUE LABELS educ maeduc paeduc speduc

97 'Not appropriate person'
98 'Do not know'
99 'Not applicable'.

Missing Values

Your data may well have some data missing unless you are very fortunate. Data may be missing for a number of reasons and can have varying effects upon your analysis. While it is not within the remit of this book to go into the varying methods of dealing with missing values we will address issues associated with 'USER-MISSING' data. SYSTEM-MISSING data is data where there is just a blank entry in the datasheet rather than a value. In SPSS, in the Datasheet View, each piece of SYSTEM-MISSING data is represented by a dot. USER-MISSING data should be allocated a value and that value is identified as representing missing data. Unless you plan to impute a value for the missing data you need to classify USER-MISSING data as 'missing' (this is carried out using the MISSING VALUES command) and also to label any values that represent the missing data (using VALUE LABELS as in Syntax 3:3).

Allocation of missing values requires a common-sense approach whereby if a value could possibly occur within a variable, then that value must not be selected to represent missing values within that variable. This remains true whether you use syntax or the drop-down, menu-driven method. For example, if you are selecting a missing value for age, then 99 is an unlikely but still feasible value for a participant's age, thus 99 is not an ideal missing value. Minus numbers are not possible for an individual's age, so –1, –2, –99, etc., are suitable missing values.

This time the command is MISSING LABELS, followed by the variable name, then either an opening bracket, then up to three discrete values that you wish to represent the missing values, then a closing bracket and a full stop.

Following on from Syntax 3:3 the example below will use SPSS sample dataset testmarket.sav and classify as missing some values in a variable (**marketid**). I am fairly certain that these values do not represent missing values, but this is just an example to illustrate the syntax that can be used.

Syntax 3:4 Indicating missing data with the MISSING VALUES command (using discrete numbers)

The SPSS sample dataset testmarket.sav was used.

GET FILE='C:\Program Files\SPSSInc\SPSS16\Samples\testmarket.sav'.

MISSING VALUES marketid (8, 9, 10).

COMMENT As a matter of good practice you can immediately type in the labels (as above in Syntax 3:3) for the missing values you have just allocated.

VALUE LABELS marketid
-8 'not completed'
-9 'none applicable answer'
-10 'answer illegible'.

The **GET FILE** command opens the datafile if not already open.
The command is **MISSING VALUES** which is then followed by the variable name, then a bracket followed by the values that you want to represent missing data. The values should be separated by a comma, and there can be no more than three values.

Just as value labels can be allocated to more than one variable, so can missing value status. Simply list the three variables which share the same missing values on the MISSING VALUES command line as below.

MISSING VALUES marketid locid ageloc (8, 9, 10).

COMMENT Note that allocating these values as missing within these variables is pure fantasy; the point is to illustrate how to allocate missing values to more than one variable simultaneously.

Up to three discrete, separate missing values can be allocated. If you want to use a greater number then you will need to use a *range* of numbers using the range indicator THRU (meaning 'through'). The main ways for indicating missing value ranges are shown below (*n* THRU *n*, LOWEST THRU *n*, *n* THRU HIGHEST).

Syntax 3:5 Indicating missing data with the MISSING VALUES command (using ranges)

The SPSS sample dataset testmarket.sav was used.

COMMENT Example 3:5:1 Missing values ranges *n* THRU *n*, the following command allocates a specific range (here 7, 8, 9 and 10) as missing values.
MISSING VALUES marketid (7 THRU 10).

COMMENT Example 3:5:2 Missing values ranges LOWEST THRU *n*, the following command allocates all numbers with a value of 4 or lower as missing values (in **marketid** this covers the values 1, 2, 3, 4).
MISSING VALUES marketid (LOWEST THRU 4).

COMMENT Example 3:5:3 Missing values ranges LOWEST THRU *n* (as per 3:5:2) as well as the number 99.
MISSING VALUES marketid (LOWEST THRU 4, 99).

COMMENT Example 3:5:4 Missing values ranges *n* THRU HIGHEST, the following command allocates all numbers 6 and greater as missing values (in **marketid** this covers the values 6, 7, 8, 9, 10).
MISSING VALUES marketid (6 THRU HIGHEST).

You can also vary the missing values for differing variables within one command line, as below.

MISSING VALUES marketid (6 THRU HIGHEST) locid (1, 2, 3) ageloc (LOWEST THRU 5, 20).

COMMENT Again note that allocating these values as missing within these variables is pure fantasy; the point is to illustrate how to allocate differing missing values to more than one variable simultaneously.

ERROR ALERT for Syntax 3:4 and Syntax 3:5

Values allocated as missing data must always be listed in ascending order (smallest first) within the MISSING VALUES syntax command. See Syntax 13:1 in the error chapter for an example of what happens when they are not listed in the correct order.

Checking the Datafile Layout and Variable Content

After creating the datafile it can be useful to print out a list of the variables, their names, value labels, missing values, etc. You can use the drop-down menu FILE → DISPLAY DATA FILE INFORMATION → WORKING FILE (for an open datafile) or select EXTERNAL FILE to select a datafile that is not currently open. Using this method the variable information for the whole file will print on the output viewer screen. Using syntax can do this also, but additionally gives you the option to print for specified variables only and this facility is only available through syntax.

Using the drop-down, menu-driven method, using FILE → DISPLAY DATA FILE INFORMATION → WORKING FILE will produce the entire file variable information. You should also see the DISPLAY DICTIONARY command preceding the file information, printed in the Log.

Syntax 3:6 Printing the variable information for a file using the DISPLAY DICTIONARY command

The SPSS sample dataset testmarket.sav was used.

GET FILE='C:\Program Files\SPSSInc\SPSS16\Samples\testmarket.sav'.
DISPLAY DICTIONARY.

The first command **GET FILE** opens the file if not already opened.

The command is **DISPLAY DICTIONARY**. This will print the information for all variables in the file.

OPTIONS
You can specify a list of variables for which you require the information to be printed in the output viewer sheet; this is only available through syntax. In the example below, the information is specified only for the first three variables in the file.

DISPLAY DICTIONARY
/ VARIABLES = marketid mktsize locid.

The command **DISPLAY DICTIONARY** will result in the variable information being displayed with the variables in the order in which they are found in the file. A further refinement only available through syntax is to include a command so that the variable information is reported in alphabetical variable order. This is achieved simply by adding the word **SORTED** after the **DISPLAY** command.

DISPLAY SORTED DICTIONARY.

Neither of these options is available using the drop-down, menu-driven method.

Summary

Datafile construction involves not only data entry but also making the datafile as user-friendly as possible. Increasing the usability of your datafile will enable you, and others, to access the data at any point in the future and still be able to make sense of it.

Correct labelling of variables and coded data will make the analysis easier to carry out and to discuss with others such as supervisors. Missing values need to be identified, classified as such, and labelled well.

Syntax commands for variable names and labels, value labels and missing values enable multiple variables to be renamed, or labelled at the same time. Syntax can save you time and effort, reduce repetition, and provide a clear audit trail of activity. Syntax is a valuable tool when making your datafile more user-friendly. If you save your syntax for labels etc. with clear explanatory names you can begin to build a 'library' of syntax files which can be adapted and amended in the future.

Useful Tips
- Remember to put the full stop at the very end of your command, not following each label or name being given.
- Variable names need to be systematic and indicative of the variable's content; variable labels will be seen on the outputs and graphs, so can be more informative.
- If you use older versions of SPSS do not forget the S at the end of VALUE LABELS, VARIABLE NAMES, RENAME VARIABLES, MISSING VALUES even when only dealing with one label, name, value, etc.

4

Amending the Datafile

Examples in this chapter will use the SPSS sample datasets
GSS 93 for Missing Values.sav
GSS93 subset.sav

This chapter will cover: creating a smaller file from a much larger one; adding new cases to data for existing variables; and adding new variables' data to existing cases.

There may be times when you wish to create a smaller datafile from variables extracted from a very large datafile, leaving the large 'master' file untouched. There is no easy way to do this with the drop-down menu method; you would have to copy the variables you want into a new dataset or delete the ones you do not want from the original. This task is much easier with syntax. There may be circumstances when you need to add new cases or add new variables to an existing datafile from another data source. These actions can be carried out easily using the drop-down, menu-driven method, but using syntax will allow you to keep track of what was included and/or removed.

Good Practice

- Always retain a copy of the original data.
- When transforming or recoding variables, do not overwrite the existing ones, instead create new variables and label original and recoded ones accordingly.
- Use the COMMENT command to note in your syntax files the purpose and rationale of transformations/recoding.

Examples of Usefulness

Consider extracting a limited number of variables from a British Birth Cohort dataset. In the BCS70 dataset there are thousands of variables for each case in the officially available datafile. I extract the variables I require (which have numbered more than 300 for some research projects) from this original 'master' datafile, and leave the original data untouched. I then have a working datafile, with the data's origin clearly documented, and all transformations, manipulations and analyses being carried out on this.

A different situation occurs when I wish to provide a limited amount of information to an external source that I do not want (or am not permitted) to give access to my full dataset. This arises when I am trying to gain externally available information such as deprivation data associated with postcodes. I have done this for myself with some regional deprivation data, but for other regions I have had to provide the postcodes to a third party. In the latter circumstances the best way has been to provide a file with just an ID and postcode for each case.

Extracting to a Smaller Datafile

Sometimes it may be useful to create a smaller datafile containing a number of the variables from a main datafile. For me this has predominantly been under two circumstances: (1) when requiring a very small proportion of data variables from a very large datafile, and (2) when I need to supply a limited number of data variables to somewhere else.

It is possible to create a new datafile from an existing one but it is very important that the newly created file is saved under a new name to avoid overwriting the original. If you look back to Chapter 2 you will see examples of saving a new file (Syntax 2:4) and of saving files generally (Syntax 2:6). Both use the syntax command SAVE OUTFILE. In the example below we will use the SAVE OUTFILE command to save a smaller dataset extracted from a larger one. The data being extracted contains the unique identifier variable (**id**) and then eight variables that could (for example) be

---

Syntax 4:1 Creating a new dataset using the SAVE OUTFILE command

The SPSS sample dataset GSS93 subset.sav was used.

GET FILE='C:\Program Files\SPSSInc\SPSS16\Samples\GSS93 subset.sav'
   /KEEP id wrkstat marital childs age sex race income91 region.

SAVE OUTFILE
   'C:\Documents and Settings\User\My Documents\GSS93_represent.sav'.

> Note new filename

The **GET FILE** command accesses the original master datafile (named GSS93 subset. sav).

The **/KEEP** sub-command then retains or 'keeps' the nine listed variables (**id wrkstat marital childs age sex race income91 region.**) and the full stop is required to complete the **GET FILE** command.

The **SAVE OUTFILE** command saves the new datafile to the required location and with a new name. A full stop completes this command.

OPTIONS
It is possible to save a new datafile from an already open dataset. If the dataset GSS subset.sav was already open then the following syntax would create the new dataset GSS_represent2.sav containing just the nine variables listed.

SAVE OUTFILE
  'C:\Documents and Settings\User\My Documents\GSS93_represent2.sav'
  /KEEP id wrkstat marital childs age sex race income91 region.
  This time the **SAVE OUTFILE** command requires the appropriate datafile to be open already. It is crucial to avoid overwriting the original dataset, so the filename and location immediately following the command **SAVE OUTFILE** need to be different to the name of the open file or that open file will be overwritten.

sent off for someone to check the representativeness of your sample compared to the regional populations.

A unique identifier is required if you need to re-merge data later. The unique ID enables the correct data to be matched to the correct case.

Adding New Variables to a Dataset

Sometimes there is a need to merge data from two datafiles. You may need to add new data variables to existing cases. You can do this with the drop-down menu method, which works well. It is found under the main menu (DATA → MERGE FILES → ADD VARIABLES). This method can be used with the PASTE button being used to create the syntax initially and adapted if required.

In syntax the command MATCH FILES is used to add new data for existing cases. The language of the syntax suggests what happens when data is added in this way. The files need to be 'matched' case by case to enable the data in both datafiles to be matched appropriately with the correct data matched to the correct case. Thus, there must be a unique identifier for each case and any given value in that variable occurs once and once only. SPSS requires the data in both datafiles to be sorted in ascending order by the unique ID variable. This sorting is a prerequisite for any matching to occur.

The syntax below takes data from variables available in a separate datafile (which I will call the donor datafile for ease of understanding) and adds those variables, and the data therein, to an already open (active) datafile. You need to add information

Syntax 4:2 Adding variables to existing cases using the MATCH FILES command

The SPSS sample datasets GSS 93 for Missing Values.sav and GSS93 subset.sav were used.

GET FILE='C:\Program Files\SPSSInc\SPSS16\Samples\GSS 93 for Missing Values. sav'.

```
MATCH FILES
   /FILE=*
   /FILE='C:\Program Files\SPSSInc\SPSS16\Samples\GSS93 subset.sav'
   /BY ID.
EXECUTE.

SAVE OUTFILE
   'C:\Documents and Settings\User\My Documents\GSS93_merge2.sav'.
```

The first command **GET FILE** gets the original master datafile, and this becomes the active datafile – indicated thereafter as **FILE=***.

The next line has the **MATCH FILES** command which will match up the two files and allow the additional variables to be added. It has two **/FILE** sub-commands.

Each **/FILE** sub-command is followed by the name of a file to be matched **FILE=*** for the active file and the full name and location of the donor datafile.
/FILE='C:\Program Files\SPSSInc\SPSS16\Samples\GSS93 subset.sav'

In this example two files are used, but as many datafiles can be used as you need to combine (up to a maximum of 50 datafiles).

The third sub-command **/BY** matches the two datafiles using the specified variable **ID** to match the cases correctly. This allows data in the variables in the donor datafile to be matched to cases in the active dataset by their unique identifier. A full stop finishes the **MATCH FILES** command.

The **EXECUTE.** command then actions the preceding syntax.

The final **SAVE OUTFILE** command saves the newly combined data with a different name so that you don't jeopardise the original datafile.

to specific cases using a unique identifier available in both the donor datafile and the active datafile. In SYNTAX 4:2 GSS93 subset.sav is the donor file.

It is absolutely imperative to sort both files by the unique identifier when using the merge facility to add data to existing cases. If this is not carried out the merging of the datafiles will not be executed.

You will find that if you try and merge the variable data and it turns out that you have not sorted both datasets correctly, it does not work. Using the drop-down, menu-driven method you would have to go through the process of opening each datafile, sorting and saving each one, and then start the merge procedure again, clicking back through the DATA → MERGE FILES → ADD VARIABLES menu. However, if you are using syntax you can add in a line for each file to ensure they are sorted correctly. Sorting cases is a very useful thing to be able to add to your syntax. The SORT CASES command will apply to the active dataset. If you have only one dataset open, that is automatically the active dataset. If you have more than one dataset open, the most recently 'used' one will be the active one (by 'used' I mean opening a file, running analysis, etc., or clicking on the Data Editor view). The last file to be sorted will be 'active' so you will need to ensure that the last datafile that you sort is the one that you want the data added to.

See Syntax 4:3 below, where the additional sort commands are highlighted

---

Syntax 4:3 SORT CASES (example embedded in Match Files)

The SPSS sample datasets GSS 93 for Missing Values.sav and GSS93 subset.sav were used.

GET FILE='C:\Program Files\SPSSInc\SPSS16\Samples\GSS93 subset.sav'.
SORT CASES BY id (A).

GET FILE='C:\Program Files\SPSSInc\SPSS16\Samples\GSS 93 for Missing Values. sav'.
SORT CASES BY id (A).

MATCH FILES
   /FILE=*
   /FILE='C:\Program Files\SPSSInc\SPSS16\Samples\GSS93 subset.sav'
   /BY ID.
EXECUTE.

SAVE OUTFILE
   'C:\Documents and Settings\User\My Documents\GSS93_merge2.sav'.

In the example above, each of the datasets is in turn opened with the **GET FILE** command then sorted using the **SORT CASES** command. They are both sorted **BY** the unique identifier **ID** in ascending order **(A)**.
   All the sorting is carried out in advance of the **MATCH FILES** syntax.
   Note that the dataset **GSS 93 for Missing Values.sav** is opened last to make it the active dataset in the **MATCH FILES** syntax, and represented by **FILE=***.

An alternative type of merged data from two datafiles can arise if you add new *cases* (rather than variables) into an existing datafile.

Adding New Cases to an Existing Datafile

You can add new cases via the drop-down menu method, which again works well. It is found under the main menu (DATA → MERGE FILES → ADD CASES). This method can be used with the PASTE button being used to create the syntax initially and adapted if required.

In syntax the command ADD FILES is used to add new data for new cases. Again, the language of the syntax gives a big clue as to what happens – the files are adding data from other datafiles. Here data does not need to be matched appropriately to each case, but needs to be matched instead to each variable.

Variables that are named the same must contain the same type of data; that is, (1) if a variable named **AGE** is in months in one file, then check that the variable named **AGE** is in months in the second datafile, and (2) if a variable named **DATE** represents the date of birth in one file, then check that the variable named **DATE** represents the same (e.g. it is not the date of survey completion) in the second data-file. This is common sense but needs checking.

Once you have checked that the variables with the same names contain the same data, you need to check their compatibility of format. Variables that are to be supplemented with data from new cases from another file must share an identical format in both datasets. If **AGE** is numeric in one file and string in another, that will not work. Even if **AGE** is numeric in both datasets, the formats need to be shared also. In short, variables with identical names need to have identical formats. You can check the compatibility of the file formats by using the DISPLAY DICTIONARY command for each file, as described in Syntax 3:6.

If you need to amend the format of any of the variables, then you may decide to identify one of the datasets as a 'template' and then alter the second datafile to match the 'template' file's format. The syntax command is quite straightforward. Open the datafile you wish to alter and then use the FORMATS command to amend the format of variables so that they match the same named variables in the other dataset. Changing the details of a variable's format is relatively straightforward. The FORMATS command is suitable for altering the length of a numeric variable or of a string variable. It can also alter the format in which date and time variables are displayed. However, it cannot be used to convert a number into text or date, or vice versa.

Syntax 4:4 Changing the variable format using the FORMATS command

The SPSS sample dataset GSS93 subset.sav was used.

GET FILE='C:\Program Files\SPSSInc\SPSS16\Samples\GSS93 subset.sav'.

FORMATS ID (F5.1) / wrkstat marital (F2) / agewed (F4).
EXECUTE.

The **GET FILE** command opens the datafile if not already open.

The **FORMATS** command is then followed by the variables to be altered and their allocated format – the first variable following straight on from the command, all others separated by the forward slash. If more than one variable is to have the same format then these can be listed prior to the format, see **wrkstat marital** above.

If you look back at page 22 , Syntax 2:2 explains that numeric variables have a specified format (e.g. F2.1, F3, A20). In Syntax 4:4, for ID the F indicates it is numerical, the 5 indicates the variable will be a maximum of five characters long, including an option for one decimal place.

Once you are confident that same named, same content variables all share the same format then you can go ahead and merge the datasets, bringing in data for new cases. In the example below a hypothetical survey from 2007 has been repeated in 2008 and the data for the new cases needs to be combined (or merged) with the existing 2007 data. The syntax is similar to the MATCH FILES syntax above, but obviously has ADD FILES rather than MATCH FILES.

In effect this syntax adds, to the active datafile, all the information for the new cases in the second file and then saves it.

Syntax 4:5 Adding new cases to an existing datafile using the ADD FILES command

This command will not work on any sample dataset, it refers to two hypothetical datafiles.

GET FILE='C:\datafiles\data2007.sav'.

ADD FILES
   /FILE=*
   /FILE='C:\datafiles\data2008.sav'.
EXECUTE.

SAVE OUTFILE='C:\datafiles\data2007_8.sav'.

The first command gets the original master datafile
GET FILE='C:\datafiles\data2007.sav' which becomes the active datafile (indicated thereafter as **FILE=***).
   The second command **ADD FILES** will add the new cases to the existing file and it has two **/FILE** sub-commands.
   Each **/FILE** sub-command is followed by the name of a file to be matched; **FILE=*** for the active file and the full name and location of the donor datafile **/FILE='C:\datafiles\ data2008.sav'**. The full stop finishes the **ADD FILES** command.
   The **EXECUTE.** command actions the preceding commands.
   The final **SAVE OUTFILE** command saves the newly combined data with a different name **SAVE OUTFILE='C:\datafiles\data2007_8.sav'.** so that you do not jeopardise the original datafile. This command is completed with the full stop.

Sometimes variables containing compatible data do not share the same name across different datafiles. To be able to merge the data within such variables they need to be linked via the same name in both datafiles (e.g. earnings may be named as **wage** in one datafile and as **salary** in the second). You can easily address any variable name mismatches within the syntax, as shown below in Syntax 4:6.

If, for example, the variable name for gender is recorded as sex in the 2008 datafile and wage is recorded as salary, then the inclusion of a /RENAME sub-command as shown below will allow the variables to be matched in the datafiles and combine as if the names were identical in the two datafiles.

SYNTAX 4:6 Adding new cases to an existing datafile where variable names differ using RENAME command (embedded in ADD FILES)

This command will not work on any sample dataset, it refers to two hypothetical datafiles.

GET FILE='C:\datafiles\data2007.sav'.
ADD FILES
   /FILE=*
   /FILE='C:\datafiles\data2008.sav'
   /RENAME gender=sex wage=salary.
EXECUTE.

SAVE OUTFILE='C:\datafiles\data2007_8.sav'.

The syntax is the same as 4:5 but with the addition of the **/RENAME** sub-command within the ADD FILES command.

Following the **/RENAME** sub-command you need to list each name that you want to change (usually this is the variable name as it appears in the donor dataset) followed by an equals sign and then the new name (usually as it appears in the active dataset). Note that the name after the equals sign is how the variable will be named in the merged dataset.

Using syntax you can add in a single command line to rename all of the misnamed (but matching in format and content) pairs of variables. Again when linking two variables this way, you need to be sure that the details of their formats are the same and the content is of the same nature.

Summary

The drop-down, menu-driven method of using SPSS is quite adequate for adding cases and for adding variables through the DATA → MERGE FILES options. However, using syntax has advantages over the drop-down, menu-driven method of using SPSS; especially where the datafiles are not exactly matching in their compatibility. Syntax can assist in preparing the datafiles for merging (by sorting or altering formats) and this is best incorporated in an overall set of syntax commands.

Closely reviewing a set of pasted syntax commands from the drop-down, menu-driven method is an excellent starting point for writing the syntax. When a set of pasted commands is viewed and analysed line by line, you can begin to see what each of the commands and sub-commands mean and what they will do. Adding your own additional command lines to sort, rename, etc., can ensure the merging of data works. Matching formats prior to a merge is vital and can be much easier using syntax.

Being able to extract a specified set of variables to create a new dataset is a valuable function of SPSS which is not easily done without syntax. Here syntax is a great time saver.

Useful Tips

- Make sure that you save any new outfile (new file) under a *different name* or location to the original one, otherwise the original datafile will be overwritten.
- Ensure each case has a unique identifier in all files in case you need to match the data at a later date.
- Start with the drop-down, menu-driven method, paste the command and then work with this, rather than starting from scratch.
- Use the SORT CASES command within MATCH FILES to avoid one of the most common errors found when trying to merge data in SPSS.
- The FORMATS command, used in conjunction with the information provided from the DISPLAY DICTIONARY command, can save a lot of time when trying to attain data compatibility for merging.

5

Syntax Involving String Variables

Examples in this chapter will use the following SPSS sample datasets
stroke_valid.sav
demo.sav
World95.sav
ceramics.sav

SPSS documentation and commands refer to text data as being in a **string** format and such data are found in **string** variables.

This chapter will explain how to use syntax to assist in dealing with text or 'string' data and variables. It will cover the coding of string variables into numeric variables and vice versa, as well as manipulating string variables This section will also feature using Excel to assist with writing a long and repetitive series of syntax commands when coding multiple text entries.

When entering your own data it is possible to enter all the data in the format that you will require for analysis. However, there are various circumstances when the data is made available in a 'less than ideal' state. Data that originated in other programs such as Excel may not import into SPSS in exactly the format that you need, for example data which appears to be standard numerical numbers can transfer in as text. This also applies to information about date and/or time. You may be able to ensure the format is correct before importing into SPSS, but sometimes that is beyond your control and you have to accept the data as it is.

When imported data is supposed to be numeric (or date or time) but instead imports in a text format, it will need to be converted into the correct format rather than left in text format. A further circumstance for converting text to numeric is when data is in the SPSS dataset as free text or categorical text format. While the text conveys information, it limits the use of the data in your analysis, either because the test you wish to carry out will not accept string variables to be used, even for the grouping variable (e.g. Mann–Whitney U test), or because the entries are too numerous to use as meaningful categories (e.g. the variable 'country' which lists 109 countries in the SPSS sample dataset World95.sav).

Good Practice

- Always retain a copy of the original data.
- Do not overwrite the original variable, instead when transforming or recoding variables create new variables and label original and recoded ones accordingly.
- Save syntax files for routine data manipulation and build a syntax library – you might need them again.
- When recoding variables name them in a way that 'ties' them to the old one, for example **q1** to **q1_recode** or **q1** to **new_q1**.
- Label the codes clearly.
- When importing data spend some time ensuring that the data is in the correct and appropriate format for your analysis.

Most of the syntax in this chapter will be adapted from commands copied and pasted from the COMPUTE VARIABLE and RECODE options available within the TRANSFORM drop-down menu. At the end of this chapter I will describe how you can use Excel to assist the coding of multiple varied text entries into a limited number of the numeric codes.

Converting Numeric Values to Text Representations of Numbers

This chapter will predominantly focus on getting text into a numeric format, to enable the data to be used by SPSS. It may seem strange then to begin by explaining how to convert numeric values to text representations of numbers. However, sometimes data does need to be in a string format and to be able to convert data from numeric to string can be useful. The main reason is that because few of the SPSS sample datasets have text representations of numbers in them, I am limited in the examples I can show you using easily accessible datasets. So, in order to provide sufficient examples for you to see and use in this chapter, we will start with a command to create variables with text representations of numbers, so that I can base examples on these string variables later in the chapter.

It is important to note that SPSS requires a string variable to be in existence before any data can be entered into it. Thus the first step is to create a new 'empty' string variable.

In the example below two new string variables will be created in the SPSS sample dataset stroke_valid.sav. For more information on the COMPUTE command see Chapters 6 and 7. As we will use this amended dataset later, you may wish to save the dataset somewhere on your computer, with a new name such as stroke_amended. sav perhaps.

Syntax 5:1 Creating a string variable using STRING and converting numeric values to text

The SPSS sample dataset stroke_valid.sav is used.

```
GET FILE='C:\Program Files\SPSSInc\SPSS16\Samples\stroke_valid.sav'.
STRING cost_txt agecat_txt (A9).

COMPUTE cost_txt=STRING(cost,f8.2).
COMPUTE agecat_txt=STRING(agecat,f4.0).
EXECUTE.

VARIABLE LABELS cost_txt 'cost as a string variable'.
VARIABLE LABELS agecat_txt 'agecat as a string variable'.

SAVE OUTFILE='C:\Documents and Settings\User\My Documents\stroke_amended.
sav'.
```

The **GET FILE** command opens the datafile if not already open.

The **STRING** command creates the two string variables **cost_txt agecat_txt** allowing each to have nine alphanumerical text characters **(A9).** and the command is completed with the full stop.

Each **COMPUTE** command is followed by the name of the string variable (this variable must exist already) followed by an equals sign **cost_txt=** and then the string function **STRING**. The string function requires brackets to enclose the numeric variable to be converted and its current format **STRING(cost,f8.2).**.

The **EXECUTE.** command then actions the preceding syntax commands.

In accordance with good practice I have then labelled the new variables (see SYNTAX 3:2).

The final **SAVE OUTFILE** command saves the amended dataset with a different name so that you can use it later – choose a location and name that works for you.

OK, now we have some text representations of numbers to work through the examples with.

Converting Text Representations of Numbers to Numeric Values

In many programs (Excel, SPSS, etc.) when you view numbers in datasheets they can be in either a text format or in a numeric format. This can be confusing if you do not realise that text 'numbers' are not treated the same as numerical data; instead they are treated as any other alphabetical piece of information. In SPSS if you attempt to carry out data analysis on a text variable that you erroneously believe to be numeric then either (1) SPSS may not let you do it (e.g. when using the drop-down menu you cannot put a string variable in as a grouping variable in Mann–Whitney, or use a string variable for the Factor in the ANOVA) or (2) you may use syntax and try to run a command and you will see a warning that a string variable was present where only numeric variables are allowed and SPSS will not execute the command. So, it is important to have numerical data in the numeric format for numeric data analysis.

There are two main ways to convert string (text) representations of numbers to numeric values, by using RECODE with or without the keyword (CONVERT).

The RECODE function is found in the TRANSFORM drop-down menu and, as with most actions in SPSS, using the paste function is a useful place to start your syntax. In RECODE each individual value need recoding so it is useful mainly when there are few values to recode. The following syntax is pasted from recoding string numbers into a numeric format via TRANSFORM → RECODE INTO DIFFERENT VARIABLES.

Syntax 5:2 Converting text numbers to numeric format using the RECODE command

This uses the amended dataset stroke_amended.sav created in Syntax 5.1.

GET FILE='C:\datafiles\s''troke_amended.sav'.

RECODE agecat_txt (' 1'=1) (' 2'=2) (' 3'=3) (' 4'=4) INTO agecat_num.
EXECUTE.

COMMENT as per Chapter 3's guidance all new variables are fully labelled.

VARIABLE LABELS agecat_num 'agecat_txt recoded into numeric format'.
VALUE LABELS agecat_num
  1 '45-54'
  2 '55-64'
  3 '65-74'
  4 '75+'.

The **GET FILE** command opens the datafile if not already open.

The **RECODE** command is followed by the existing variable that you wish to recode **agecat_txt** followed by a list of criteria and resulting recode value, each set within brackets (e.g. (' 1'=1)); each string element to be recoded is enclosed in inverted commas and this has to include all of the string element including any leading spaces.

At the end of the list is the keyword **INTO** followed by the name of the variable where the new derived values are to go **agecat_num.**. The full stop follows this to complete the **RECODE** command.

The **EXECUTE.** command then actions the preceding syntax commands.

In accordance with good practice I have then labelled the new variable and the values (see Syntax 3:2 and Syntax 3:3).

ERROR ALERT
The INTO sub-command is very important. If you do not add this sub-command followed by a new derived variable name **INTO agecat_num** then the recode will still go ahead, but will overwrite your existing variable **agecat_txt**. This would be the same as selecting TRANSFORM → RECODE INTO SAME VARIABLES instead of selecting TRANSFORM → RECODE INTO DIFFERENT VARIABLES.

The above syntax is very helpful when the different values in the variable are limited. However, it is common for there to be numerous text numbers in the variable. A very efficient syntax exists for converting text representations of numbers to exactly the same numeric values via use of a keyword (CONVERT).

Syntax 5:3 Converting text numbers to numeric format using the RECODE command and the (CONVERT) keyword

This uses the amended dataset stroke_amended.sav created in Syntax 5.1.

GET FILE='C:\datafiles\stroke_amended.sav'.

COMMENT this syntax converts each and every individual number into a numeric value and ignores any leading spaces, etc.

RECODE cost_txt (CONVERT) INTO cost_num.
EXECUTE.

VARIABLE LABELS cost_num 'cost_txt converted from string to numeric'.

The **GET FILE** command opens the datafile if not already open.

The **RECODE** command is followed by the existing string variable **cost_txt** that you wish to recode followed by the CONVERT keyword in brackets **(CONVERT)**, then the keyword **INTO** and the name of the new numeric variable **cost_num.**. The full stop follows this to complete the **RECODE** command.

The **EXECUTE.** command then actions the preceding syntax commands.

In accordance with good practice I have then labelled the new variable (see Syntax 3:2).

OPTIONS

This automatic recoding of data into numeric format has a default format of F8.2 but still seems happy to convert numbers larger than that. Try converting the variable **patid**, which has 10 digits, and you will see that the data is still converted. If you want the converted number to have a different format to F8.2 (e.g. with more or fewer decimal places) add a FORMATS command line (Syntax 4:4) after the RECODE, see example below.

COMMENT the additional FORMATS line will mean no decimal places are displayed.
RECODE cost_txt (CONVERT) INTO cost_num2.
FORMATS cost_num2 (F8).
EXECUTE.

There is the additional facility to specify non-direct conversions in the recoding, for example you could specify that the **cost_txt** value 0 should be converted into -99 and made into a missing value. This is something that syntax can record for audit. Just add any specific recode values prior to the (CONVERT) keyword. Note that in **cost_txt** the zero values are actually represented as text by five spaces, then a decimal point, then two noughts.

RECODE cost_txt ('   .00'=-99) (CONVERT) INTO cost_num3.
MISSING VALUES cost_num3 (-99).
EXECUTE.

Converting Categorical Text to Numeric Values

Text categories, such as male/female, are frequently useful as grouping variables in analysis. However, as mentioned earlier, string variables are not always accepted as grouping variables in SPSS (e.g. for Mann–Whitney, ANOVAs) so you need to be able to convert such text data into numeric format.

As well as RECODE you can use AUTOMATIC RECODE which is also found under the drop-down TRANSFORM menu. AUTOMATIC RECODE, as the name suggests, recodes a variable by automatically assigning a numeric codes, one per each variation of a text entry in the variable. It is useful to carry this out using the drop-down, menu-driven method and then paste the command. The following syntax will recode string numbers or text into a numeric format and will assign one numerical value per each variation of text found. Note that the original values are assigned as value labels for the numeric codes in the new variable.

Syntax 5:4 Converting text categories to numeric format with AUTORECODE

The SPSS sample dataset stroke_valid.sav is used.

```
GET FILE='C:\Program Files\SPSSInc\SPSS16\Samples\stroke_valid.sav'.

AUTORECODE VARIABLES=hospid
    /INTO hospid_num.
EXECUTE.

VARIABLE LABELS hospid_num 'hospid as a numeric variable'.
```

The **GET FILE** command opens the datafile if not already open.

The **AUTORECODE** command is followed by the keyword VARIABLES and an equals sign and then the name of the variable to be recoded **hospid**.

Following this is the **/ INTO** sub-command and the name of the variable where the new derived values are to go **hospid_num.** and the full stop follows this to complete the **AUTORECODE** command.

The **EXECUTE.** command then actions the preceding syntax commands.

OPTIONS

The inclusion of a sub-command /BLANK=MISSING will allow blanks to be assigned the last (highest) value and this will be classified as a missing value.

```
AUTORECODE VARIABLES=hospid
    /INTO hospid_num2
    /BLANK=MISSING
    /PRINT.
```

The inclusion of the **PRINT** command means that the values and the labels (original text values) will be listed in the output file (see below).

```
hospid into hospid_num2 (Hospital ID)
Old Value   New Value   Value Label

ALK                1    ALK
BLA                2    BLA
EFX                3    EFX
GFG                4    GFG
IZO                5    IZO
NHV                6    NHV
NSR                7    NSR
OZN                8    OZN
PBW                9    PBW
QWS               10    QWS
RLD               11    RLD
SLB               12    SLB
WPA               13    WPA
WWL               14    WWL
YYH               15    YYH
```

AUTORECODE VARIABLES can be used to allocate values according to the *rank order* of text numbers, rather than their numerical values.

Note: if you wish to specify which numeric codes are to be allocated when converting text to numerical values then you will need to use alternative methods rather than accept the AUTOMATIC RECODE allocations. As well as using the RECODE (as per Syntax 5:1) you can use the IF command, accessed via the TRANSFORM drop-down, menu-driven method and using the `If...` (optional case selection condition) button found in the bottom left of the COMPUTE VARIABLE dialogue box.

The following syntax will recode a string variable **gender** as found in the SPSS sample dataset demo.sav into a numeric format.

Syntax 5:5 Converting text categories to numeric format using the IF command

The SPSS sample dataset demo.sav is used.

GET FILE='C:\Program Files\SPSSInc\SPSS16\Samples\demo.sav'.

IF (gender ='m') gender_num = 1.
IF (gender ='f') gender_num = 2.
EXECUTE.

VARIABLE LABELS gender _num 'sex of employee recoded from gender'.
VALUE LABELS gender_num 1'male' 2'female'.

The **GET FILE** command opens the datafile if not already open.

The **IF** command is followed by criteria (variables and values) that need to be met **(gender ='m')**. Note that the text value must be enclosed single quotes. This is followed by the name of the variable to be affected **gender_num** which in turn is followed by an equals sign and the value assigned to cases where the criteria are met **= 1. IF (gender ='m') gender_num = 1.**

Each **IF** command requires the criteria, the affected variable and the outcome, and each **IF** command must finish with a full stop.

The **EXECUTE.** command then actions the preceding syntax commands.

In accordance with good practice I have then labelled the new variable (see Syntax 3:2).

Alternatively, you can use the RECODE method as in Syntax 5:2, making sure you enclose the text to be recoded in inverted commas as below.

RECODE gender ('m'=1) ('f'=2) INTO gender_num2.

EXECUTE.

Changing the Case in a String Variable

There are times when it is advantageous to reformat the case of the text in a string variable; primarily because lowercase letters and uppercase letters within a string variable are treated as being different, for example 'M' will not be seen as 'm' in Syntax 5:5. Fortunately in demo.sav all the text entries are consistently entered as 'm' but datafiles I have used have sometimes come with inconsistent text entries (e.g. 'Mother', 'MOTHER' or 'mother' as entries for maternal next of kin). If you are recoding a text variable into a numeric one and the data entry has not been consistent in the use of case, you can either (1) have separate command lines for all text options, or (2) run a command to ensure consistency of case before starting to convert to numeric.

The sample files with SPSS do not have such inconsistencies, but World95.sav has a variable for country, which has capitals and lowercase. This can be used for demonstration purposes.

Syntax 5:6 Changing case within string variables using the COMPUTE command, plus LOWER and UPCAS subcommands

The SPSS sample dataset World95.sav is used.

GET FILE='C:\Program Files\SPSSInc\SPSS16\Samples\World95.sav'.

STRING country_case (A20).
COMPUTE country_case=UPCASE(country).
EXECUTE.

The **GET FILE** command opens the datafile if not already open.

The **STRING** command creates the string variable **country_case** with a maximum of 20 text charaters **(A20).** and the command is completed with the full stop.

The **COMPUTE** command is followed by the name of the string variable (this variable must exist already, here created by the previous command line), followed by an equals sign **country_case=** and then the 'convert to uppercase' function **UPCASE**. The function **UPCASE(country)** requires brackets to enclose the variable to be converted.

For conversion to lowercase use the LOWER function instead, see below.

```
STRING country_case2 (A20).
COMPUTE country_case2=LOWER(country).
EXECUTE.
```

Converting Categorical Text with Multiple Variation Entries to Numeric Values

There are times when you may be faced with a datafile which has a text variable with many different text entries and, instead of a code for each text value, these need coding down to a limited number of numeric codes. Here the task is to assign the numeric codes as efficiently as possible.

Using the drop-down, menu-driven method (RECODE or COMPUTE VARIABLE with **IF**) you would need to enter each different text variation individually and allocate it the appropriate numeric code. This is very time consuming. Using syntax in the standard way would be a little quicker: just use the paste method for the first text variation and code and then copy and paste that line, replacing the text and code etc. for each text variation that you have. This is still quite a long-winded way of doing it and leaves scope for human error as with most repetitive tasks.

What I do here is to use the best of Excel and SPSS syntax together. You can use the 'Fill Down' capabilities of Excel to assist you in writing a long syntax file in a very time-efficient way. First, you should minimise the combinations of upper- and lowercase combinations where possible and legitimate, using Syntax 5:6. Here is a worked example.

Go to World95.sav. You will see that the first variable in this datafile is the variable **country**. There are 109 different countries listed in this variable, but imagine that you would like the analysis to be available by economic region. To do this you will need to code each country to one of the six regions you wish to classify by (Organisation for Economic Co-operation and Development [OECD], East Europe, Pacific/Asia, Africa, Middle East, Latin America). *Note that there is a variable called region in the SPSS dataset already, so I have used those values as neither geography nor world economics are my forte.*

1. Paste the first command using the drop-down, menu-driven method (as per Syntax 5:5)

```
IF (country="Afghanistan") region_code = 3.

EXECUTE.
```

2. Take the first line **IF (country='Afghanistan') region_code =3.** and identify which elements of its component parts are 'constant' and which are 'changing' (my phrasing); you need to identify those parts that will change on each command and those that will stay constant. In this example the changes for each command line are the text of the country listed, and the code assigned to that country. For illustration the text below shows the 'constant' elements in normal text and the 'changing' elements in bold, just for illustration purposes.

    IF (country="**Afghanistan**") region_code =**3**.

    IF (country="**Argentina**") region_code =**6**.

    IF (country="**Armenia**") region_code =**5**.

    IF (country="**Australia**") region_code =**1**.

    IF (country="**Austria**") region_code =**1**.

    And so forth.

    Once you have identified the constant and the changing elements, go to a blank Excel spreadsheet. You will need to allocate a column for each component block of text, leaving the 'changing' ones empty. In the example above:

    *   The first component part is the constant IF(country=" this will go in column A.
    *   The next component part is the first changing component (the name of each country) so leave column B empty.
    *   The third component part is the constant ")region_code =, this will go in column C.
    *   The next component part is the second changing component (the allocated code) so leave column D empty.
    *   The third component part is the constant full stop ⊡ ; this will go in column E.

    The spreadsheet should now look something like Figure 5.1. Save the spreadsheet.

3. Next, in SPSS, run a frequency table for the text variable, then in the output file double-click on the pivot table and highlight the text column (see Figure 5.2). Then copy this highlighted text (use any method: CTRL+C; or right mouse click and select COPY; or the EDIT drop-down menu and COPY option).

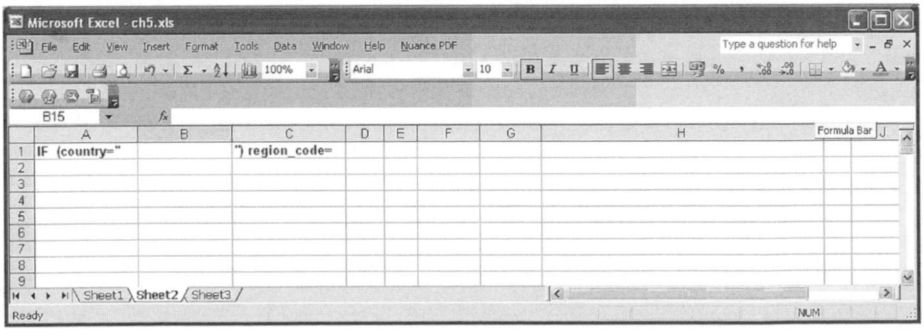

Figure 5.1

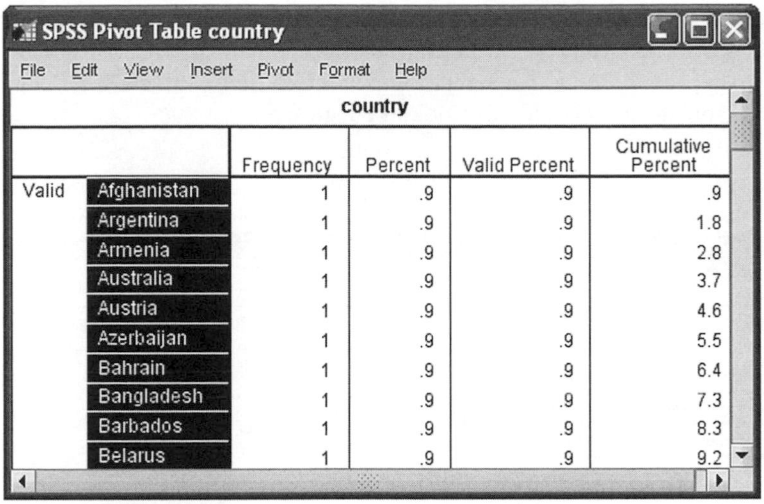
SPSS Pivot Table country

country

		Frequency	Percent	Valid Percent	Cumulative Percent
Valid	Afghanistan	1	.9	.9	.9
	Argentina	1	.9	.9	1.8
	Armenia	1	.9	.9	2.8
	Australia	1	.9	.9	3.7
	Austria	1	.9	.9	4.6
	Azerbaijan	1	.9	.9	5.5
	Bahrain	1	.9	.9	6.4
	Bangladesh	1	.9	.9	7.3
	Barbados	1	.9	.9	8.3
	Belarus	1	.9	.9	9.2

Figure 5.2

4. Next return to the Excel spreadsheet and paste the text into the second column, B, between the two constant components (see Figure 5.3).

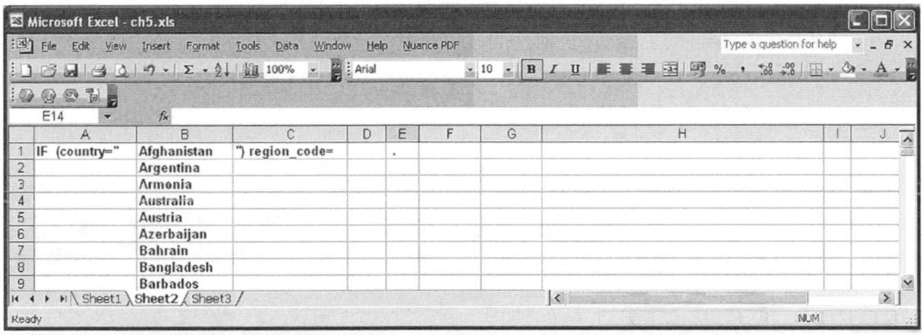
Microsoft Excel - ch5.xls

	A	B	C	D	E
1	IF (country="	Afghanistan	") region_code=		.
2		Argentina			
3		Armenia			
4		Australia			
5		Austria			
6		Azerbaijan			
7		Bahrain			
8		Bangladesh			
9		Barbados			

Figure 5.3

5. Now you need to code each country according to the region you wish it to be assigned to. In this example, type each code into column D, the second changing component (see Figure 5.4).

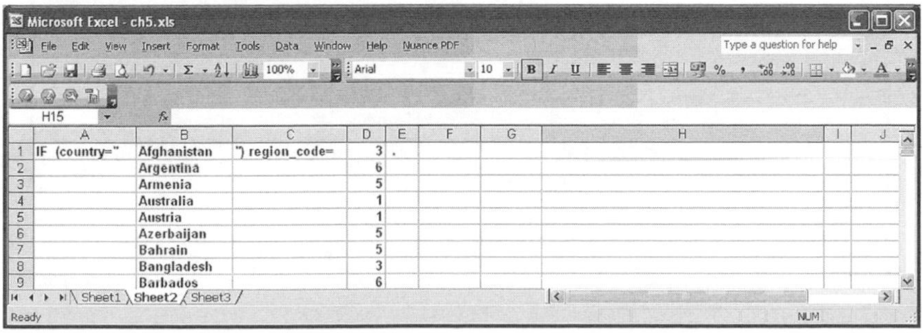
Microsoft Excel - ch5.xls

	A	B	C	D	E
1	IF (country="	Afghanistan	") region_code=	3	.
2		Argentina		6	
3		Armenia		5	
4		Australia		1	
5		Austria		1	
6		Azerbaijan		5	
7		Bahrain		5	
8		Bangladesh		3	
9		Barbados		6	

Figure 5.4

6. Highlight a 'constant' component column, then using Excel's EDIT → FILL → DOWN facility you can fill the constant component columns with the repeated text. Repeat for each 'constant' component column, so columns A, C and E. Your spreadsheet should now look like Figure 5.5.

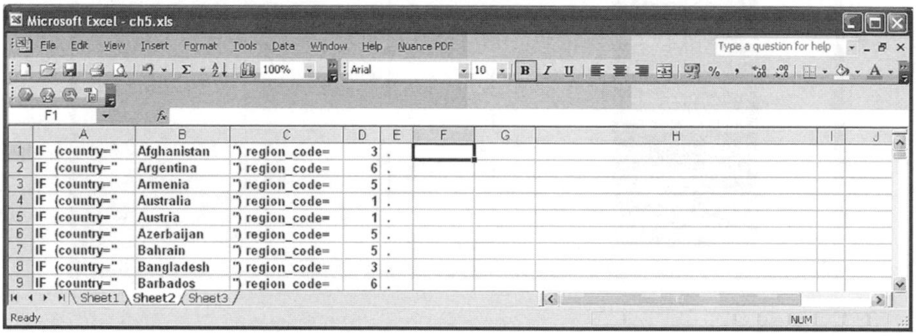

Figure 5.5

7. In the next empty column's first row (here cell F1) insert the concatenate function, by drop-down INSERT→ FUNCTION, and then select concatenate. Enter each column of text (constant and changing) in the correct order as in Figure 5.6. Then click OK.

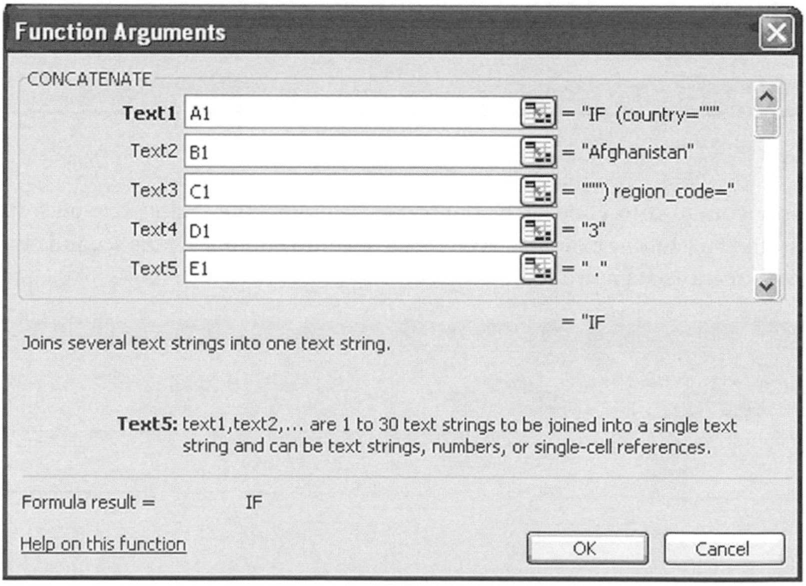

Figure 5.6

8. Highlight the column with the concatenate function in, then using Excel's EDIT → FILL → DOWN facility you can fill the cells with the concatenate function. Your spreadsheet should now look like Figure 5.7. Note that although each cell in column F appears to be full of text, they are actually filled with the concatenate formula.

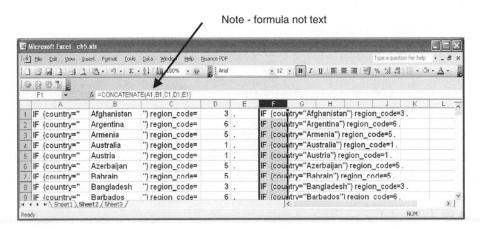

Figure 5.7

9. The last task in Excel is to copy the concatenate column and then use PASTE SPECIAL to paste the *values only* into an empty column, here column G.

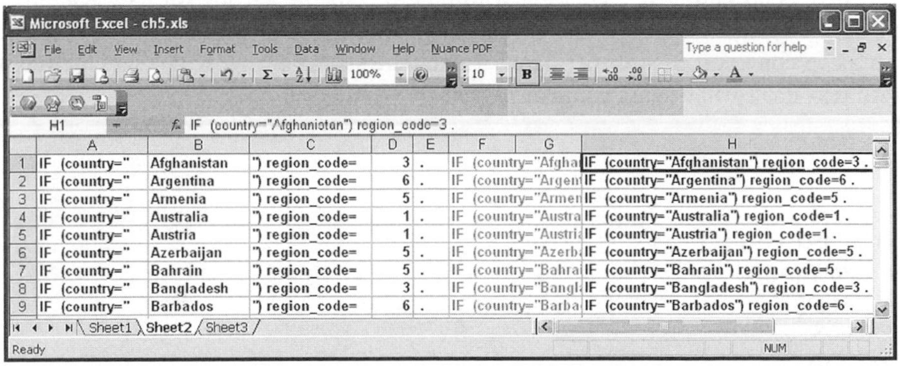

Figure 5.8

10. You can see in Figure 5.8 that the values in the cells in column G are now the text you require for your syntax. Copy this column and paste into your syntax sheet, complete with an EXECUTE command and final full stop. Just run ALL syntax (see Figure 5.9) and all 109 countries will be coded as per your assigned codes, without having to copy and paste 109 times, etc.

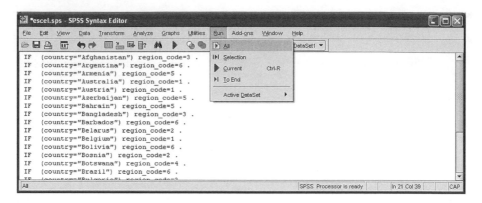

Figure 5.9

This process is worthwhile when multiple variations of text entries are to be assigned to each numeric code as in the example above where there are between 14 and 21 text options assigned to each of the six codes.

Date as Text into Date Format

A further situation in which you may need to alter the data's format concerns date and time variables which have string representations of date or time rather than recognised date formats. Chapter 6 will show why this formatting is important for date calculations.

There is no sample SPSS dataset with date or time in a string format. Therefore we need to create a dataset with date in text format, so that I can show how to use syntax to convert it to a proper date format. The syntax below will create a dataset with text dates using syntax similar to that in Syntax 2:2.

```
DATA LIST LIST
    / date (A8).
BEGIN DATA
12/09/08
03/08/07
04/06/06
21/05/94
END DATA.
SAVE OUTFILE='C:\Documents and Settings\User\My Documents\date_as_text1.
sav'.
```

Hopefully you now have the datasheet available that has the following Data View and Variable View (Figure 5.10).

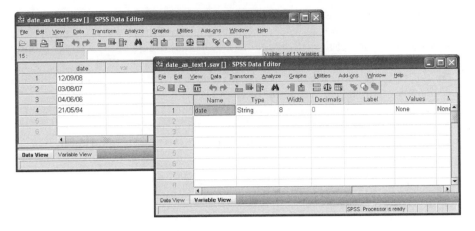

Figure 5.10

The date variable in this format is not usable in date calculations so you will need to change from a string variable to a date one. The following syntax will use the date string variable in date_as_text1.sav and convert it into a date format.

Syntax 5:7 Changing date string variables (in recognised formats) with COMPUTE command

Use the dataset created above, date_as_text1.sav.

GET FILE='C:\Documents and Settings\User\My Documents\date_as_text1.sav'.

COMPUTE date2 = NUMBER(date,EDATE10).
FORMATS date2(EDATE10).
EXECUTE.

VARIABLE LABELS date2 'date variable in date format'.

The **GET FILE** command opens the datafile if not already open.

The **COMPUTE** command names the variable to be created **date2** followed by an equals sign and then the **NUMBER** function which converts the string variable enclosed in brackets **date** to a numerical format, and this string variable is flagged up **EDATE10** as being laid out as a date layout. The full stop follows this to complete the **COMPUTE** command.

The **FORMATS** command specifies that the newly created variable is to have a date format.

The **EXECUTE.** command then actions the preceding syntax commands.

In accordance with good practice I have then labelled the new variable (see Syntax 3:2).

Syntax 5:7 will work as long as the string date variable is in a recognised SPSS date layout. The string date variable must contain days, months and years separated by spaces, dashes, slashes, full stops or commas. Note that American style dates (month/day/year) can be read using the ADATE format rather than the EDATE.

In the example above the data is already laid out in the European date format (day then month then year) required for EDATE, with an accepted divider **/**.

Months can be represented in digits or text (in full or with the first three letters), text must be in English; month names in other languages are not recognised. The same syntax will work if the datafile had been created with the following format for the dates:

12-Sep-08

03-Aug-07

04-Jun-06

21-May-94

Manipulating String Variables

You may sometimes need to manipulate 'parts' of a string variable. Data sometimes comes in text arrangements/formats that you do not want and therefore need to alter. When this occurs there are several commands which allow you to manipulate the string variables; most of these can be found in the TRANSFORM drop-down menu. If you open the SPSS sample dataset ceramics.sav and then go to TRANSFORM → COMPUTE VARIABLE you can select the STRING function group in the right-hand box and you will see the STRING options in the box below (see Figure 5.11).

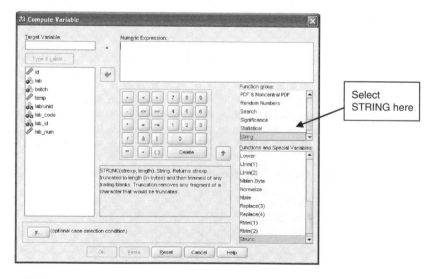

Figure 5.11

Using the drop-down, menu-driven method to manipulate string variables via these string options is fine, but remember to paste the commands into your syntax sheet. Syntax has an advantage – access to the SUBSTRING function. This is a sub-command which is only available through syntax and does not appear as a function in the dialogue box above, but it is a very useful sub-command which allows you to extract smaller strings from an existing one.

In ceramics.sav the variable **labrunid** has a letter, then three more characters, made up of two spaces and a number, or one space and two numbers, or of three numbers. Imagine we want to separate the letter from **labrunid** perhaps to use as a grouping variable. We may also want to retain the ID number separate to the group letter.

Syntax 5:8 Extracting elements of string variables using SUBSTRING

The following syntax will split a string variable, using the SPSS sample dataset ceramics.sav.

GET FILE='C:\Program Files\SPSSInc\SPSS16\Samples\ceramics.sav'.

COMMENT Here a substring is taken from string variable **labrunid**, starting from the character in position 1, and extracting just that one character; the first one, the letter
Note the new string variable is created first using the STRING command.
STRING lab_code (A1).
COMPUTE lab_code= SUBSTRING (labrunid,1,1).
EXECUTE.

COMMENT Here the substring is again from string variable **labrunid**, this time starting from the character in position 2, and for three characters inclusive, extracting the three numbers, as text.
Note the new string variable is created first using the STRING command.
STRING lab_id (A3).
COMPUTE lab_id=(SUBSTRING (labrunld,2,3)).
EXECUTE.

COMMENT An alternative way to manipulate the id number, separated from the letter part of the string, is to create a numerical not string version – here you need to specify that the string is being made into a NUMBER before the substring sub-command is given, followed by the format of the new numeric variable; here it is F8 (see brief explanation of formats in Syntax 2:2).
COMPUTE lab_num=NUMBER(SUBSTRING (labrunid,2,3), f8).
EXECUTE.

In the first two examples in Syntax 5:8 each first line creates a new string variable (see Syntax 5:1); all of the examples create (compute) the data by creating a sub-string from an existing string variable **labrunid**. Inside the brackets you list first the existing string variable, then the character position you wish the substring to start from, and then you finish with the number of characters you want to extract for the new substring.

Summary

String variables are an inevitable part of most researchers' data and where it is present the identification and formatting of string data is an important part of data management. Robust labelling, consistent use of codes, and the creation of new variables rather than overwriting original variables are key elements. Syntax can help with all of these processes. Where massive numbers of text entries require reducing down to a smaller set of meaningful categories, then SPSS can be used in tandem with Excel to make this a much more efficient process.

Useful Tips

- If a command appears in the Log but does not produce any 'action' when you run it you have probably omitted the EXECUTE command which is required before SPSS will perform some commands. Just type EXECUTE followed by a full stop and run that line.
- When numerical data has been imported into SPSS in text format, conversion is quick and accurate using the (CONVERT) keyword in the RECODE command.
- AUTOMATIC RECODE is an excellent way to convert text to numerical codes, even placing the original text in the value label for the number that has been used to recode it.

6

Syntax Involving Date and Time Variables

Some examples in this chapter work with SPSS sample dataset marketvalues.sav

This chapter will go through the syntax involved in manipulating the format of date and time variables, as well as using date and time calculations to derive new variables.

The chapter will explain: how SPSS handles time data; the difference between the main date/time syntax commands; the syntax for calculating time between events; converting between units of time (e.g. hours, days, months, etc.); how to output date variables in differing formats, how to extract the day of week, month of the year, etc., from a full date format.

'Simple' manipulation of date and time variables is often more complicated than for other numeric variables and, in recognition of this, SPSS has a special 'Date and Time Wizard'. We will use this later to produce initial syntax to PASTE into the syntax sheet and work with. In order for the SPSS program to be able to manipulate date and time variables it handles them in a method that (for a computer) is very straightforward even though it may seem slightly long-winded to us humans.

How SPSS Works with Dates and Time

SPSS stores all date and time values as the number of seconds since midnight on 14 October 1582. The rationale for the selection of this particular date is that it marks the start of the Gregorian calendar, and since this date we have been working to a 365 day year, with the exception of leap years which of course have 366 days.

To process data as date and time, SPSS requires the data to be in a date and time layout that it recognises. There are different ways to display date and time variables in data files, but their underlying format (of seconds since midnight on 14 October 1582) remains constant. If data is imported into SPSS in a different format, for example from Excel, you need it to be converted into the correct date/time format.

Good Practice

- Look through all date and time variables in the Variable View or with the DATA DICTIONARY (see Syntax 3:6) to identify whether they are in a date/time format.
- Ensure that all date and time variables are in the correct format.
- Try to use four digits to represent years (e.g. 2008 not 08).
- When years are represented by two digits (e.g. 63, 94, 27 or 08) ensure they are in the correct century (e.g. 1927 not 2027).

Date and Time Wizard

The date and time wizard can be accessed via the TRANSFORM drop-down menu. If you started this book at the beginning (which is not necessarily the case) you may recall how in Chapter 1 I outlined that the approach in this book is not an either/or approach to using SPSS with the drop-down, menu-driven method or syntax. Rather to use them alongside each other to optimise their usefulness and tailor the complexity to the level of the user's expertise. This allows you to take the most useful or suitable elements from the two methods of using SPSS. A good way to start creating syntax files is by using the PASTE function, and in time beginning to add to and amend commands. Date and time commands are an area where the commands can seem quite complicated and the paste facility from the Date and Time Wizard can be very useful indeed.

The SPSS sample dataset marketvalue.sav is used to illustrate the use of the Date and Time Wizard in a series of screenshots below. Figure 6.1 shows the options that are available.

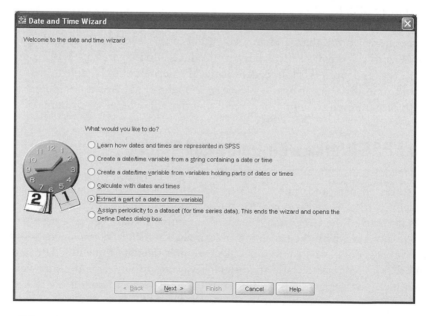

Figure 6.1

Next, Figure 6.2 shows the dialogue box presented if the option EXTRACT A PART OF A DATE OR TIME VARIABLE has been selected and the variable **sell-date** moved across as the Date or Time variable selected. Once you move a date or time variable across then the choice of unit to be extracted can be seen in Figure 6.2 in the drop-down element of the Unit to Extract option.

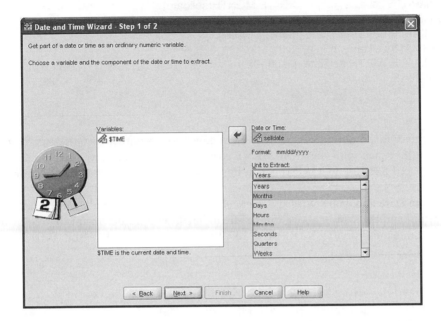

Figure 6.2

You have the option to PASTE commands into the syntax window rather than carried out immediately. This is not in the usual place with a PASTE button alongside the OK or Finish button, rather it is a separate EXECUTION section just above the Wizard's Finish button. This is shown with an arrow on Figure 6.3.

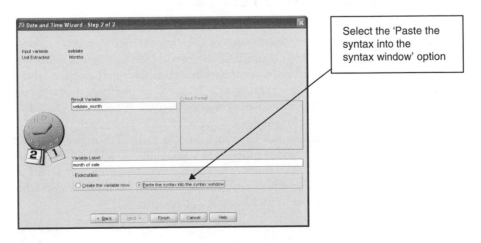

Figure 6.3

The syntax sheet then shows the syntax pasted in, which is usefully indicated as originating from the Date and Time Wizard.

```
* Date and Time Wizard: selldate_month.
COMPUTE selldate_month=XDATE.MONTH(selldate).
VARIABLE LABEL selldate_month "month of sale".
VARIABLE LEVEL selldate_month(SCALE).
FORMATS selldate_month(F8.0).
VARIABLE WIDTH selldate_month(8).
EXECUTE.
```

Note that, in this auto-generated syntax, comments start with an asterisk (see Syntax 2:6) rather than with the COMMENT command. This is perfectly acceptable and effective; I have used COMMENT in this book rather than an * for clarity for the reader.

The Date and Time Wizard is meticulous in its coverage of all elements of formatting and the syntax above can be streamlined, with no detriment, by removing the commands for the VARIABLE LEVEL and for the VARIABLE WIDTH as below.

```
COMPUTE selldate_month2=XDATE.MONTH(selldate).
VARIABLE LABEL selldate_month2 "month of sale".
FORMATS selldate_month2(F8.0).
EXECUTE.
```

Setting the Date and Time Formats

Chapter 5 showed how text representations of date information can be converted from string to date format (see Syntax 5:7). Now we will look at how date information that is in numeric format can be converted into date format. This may arise if date information is inputted or imported as a 'stream' of numbers, for example 23061995 (for 23 June 1995), as 19950623 or possibly even as 06231995 based on the American convention of writing dates.

The sample SPSS datasets do not have any date or time data in the incorrect format for us to reformat, so you can either: type some data into a blank SPSS dataview (230695, 25062001, 12021963, etc.); or run the syntax within Syntax 6:1 to create a datafile to practise the syntax on. This syntax can be downloaded from www.sagepub.co.uk/colliersyntax (see Resource 2, page 30).

Syntax 6:1 Converting date in numeric format to date format

COMMENT This will create a variable DATE_NUM with numbers to convert to date format or you can just type some into SPSS yourself.
DATA LIST LIST
  / date_num (F8).
BEGIN DATA
23061995
25062001
12021963
END DATA.

STRING date_txt (A9).
COMPUTE date_txt=STRING(date_num,F8.2).
EXECUTE.

COMPUTE date_day =NUMBER(SUBSTRING (date_txt,1,2), F8.0).
COMPUTE date_month =NUMBER(SUBSTRING (date txt,3,2), F8.0).
COMPUTE date_year =NUMBER(SUBSTRING (date_txt,5,4), F8.0).
EXECUTE.

COMPUTE date_2 = DATE.DMY (date_day,date_month,date_year).
FORMATS date_2(EDATE10).
VARIABLE LABELS date_2 'date_num converted into tdate format'.
EXECUTE.

DELETE VARABLES date_txt date_day date_month date_year.

The first set of commands DATA LIST LIST and BEGIN DATA creates the variable **date_num** with numbers suitable to convert to date format.

The **STRING** command creates a string variable **date_txt**.

The **COMPUTE** command then converts the data in **date_num** into a string format using the **STRING** function and puts it into the string variable **date_txt** (see Syntax 5:1). This step is required to enable the partitioning of the data via the **SUBSTRING** function (see Syntax 5:8).

There are three **COMPUTE** commands, one each to create a variable for day, for month and for year using the **NUMBER** and **SUBSTRING** functions (see Syntax 5:8).

The last **COMPUTE** command creates a new date variable **date_2** with the date format specified **DATE.DMY** and created from the three previously created string variables **(date_day,date_month,date_year)**. This will make the date in date format from the three variables above, and label it with its origin.

The **DELETE VARABLES** command will delete the interim string variable, and the three day, month and year variables as they are only temporary steps. This is optional, it just depends whether you prefer a 'comprehensive' dataset or a 'tidy' one.

While this syntax looks very long-winded it runs in a second, and is ideal for your syntax library, saved in a syntax sheet called something like date_numerical_to_ date_format.sps.

To use it in the future you just need to copy it into the project's syntax file, put in the correct name of your numerical date variable instead of **date_num** and the desired name for your new date formatted date instead of **date_2**, run it and, before you know it, you will have the date in the correct format.

Sometimes you may have dates entered as two-digit years not four-digit years (e.g. 63, 94, 27 or 08). This is fine as long as your years do not extend over more than 100 years; you simply have to ensure that the century allocated to the two digits is correct. SPSS has a default setting of 69 years prior to and 30 after the current year for two-digit numbers, but you can change that in the drop-down menu settings option via EDIT → OPTION → DATA shown in Figure 6.4.

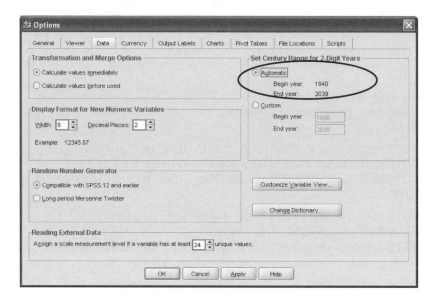

Figure 6.4

You can opt to set your own custom settings using this dialogue box. These remain the settings for all datasets opened after this time until you change it again. Alternatively you can use syntax to specify the years you wish the timespan to cover. Again, this setting will remain in place until you change it.

Syntax 6:2 Setting the span for two-digit years using SET EPOCH

SET EPOCH = 1990.

This single-line command **SET EPOCH** allows you to specify the earliest two-digit year to be recognised, and will automatically allocate all two-digit year dates to the 100 years that include and follow the year stated in the command. The command **= 1990.** is completed with a full stop.

To reset back to the Automatic setting is simply a case of running the single command line below.
SET EPOCH = Automatic.

If your data has years spanning more than 100 years then use of the four-digit year is required, not just because of SPSS but for common-sense reasons. How else will you know whether 12 May 04 is referring to 1904 or 2004? You may know

now, but the datafile should be set up for others also to be able to access the data meaningfully. Also, if you need to return to the data after a long break then data still needs to 'make sense' to you.

Other factors also affect how you want the data to be displayed including: personal preference; matching to existing variables/datasets; and local convention. How the date and time look in SPSS will depend on the setting used. SPSS has many options allowing you to display the dates: in American convention (mm/dd/yyyy) or the European convention (dd/mm/yyyy); using numbers for the month or using letter abbreviations; with two-digit years or four-digit years; and so forth.

ADATE is for the American date format, EDATE is for the European format. Numbers indicate the number of characters in the displayed date. ADATE10 has 10 characters: 2 for the month, 1 for the /, 2 for the day, 1 more for the second /, and four for the year; ADATE8 has 2 for the year; EDATE has the same numbers (10 or 8). DATE uses three letters for the month (JAN, FEB, etc.) so DATE needs to be DATE11 or DATE 9 for four- and two-digit year display formats, as the month needs 3 characters not 2. For a full list of options look up FORMATS in the *Command Syntax Reference* guide (see the Resources section, page 30).

Extracting Month, Day of Week, Year

On occasion you may wish to identify which day of the week is being referred to in a date. This is quite a simple task using XDATE (think of it as eXtracting part of a DATE).

Syntax 6:3 Creating a new variable with the day of the week from a date variable using COMPUTE and the XDATE function

The following syntax will extract the day of the week from **selldate** as found in the SPSS sample dataset marketvalues.sav.

GET FILE='C:\Program Files\SPSSInc\SPSS16\Samples\marketvalues.sav'.

COMPUTE dayofwk = XDATE.WKDAY(selldate).

VARIABLE LABEL "dayofwk the day that the sale took place".
VALUE LABELS dayofwk 1'Sun' 2'Mon' 3'Tue' 4'Wed' 5'Thu' 6'Fri' 7'Sat'.
EXECUTE.

The **GET FILE** command specifies the datafile to be opened.

The **COMPUTE** command names the variable to be created **dayofwk** followed by an equals sign and then the **XDATE.WKDAY** function which extracts the weekday from the variable enclosed in brackets **(selldate).**. The weekdays are returned as a numeric value of 1 to 7, with day 1 being Sunday. This allocation of numbers is set by SPSS automatically. The full stop follows this to complete the COMPUTE command.

In accordance with good practice I have then labelled the new variable and the values (see Syntax 3:2 and Syntax 3:3).

The **EXECUTE.** command then actions the preceding syntax commands.

OPTIONS

You can use a FORMATS command to format the extracted variable with a date format which shows the day of the week. (For some reason, on my PC this needs to be viewed without using labels.)

COMPUTE dayofwk2 = XDATE.WKDAY(selldate).
FORMATS dayofwk2(WKDAY2).
VARIABLE LABEL dayofweek2 "the day that the sale took place".
EXECUTE.

   Likewise you can retrieve the year or the month from a date by using **XDATE.YEAR** or **XDATE.MONTH**. You can also find out which quarter (1–4) or day of the year (1–366), or week of the year (1–53) a date is in by using **XDATE.QUARTER**, **XDATE.JDAY** or **XDATE.WEEK**.

Calculations Including Both Date and Time

It is not uncommon to need to calculate the time interval between two dates and/or times in separate variables. Straightforward calculations do not involve both date and time, but more complex ones do. There is not a sample SPSS dataset which has two date variables and two time variables, so we need to create a datafile. You can either: type some data into a blank SPSS dataview; or run a syntax, as below, to create a suitable datafile. This syntax can be downloaded from www.sagepub.co.uk/colliersyntax (see Resoure 2, page 30).

COMMENT This will create two date variables (date_buy & date_sell) and two time variables (time_buy & time_sell) and save as a file date_time.sav.
DATA LIST LIST
    / date_buy(EDATE10) time_buy(TIME) date_sell(EDATE10) time_sell(TIME).
BEGIN DATA
12-Sep-08 12:25 15-Oct-08 13:30
03-Aug-07 22:10 04-Aug-07 06:40
04-Jun-06 11:05 04-Jun-06 15:05
21-May-94 06:45 25-May-94 08:20
END DATA.
SAVE OUTFILE='C:\Documents and Settings\User\My Documents\date_time.sav'.

The syntax below can be pasted using the TRANSFORM → COMPUTE VARIABLES drop-down, menu-driven method, selecting the DATEDIF function from the function list.

Syntax 6:4 Calculating a date or time interval using COMPUTE and the DATEDIFF function

This works on the SPSS dataset date_time.sav created from the syntax above.

GET FILE ='C:\Documents and Settings\User\My Documents\date_time.sav'.

COMPUTE Days=DATEDIFF(date_sell, date_buy, "days").
VARIABLE LABEL Days "days between buying and selling".
EXECUTE.

The **GET FILE** command specifies the data file to be opened.

The **COMPUTE** command names the variable to be created **Days** followed by an equals sign and then the **DATEDIF** function which calculates the difference between the two date variable enclosed in brackets **(date_sell, date_buy, 'days').** and reports this difference in the units stated within the brackets.

The full stop follows this to complete the **COMPUTE** command.

In accordance with good practice I have then labelled the new variable (see Syntax 3:2).

The **EXECUTE.** command then actions the preceding syntax commands.

Additionally, you can calculate the number of hours or minutes that have elapsed using a similar single line syntax to that above, although this will only work accurately if there are no days to take into account in the time interval. In our data, above, to find the exact time elapsed using the hours/minute information, you cannot just carry out a calculation on the **time_buy** and **time_sell** variables because this will not take into account the number of days that have also elapsed. You first need to make a new variable which contains all the date and time information for the two timepoints, that is for buying and for selling.

Syntax 6:5 Creating a variable with both date & time using COMPUTE and then FORMATS

This works on the SPSS dataset date_time.sav created from the syntax above.

GET FILE ='C:\Documents and Settings\User\My Documents\date_time.sav'.

COMPUTE date_time_buy = date_buy + time_buy.
FORMATS date_time_buy (datetime).

COMPUTE date_time_sell=date_sell + time_sell.
FORMATS date_time_sell (datetime).

EXECUTE.

The **GET FILE** command specifies the datafile to be opened.

Each **COMPUTE** command makes a new variable (e.g. **date_time_buy**) by adding a date and a time variable together (e.g. **date_buy + time_buy.**).

The **FORMATS** command correctly formats the newly created variables in an SPSS format which allows both the date and the time element **(datetime).** to be included.

Using the datafile created at the beginning of this section, date_time.sav, Syntax 6:5 will make new variables containing all the date and time information for the two timepoints, buying and selling. Note that this syntax relies on the variables both being in recognised DATE formats already (as ours are).

Once you have the date and time in one date formatted variable you can carry out a simple COMPUTE command to take one timepoint from another. However, because SPSS stores all date and time information as the number of seconds since midnight on October 14, 1582 SPSS will return the difference between the two timepoints as seconds. For many time calculations, seconds are not the most useful measure, so you just divide by 60 to get the time interval in minutes, by 3600 (60 × 60) to get the time interval in hours, by 86,400 (60 × 60 × 24) to get the time in days, and so forth. See an example below of syntax calculating time in hours.

COMMENT the syntax below will give the time difference between buying and selling in hours.
COMPUTE time_owned=(date_time_sell – date_time_buy)/3600.
EXECUTE.

Note that because the format of the computation is the default numeric (F8.2), the resulting data from this will be presented as units and their decimal parts, so 1 hour 30 minutes will be 1.5 not 1:30.

Find a Date/Time from One Date/Time Variable and One 'Duration' Variable

Datasets may have variables containing data about duration (period of time, time intervals) which is entered as a numeric value (e.g. number of days or hours). To calculate a new date or time from a date variable and a 'duration variable' you need to identify the unit of time that the 'duration variable' is in and whether you wish to add or subtract the value from the specified date/time variable.

Using the SPSS sample dataset marketvalues.sav it is possible to show how to use a date variable and a duration variable in order to calculate a new date variable. The variable **selldate** is the date that a property has been sold, and **marktime** is the number of days that the property was on the market (our 'duration variable'). We can use these to calculate the date that the property went onto the market.

Syntax 6:6 Creating a new date from a date variable & 'duration' variable using COMPUTE command and the DATESUM function

The SPSS sample dataset marketvalues.sav is used.

```
GET FILE='C:\Program Files\SPSSInc\SPSS16\Samples\marketvalues.sav'.
COMPUTE market_date=DATESUM(selldate, -marktime, "days").

VARIABLE LABEL market_date "sell date minus days on market".
FORMATS market_date(ADATE10).
EXECUTE.
```

The **GET FILE** command specifies the data file to be opened.

The **COMPUTE** command makes a new variable **market_date** by taking a date **sell-date** and subtracting a duration variable from it **-marktime** the unit of which is indicated within the brackets **"days")**..The subtraction element occurs because the duration variable **marktime** is preceded by a minus sign. You can test this by re-running the syntax but omitting the minus sign and you will see that it adds the days onto **sell_date** instead.

The **(FORMATS market_date(ADATE10).** command correctly formats the newly created variable in a standard SPSS date format.

Note that in the example above **marktime**, the duration variable is in 'days' so the calculation is also in days. Acceptable units are years, quarters, months, weeks, days, hours, minutes, seconds – just select the one that is appropriate for your duration variable and amend the unit specified in the formula. As with other date/time calculations the value returned has an underlying date/time value expressed as a number of seconds. To display the value as a date, an appropriate format has been assigned to the variable. Because the dates are displayed according to the American style mm/dd/yyyy in this dataset, for consistency I have selected ADATE10 (American date) in the FORMATS.

Summary

At a core level, SPSS treats date and time variables simply as very large numbers – the number of seconds since the beginning of the Gregorian calendar, but thankfully SPSS is able to display the date in a much more usable format for its users. See below for a short bit of syntax which can be run to illustrate this point, converting a given

```
DATA LIST LIST
    / kickoff(f20).
BEGIN DATA
13495586400
END DATA.
FORMATS kickoff (datetime).
```

number of seconds to a date and time format that we can all easily understand. In this example, 13,495,586,400 seconds is converted to 10 June 2010 at 22:00 GMT which happens to be the date and time that the FIFA webpage gives for the 2010 World Cup tournament kickoff.

SPSS can manipulate and analyse dates and times as long as the information is inputted correctly and is formatted as date and time enabling SPSS to work with this 'number of seconds since the beginning of the Gregorian calendar' system of treating both dates and times as numerical data.

Useful Tips

- Date and time calculations can exercise the mind and try your patience. They are therefore ideal for recording in your syntax library when you get them right.
- Use the Date and Time Wizard (under TRANSFORM) to begin with – read the pasted syntax carefully so that you understand it and can adapt it.
- Use the *Command Syntax Reference* guide to see options available for each command.
- Remember that all date and time variables have seconds as the underlying unit. If you carry out a transformation or calculation and get a really large number (like millions and millions), then it *may* just be the format that you need to correct rather than anything being fundamentally wrong with the transformation or calculation.

7

Syntax for Manipulating Numeric Variables

All examples in this chapter work with SPSS sample datasets
nhis2000_subset.sav
satisf.sav

This chapter will explain the syntax commands that enable the user to recode from existing data variables into both existing and new variables, to count values in existing variables, and to compute new variables. Some of the options available to manipulate and compute numerical data will be explored, but the main focus will be on the principles required to: carry out the various ways of carrying out *basic* mathematical tasks; select between similar commands; apply calculations to specific cases only; and use some less common but very handy commands. This chapter will reiterate the value in using syntax as it clearly records how data variables are created and enables a data audit trail.

Variables that are created from existing data in the dataset rather than being directly entered are known as *derived* variables.

SPSS is a powerful program for the manipulation of numerical data. When you have a datafile with raw data in it, SPSS can be used to manipulate the data for you rather than you manipulating the data by hand first and then entering it into the program in that processed state. The computer is able to do this much more consistently than a person can. As a user of SPSS you will have probably realised the benefits of using SPSS's powerful facilities to do such tasks through the drop-down, menu-driven method of using the program. Using syntax to support you in carrying out these tasks can increase the efficiency and robustness of your data handling. Whichever method of SPSS is used, if we input the correct commands the program will get it right. The advantage of syntax is that even if we input an incorrect command and get it wrong, it is done in an auditable way where we can track back exactly what has been done and where we went wrong. Of course, even if you do not use syntax fully it will be auditable if you are using the Journal and Log correctly (see Chapter 1, pages 2–8). If you have skipped these two elements of SPSS use they are invaluable and should be read.

Good Practice

- Always retain a copy of the original data.
- Enter original raw data when possible, manipulating or transforming later as required.
- Do not overwrite the original variable, instead when transforming or recoding variables create new variables and label original and recoded ones accordingly.
- Provide evidence of reasons, processes and outcomes through the COMMENT facility, which enables you to write notes into the syntax.
- Save syntax files used for routine data manipulation and build a syntax library – you will need them again.
- When creating new variables (e.g. recoded or derived ones) then name them in a way that 'ties' them to the old one (e.g. **q1** to **q1_recode** or **q1** to **new_q1**).

Basic Principles to Observe in Transforming Data and Creating Variables

You may have noted that the first two points in the Good Practice box are exactly the same as for Chapter 4. This is not an oversight or a sloppy copy and paste error – it is that these two points are so important when you are altering any data. You can have some really good data, but then inadvertently 'mess it up' and risk getting 'garbage out' despite starting with good data that could help identify or explain significant issues.

Whichever method of using SPSS you use, drop-down, menu-driven or syntax, if you have not kept a copy of the original data as it was entered from the raw source (before you have modified it) then it is much more difficult to be able to go back and check should you need to (or if you suspect that everything is not as it should be, or indeed if you are asked to go through data audit processes or challenged on your findings).

Recoding or transforming variables into the existing ones rather than setting up new ones can leave you open to mistakes, such as recoding a variable that does not need it because it has already been recoded and ending up with an erroneous set of data as a result. To give an example, imagine you have a survey looking at quality of life with some items that are phrased negatively and some positively. All the responses are given on a five-point scale rating responses from 'always' to 'never'. To compile the overall quality of life the scoring for some items will need reversing (some will have 1 to 5 for 'always' to 'never' and others will have values from 5 to 1 for 'always' to 'never'). You could do this by hand when entering the data, remembering which items to reverse as you go. However, this method is risky in terms of potential human error. Instead, you could enter them all as 1 to 5, and then reverse the 'negatively' phrased ones. If you carry out the reversing through the TRANSFORM function but put the reversed items back into the original variable, then it is possible to accidentally carry this out more than once. Imagine a situation where you reverse the scores for the items, then at a later data for whatever reason (bad memory, two people working on the data, returning to it having forgotten what had been done, adding new cases, etc.) someone returns to the data and reverses the variable scores again. This will render the data completely inaccurate and thus useless (or worse than useless), so it is safer to recode into a new variable and to leave the original variable intact.

I find it useful to name any new derived variable in a way that links it to the original variable (e.g. **q1** transformed into **q1_recode** or **new_q1**). I would also suggest that the label of the old variable is amended in some way if appropriate (e.g. 'do not use this **q1**, items not reversed, use **new_q1**').

Many risks in transforming data are reduced by recoding into a new variable and others are reduced further by using syntax. When transforming data, the use of syntax to code new variables is by far the most robust and safe combination of actions.

Advantages of Using Syntax

One of the advantages of using syntax is the ability to audit what has happened with your data. Furthermore, if you have the transformation commands stored in syntax (or if you can retrieve them from the Journal or from earlier Logs), you will be able to create a 'derived variables' syntax file to re-run and which will re-create all the new variables.

For each project/datafile, it is helpful to create a 'derived variables' syntax file (e.g. projectx_derived.sps). You can start by extracting the commands from the Journal or from previous Logs and pasting them onto a single syntax sheet. A 'derived variables' syntax file can also be created as you carry out the initial transformations, either via pasting the commands as you go, or (once you get to be more experienced) through a combination of pasting commands as you go and writing syntax of your own. Once you have created and saved a 'derived variables' syntax file, it is possible just to re-run the syntax to derive any variables once again if needed, perhaps if new cases, or new data, become available. Fully annotating such a file (using the COMMENT command) will increase its reuse and the 'transferability' of the commands.

Deleting Variables

It may seem strange to begin a section on creating new variables by informing you of the syntax to delete variables. However, to ensure that all the data in a new variable is refreshed at the same point it is good practice to delete previous versions of any derived variables before you re-run their creation. This syntax is best embedded in the syntax file; before each set of commands to create the variable, first put in a command line to delete the existing version of the derived variable. To delete variables is a simple one-line command which will work on the active dataset.

Syntax 7:1 Deleting variable with the DELETE VARIABLES command

The SPSS sample dataset nhis2000_subset.sav was used.

GET FILE='C:\Program Files\SPSSInc\SPSS16\Samples\nhis2000_subset.sav'.

DELETE VARIABLES region sex.

The **GET FILE** command opens the datafile if not already open.
The **DELETE VARIABLES** command is then followed by a list of the variables to be deleted **region sex** after which there is a full stop to complete the command.

Note that even though the variable names are in capitals in the dataset provided, SPSS syntax ignores whether variable names are typed in uppercase or lowercase. I have put them in lowercase to maintain the convention of commands and subcommands in uppercase, variable names in lowercase.

WARNING – if you run the DELETE VARIABLES command, SPSS will assume that you know what you are doing and you will not be asked whether you are sure you want to do this; SPSS will just delete as instructed.

Routine/Simple Data Manipulation

When we carry out manipulation of numeric variables using the drop-down menu-driven method, we usually do this through the TRANSFORM menu. COMPUTE commands can be accessed this way to carry out simple arithmetical operations upon the data, for example to calculate a mean value for a number of related variables (e.g. average weight of all piglets delivered to a sow), to sum values from specified items from psychometric measures (e.g. items on a quality of life inventory) or related data (e.g. salary 1 plus salary 2 to arrive at joint income).

To begin with, it may be best to obtain the commands to transform your data, carry out calculations, and so on, by pasting them from the drop-down menu. You will see that they begin with the main commands COMPUTE, COUNT or RECODE.

COMPUTE

There are many transformation expressions that can be used with COMPUTE. Transformation expressions include numeric expressions (e.g. addition, division), arithmetic functions (e.g. square root, base logarithms), statistical functions (e.g. mean, variance), date and time functions (e.g. date values, time intervals), string functions (e.g. concatenation, trim), logical operands (e.g. and, or) and missing value functions (e.g. system missing, user missing).

Full details of transformation expressions can be found in the *Command Syntax Reference* guide or through use of the F1 key while in the syntax editor (see the Resources section, pages 30–32).

Summing Across Variables

A common data manipulation requirement is to add things up, to 'sum' them. This is where it is very useful to be aware of how SPSS can treat data differently depending on which of two possible 'methods' is used to add things up.

We will consider a very simple example of adding two salaries together to calculate joint income. The two salaries are better entered separately whenever that information is available – the two main reasons being that adding it yourself before entry can increase the scope for human error, but also because at a later date you may want to carry out secondary analysis of the data for a different purpose where knowing the two individual incomes is of value.

The COMPUTE command is required here and there are two alternatives:

(1) using simple addition, which will add up the two variables only where all variables to be added in the formula are present;

```
COMPUTE joint_sal_add =salary1 + salary2.
EXECUTE.
```

(2) using the SUM sub-command, which will add up the two variables regardless of whether any variables to be added in the formula are missing.

```
COMPUTE joint_sal_sum =SUM(salary1, salary2).
EXECUTE.
```

Either way you should add the variable label and if you create this variable using the drop-down, menu-driven method, you might need to put the method of calculation in the variable label so that when reviewing the data you would know how this has been calculated. However, this would make the variable labels much more 'long-winded'. Syntax allows you instead to add a COMMENT with as much detail as you like in the output and syntax file (see Syntax 2:7). The COMMENT command can permit useful additional text to supplement the commands in the syntax file showing how the variable was made.

In the example below, the SPSS sample dataset nhis2000_subset.sav is used and three different 'activity' frequency variables are totalled so that an overall exercise score is calculated. There are some missing values in each of the variables.

Syntax 7:2 Adding together values in several variables using the COMPUTE command and using addition

The SPSS sample dataset nhis2000_subset.sav was used.

GET FILE='C:\Program Files\SPSSInc\SPSS16\Samples\nhis2000_subset.sav'.

COMMENT using addition to calculate the total exercise will give fewer cases but they will all have had complete data.

COMPUTE tot_ex_v1 = vigfreqw + modfreqw + strfreqw.
EXECUTE.

VARIABLE LABELS tot_ex_v1 'total exercise in last week, complete cases'.

The GET FILE command opens the datafile if not already open.

The COMMENT command allows extra information to be recorded in the Journal and in the output viewer.

The **COMPUTE** command is followed by the variable that will result from the computation. Here it is a new variable called **tot_ex_v1**, followed by an equals sign and then the method of computation **vigfreqw + modfreqw + strfreqw.** and completed with a full stop.

The **EXECUTE.** command then actions the preceding syntax.

In accordance with good practice I have then labelled the new variable (see Syntax 3:2).

Remember, when the addition sign is used to add up the values in several variables it will only add up the values when all of the variables listed for totalling are present. Sometimes it is important for your analysis to have a value for each data point in a series, at other times it is not. It is up to you as a researcher to decide in advance which of the methods is most suitable for you to use. When the inclusion of cases with missing data is acceptable, then the SUM function may be suitable.

Syntax 7:3 Adding together values in several variables using the COMPUTE command and the SUM function

The SPSS sample dataset nhis2000_subset.sav was used.

GET FILE='C:\Program Files\SPSSInc\SPSS16\Samples\nhis2000_subset.sav'.

COMMENT using the SUM function to calculate the total exercise will give more cases but will be based on incomplete data.

COMPUTE tot_ex_v2 = SUM(vigfreqw, modfreqw, strfreqw).
EXECUTE.

VARIABLE LABELS tot_ex_v2 'total exercise in last week, all cases'.

The explanation for this syntax example is pretty much the same as in Syntax 7:2 but on the **COMPUTE** command line the **SUM** function is used after the equals sign.

COMPUTE tot_ex_v2 = SUM(vigfreqw, modfreqw, strfreqw).

When the **SUM** function is used, the variables are enclosed within brackets and each separated by a comma.

You will see that with both methods a variable label has been added. Syntax also gives the possibility to expand on the rationale for the choice of method of calculation in a COMMENT (see Syntax 2:7) with as much detail as you like. This is then available in both the output and syntax file.

Creating Categories from Continuous Numerical Data

You may need to create categories from continuous numerical data, such as age bands from continuous ages. There are two ways to do this. The drop-down menu accesses these through TRANSFORM and then either COMPUTE VARIABLE or RECODE. If you paste from these methods you will see that the syntax pasted from the drop-down menu TRANSFORM → RECODE starts with the command RECODE, but that the syntax pasted from the TRANSFORM → COMPUTE VARIABLE drop-down menu does not start with a COMPUTE command, instead using the IF command.

The logical operator **IF** allows data to be given a value providing it meets specified criteria. When the criteria are met a value is allocated. In the example below the age bands are created from the continuous age variable. The variable should match exactly the existing variable **age_cat** already in the dataset.

Syntax 7:4 Use of the IF command to create categories from continuous data

The SPSS sample dataset nhis2000_subset.sav was used.

GET FILE='C:\Program Files\SPSSInc\SPSS16\Samples\nhis2000_subset.sav'.

IF (age_p >= 18 & age_p <25) age_band= 1.
IF (age_p >= 25 & age_p <45) age_band = 2.
IF (age_p >= 45 & age_p <65) age_band = 3.
IF (age_p >= 65) age_band = 4.
EXECUTE.

VARIABLE LABELS age_band 'Age category'.
VALUE LABELS age_band 1 '18-24' 2 '25-44' 3 '45-64' 4 '65+'.

The **GET FILE** command opens the datafile if not already open.

The **IF** command is followed by criteria (variables and values) that need to be met **(age_p >= 18 & age_p <25)**, followed by the name of the variable to be affected **age_band** which in turn is followed by an equals sign and then the value **= 1.** assigned for when the criteria are met.

Each **IF** command requires the criteria, the affected variable, the new variable and the outcome, and each **IF** command must finish with a full stop.

The **EXECUTE.** command then actions the preceding syntax commands.

In accordance with good practice I have then labelled the new variable (see Syntax 3:2).

Syntax can really help speed up your categorisation. Rather than having to keep going through TRANSFORM and then COMPUTE VARIABLE, enter the value, then click through the IF section, set the conditions each time and then press OK; in syntax you can just type the lines out. Indeed, rather than type each line out one after the other it is quicker to get the first line correct and then copy and paste as many times as you need, just altering the criteria for each set of conditions and for each new derived variable value. Attention to detail is required whatever method you use.

Example of Usefulness

It is very annoying when you look at your data in a newly created variable and realise that you have made a mistake. For example, when I was setting the conditionals for Syntax 7:4 I used the following conditional formulae:

age_p >= 18 & age_p <24,

age_p >= 25 & age_p <44,

age_p >= 45 & age_p <64

age_p >= 65.

I then looked at the resulting data in the Data Editor View and quickly realised that I had missing values, which I should not have had. I immediately saw that, rather worryingly, I had made a beginner's error and had given no value for 'borderline' ages 24, 44, 64. Anyway, I quickly returned to the syntax, amended the error in my formulae, deleted the **age_band** variable that I had just created and then re-ran the amended syntax. The data appeared in the newly derived variable, all present and correct. To do this with the drop-down menu method would have been much more time-consuming and much more annoying.

The second way to create categories uses RECODE. Using the drop-down, menu-driven method then RECODE is much quicker than accessing IF via the COMPUTE menu. However, there is one disadvantage – you cannot use 'or equal to' alongside a 'greater than' or 'less than'. This means that a value with decimal places can slip through the borders if you use whole number criteria (18 to 24, 25 to 44, 45 to 64, >65 would miss 24.5, 44.6, 64.8, etc.). One solution is to add a couple of decimals in your conditional values as below in Syntax 7:5 (18 to 24.99, 25 to 44.99, 45 to 64.99, >65). The danger then arises when you have existing values with more decimal places (such as if age is calculated from date of birth and date of survey) and it is still possible for cases to slip through the (narrow) boundaries. Again the choice of which method to use is based on your knowledge of the data format and source.

In the example below the age bands are created from the continuous age variable and should match exactly the existing variable **age_cat**.

Syntax 7:5 Use of the RECODE command to create categories from continuous data

The SPSS sample dataset nhis2000_subset.sav was used.

GET FILE='C:\Program Files\SPSSInc\SPSS16\Samples\nhis2000_subset.sav'.

RECODE age_p (18 thru 24.99=1) (25 thru 44.99=2) (45 thru 64.99=3) (65 thru Highest=4) INTO age_band_v2.
EXECUTE.

VARIABLE LABELS age_band_v2 'Age bands created using recode'.
VALUE LABELS age_band_v2 1 '18-24' 2 '25-44' 3 '45-64' 4 '65+'.

There is a single **RECODE** command line. Even though it 'flows' over two lines on this page, there is just one command line. The command is followed by the existing variable that you wish to recode **age_p**, followed by a list of criteria and resulting recode values, each set within brackets (e.g. **(18 thru 24.99=1)**).

At the end of the list is the sub-command **INTO** followed by the name of the variable where the new derived values are to go. The full stop follows this to complete the **RECODE** command.

This syntax example has the same GET FILE, EXECUTE, VARIABLE LABELS and VALUE LABELS commands as in Syntax 7:4.

ERROR ALERT
As mentioned in the ERROR ALERT for Syntax 5:2 the **INTO** keyword is very important. If you do not add this keyword followed by a new derived variable name **INTO age_band_v2** then the recode will still go ahead, but will overwrite your existing variable **age_p**. This is the same as selecting TRANSFORM → RECODE INTO SAME VARIABLES instead of selecting TRANSFORM → RECODE INTO DIFFERENT VARIABLES.

RECODE is a useful command for single variables, but is particularly helpful when large numbers of variables require the reversing of their scores. Many surveys and measures have a standard set of responses (e.g. strongly agree, somewhat agree, neutral, somewhat agree, strongly agree) and within their survey they alter the phrasing of the questions so that for some questions a 'strongly agree' response would indicate for example a high level of satisfaction and for other questions it would indicate a very low level of satisfaction (compare, 'The staff dealt with me politely' or 'I had to wait a long time before the assistant dealt with my query').

In SPSS sample dataset satisf.sav the last six variables all have the same five response options (strongly negative, somewhat negative, neutral, somewhat positive, strongly positive). In Syntax 7:6 imagine that we need to reverse the values for three of these variables. Syntax can do this in one go. The explanations in this example are incorporated in the example itself, via COMMENT command lines.

Syntax 7:6 Use of the RECODE to reverse scoring for several variables at once

The SPSS sample dataset satisf.sav was used.

GET FILE='C:\Program Files\SPSSInc\SPSS16\Samples\satisf.sav'.

COMMENT List all the variables to be identically recoded, then put the criteria and recode values in brackets; then put the INTO keyword followed by the names for the new recoded variables – in exactly the same order as the partnered uncoded variables.

RECODE price service quality
  (1=5) (2=4) (3=3) (4=2) (5=1) (SYSMIS=SYSMIS) (ELSE=Copy) INTO price_r
service_r quality_r.
EXECUTE.

VARIABLE LABELS
  price_r 'price reversed'
  service_r 'service reversed'
  quality_r 'quality reversed'.

VALUE LABELS price_r service_r quality_r
  1 'Strongly Negative'
  2 'Somewhat Negative'
  3 'Neutral'
  4 'Somewhat Positive'
  5 'Strongly Positive'.

COMMENT if the original variables should not be used it is a good idea to relabel them.

VARIABLE LABELS
    price 'Do not use - use price_r'
    service 'Do not use - use service_r'
    quality 'Do not use - use quality_r'.

Counting Data Values

Sometimes you may need to count the number of times a certain value is reported within a number of variables. For example, you may want to know how often your 'neutral' response was ticked for a given question or you may want to know how many times individuals selected extreme responses on items using a five-point response scale. We can do these things using the COUNT command. You can access the COUNT command via the drop-down menu TRANSFORM → COUNT VALUES WITHIN CASES and then paste the command into syntax.

Syntax 7:7 Counting the occurrence of a specified value using the COUNT command

The SPSS sample dataset satisf.sav was used.

GET FILE='C:\Program Files\SPSSInc\SPSS16\Samples\satisf.sav'.

COUNT neutral = price numitems org service quality overall (3).
EXECUTE.

VARIABLE LABELS neutral 'number of neutral answers in price numitems org service quality overall'.

The GET FILE command opens the datafile if not already open.

The **COUNT** command is followed by the name of the derived variable you are creating **neutral**, an equals sign and then a list of all the variables that you want including the count **price numitems org service quality overall**; this is followed, in brackets, by the value to be counted **(3).** and the command is completed with a full stop.

The **EXECUTE.** command then actions the preceding syntax commands.

Syntax 7:8 Counting the occurrence of multiple values using the COUNT command

The SPSS sample dataset satisf.sav was used.

COMMENT To count more than one discrete value you need to list the variables of interest followed, in brackets, by the first value to be counted – then list the variables again followed, in brackets, by the next value to be counted, and so forth.

COUNT extremes = price numitems org service quality overall (1)
  price numitems org service quality overall (5).
EXECUTE.

VARIABLE LABELS extremes 'number of extreme answers in price numitems org service quality overall'.

COMMENT To count using a range of values you need to list the variables of interest followed in brackets by the range to be counted.
COMMENT you can obtain counts for a range of values between specified values (X THRU X), from a specified value and above (X THRU highest) or from a specified value and below (lowest thru X). Note that the lowest value must come first for all of the range options.

COUNT moderates = price numitems org service quality overall (2 thru 4).
EXECUTE.

VARIABLE LABELS moderates 'number answering 2, 3 or 4 in price numitems org service quality overall'.

You can count system missing values or system and user missing values by putting the appropriate text as the 'value to be counted' within the brackets, namely (SYSMIS) or (MISSING). You can also count more than one discrete value, or can count values within a range.

Summary

Use of syntax for manipulation of numeric variables can begin with the drop-down, menu-driven method and then, via the PASTE function, it can be incorporated into a 'derived variables' syntax file for any given project. Once you have created and saved a 'derived variables' syntax file, you are able just re-run the syntax to derive the variables once again as needed, perhaps if new cases, or new data, become available. A 'derived variables' syntax file is efficient, provides a reliable repeatable pattern of variable creation, and allows a clear audit trail of variable creation.

Useful Tips

- To begin with, use the drop-down menu-driven method to transform variables and use the PASTE button to put them in a syntax file.
- Create a derived variables syntax file for a project to enable re-running later.
- Save syntax files for transformations that were very complicated or for some reason or other took you a lot of time/effort/attempts to get right – you may need them again. Add to your syntax library.
- For categorising data it may be best to use RECODE for discrete values and to use IF for numbers with many decimal places.
- If a command appears in the Log but does not produce any 'action' when you run it you have probably just omitted the EXECUTE command that is required before SPSS will perform COMPUTE, RECODE and COUNT commands. Just type EXECUTE followed by a full stop and run that line.

8

Syntax for Data Exploration

All examples in this chapter will use the following SPSS sample dataset stroke_valid.sav

This chapter will explain the syntax commands that enable the user to carry out basic data exploration, including frequencies, descriptives and cross-tabulations.

Data exploration is a process that underpins our understanding of the data obtained during our research. You can go straight to the inferential analysis, carrying out your correlations, ANOVAs and regressions, but I believe that exploratory data analysis should be carried out first. Descriptive statistics and graphs not only help you 'get a feel' for the data but also help you to understand whether parametric or non-parametric tests are appropriate. The syntax commands to assist you in creating graphs are covered in Chapter 10, but you will probably be carrying out the descriptive statistics alongside graphs.

This chapter will not go into the selection of the 'correct' statistics for your data. This book is not intended to teach you about statistics; it is written for newcomers to syntax, not newcomers to statistics or SPSS. Thus, there are assumptions made (1) that readers are already experienced and familiar with statistics and also (2) that readers are experienced and familiar with the drop-down, menu-driven methods of using SPSS.

In the examples below, there are some options which are available via syntax that are not available via the drop-down menu options. These are identified by the following shaded text only available through syntax.

Good Practice
- Base your analysis on the data analysis plan (see page 96).
- Save the syntax files with sensible names that link them to their datafile.
- Save useful syntax commands in your syntax library.
- Annotate your commands through the use of COMMENT when appropriate.
- Pay attention to the error messages and work them through – do not ignore them.

Data Analysis Plans

If a discussion about analysis plans seems like I am digressing a little in a book about syntax, please bear with me. I am a great advocate of data analysis plans, which are often underrated. A good data analysis plan can be an incredibly useful tool available to a researcher.

In my ideal world, we would compile a full data analysis plan which would be drafted before data analysis is started; in fact in a *truly* ideal world the data analysis plan would be drafted before data is collected; and in a Utopian world a data analysis plan would even be drafted as part of the project proposal.

There are different ways to draft an analysis plan, but to get you started here is an outline of how I do mine:

- In the first stage of an analysis plan I list: the key research questions that the project is to address; the main outcome; what information/data I am going to collect; and the type of data I expect to obtain. I then check that the information to be collected is the correct information to answer the specified key questions.
- Then I take the research questions that I want the data to answer (in plain English, not necessarily in 'stats-speak') and work out how I can reach an answer with the data, which enables me to identify the most appropriate graph, test or statistical analysis for each step of the way.
  - First, I start the analysis plan with basic descriptives and graphs, which will help me to 'get a feel' for the data and also to see if parametric or non-parametric tests are appropriate.
  - Second, I plan which of the relationships between variables I will need to explore and exactly how I will do that and which of the basic univariate tests and graphs will identify the associations and data patterns.
  - Third, I identify the more complex multivariate methods of data analysis methods that will help to answer any of the research questions.
- I usually have a couple of sides of A4 by the time I finish which can, in effect, tell me what to do with all that data before I even have it.

An analysis plan is useful for several reasons, but for me the main ones are:

- It helps ensure I collect the data that I need to answer the key questions.
- It helps me to stay focused, rather than go 'wandering' through the dataset.
- It reduces the risk of data trawling.
- It helps me identify which elements of my findings are hypothesis driven (usually based on the analysis plan) and which are data driven (usually based on finding something interesting while wandering around the data), which in turn will influence how I report the two different types of findings.
- A good analysis plan enables you to begin writing the syntax which will enable the analysis to be carried out. You can do this before any data has even been collected.

Drafting a data analysis plan and then converting it into the syntax can be both useful and motivating while you are waiting for your data to come in. You can even test out your drafted syntax files on dummy data – which in turn requires you to get your datafile set up, with the variables laid out and formatted, a motivating factor to get the datafile setup completed 'early'.

Exploring Categorical Data

One of the most simple ways to explore categorical data is to look at the frequencies. This is easily carried out using the drop-down, menu-driven method of using SPSS, through ANALYZE → DESCRIPTIVE STATISTICS → FREQUENCIES. The commands can then be pasted into a syntax file to create a record of your analysis; either to allow repetition if (for example) further cases are added, or for discussion with your supervisor or colleagues.

Syntax 8:1 Exploring categorical data using the FREQUENCIES command

The syntax will explore categorical data in the SPSS sample dataset stroke_valid.sav.
    You can paste the command via the drop-down, menu-driven method first and adapt as you become more confident.

GET FILE='C:\ProgramFiles\SPSSInc\SPSS16\Samples\stroke_valid.sav'.

FREQUENCIES VARIABLES=gender smoker result surgery
   /ОNDCП=ANALYΣIΣ.

The GET FILE command opens the datafile if not already open.
    The **FREQUENCIES** command must be followed by **VARIABLES** (or **VAR**) and then an equals sign followed by a list of the variables names to be analysed.
FREQUENCIES VARIABLES= gender smoker result surgery.

    The **/ORDER=ANALYSIS.** is a default sub-command and specifies how the output will be displayed. The command is completed with a **full stop**.

LAYOUT OPTIONS available via the drop-down, menu-driven method are also easily available through syntax. For the equivalent of selecting the option available in the 'Multiple variables' section of the **FORMAT** dialogue box (shown in the illustration above) use **/ORDER=VARIABLES** instead of using **/ORDER=ANALYSIS** – this would then display the outputs individually for each variable, rather than in a single-table layout.

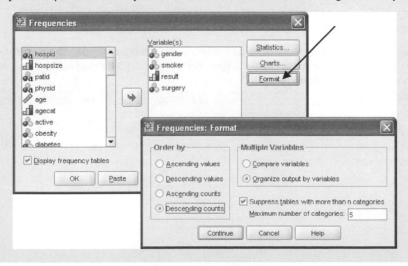

OPTIONS

As many variable names as you like can be entered with the **VARIABLES** keyword; alternatively the word **ALL** can be used to indicate that all variables should be included **VAR=ALL**. Analysis would be carried out for both string and numeric variables.

Using a further sub-command **/FORMAT** you can present the data in order of: increasing (ascending) value label (**AVALUE**)

decreasing (descending) value label (**DVALUE**)

increasing (ascending) frequency of the values (**AFREQ**)

decreasing (descending) frequency of the values (**DFREQ**)

You can also use the **FORMAT** sub-command to limit the command to only those variables which have X or less values – this is very handy when combined with the **VARIABLES= ALL** option above where it can be used to exclude numeric variables. In the example below any variable with more than five values is excluded.

```
FREQUENCIES VARIABLES=ALL
    /FORMAT=DFREQ LIMIT(5)
    /ORDER=VARIABLE.
```

The other commonly used method of exploring categorical data is via contingency tables or cross-tabulations. This is easily carried out using the drop-down, menu-driven method of using SPSS, through ANALYZE → DESCRIPTIVE STATISTICS → CROSSTABS, but it is helpful to then paste as a record.

Some useful cross-tabulation options are identified in Syntax 8:3, Syntax 8:4 and Syntax 8:5 that are not available through the drop-down, menu-driven method and which are only available through syntax.

Syntax 8:2 Simple contingency tables using the CROSSTABS command

The syntax will explore categorical data in the SPSS sample dataset stroke_valid.sav.

You can paste the command via the drop-down, menu-driven method first and adapt as you become more confident.

The syntax below is created from two categorical variables in the row selection and two in the column selection

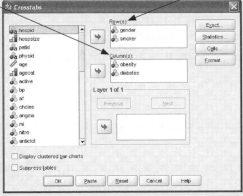

GET FILE='C:\Program Files\SPSSInc\SPSS16\Samples\stroke_valid.sav'.

CROSSTABS
    /TABLES=gender smoker BY obesity diabetes
    /FORMAT=AVALUE TABLES
    /CELLS=COUNT
    /COUNT ROUND CELL.

The GET FILE command opens the datafile if not already open.
The CROSSTABS command is followed by a series of sub-commands. Note that all the following sub-commands are indented and each is preceded by a forward slash/.

Crosstabs needs the TABLES sub-command to be followed by a list of variables to create the cross-tabulations /TABLES=gender smoker BY obesity diabetes. This example will create a series of four 2 × 2 cross-tabulations gender × obesity gender × diabetes smoker × obesity smoker × diabetes. Incidentally, as long as the list of tables is put immediately after CROSSTABS, you can leave the /TABLES= out.

The format command /FORMAT=AVALUE TABLES specifies that the tables display from the lowest to the highest value label (ascending values AVALUE); alternatively you can select from the highest to the lowest (DVALUE). The word TABLES simply tells SPSS to then show the tables in the output viewer. For basic default tables you can miss this sub-command out.

Crosstabs can display considerable amounts of information in the cells; the default in the drop-down method is simply to present the cell counts /CELLS=COUNT but you can also select the expected count (EXPECTED), the row percentages (ROW) or column percentages (COLUMN), and so forth. The *Command Syntax Reference* guide has a full list of sub-commands and options (see the Resources section, page 30). These options are available in the drop-down, menu-driven options behind the CELLS button. For tables solely with the COUNT option you don't need to put this default command for it to be performed.

The COUNT sub-command also controls how 'case weights' are handled /COUNT ROUND CELL. This is required for the statistics sub-commands (see Chapter 11) and is not required simply for tables. However, it appears in the pasted syntax as it is a default command and ensures that the accumulated weights in the cells are rounded before computing any statistics.

So, considering that three sub-commands are defaults and can be missed out when you want to produce basic tables, you could get the same output as Syntax 8:2 using the more streamlined syntax below.

CROSSTABS gender smoker BY obesity diabetes.

If you want more complex information to be displayed, there are additional options available using syntax.

Syntax 8:3 Multi-layered contingency tables using the CROSSTABS command

The syntax will use the data in the SPSS sample dataset stroke_valid.sav.

GET FILE='C:\Program Files\SPSSInc\SPSS16\Samples\stroke_valid.sav'.

CROSSTABS
  /TABLES=gender BY diabetes BY smoker BY obesity.

The difference in the syntax here (compared to Syntax 8:2) is in the **/TABLES** sub-command where there is the word **BY** between each of the variables. This produces a sub-table for each combination of values in the variables. Rather than four 2 × 2 tables gender × obesity | gender × diabetes | smoker × obesity | smoker × diabetes | being produced by Syntax 8:2, a single large cross-tabulation is produced exploring **gender** and **diabetes**, within which you can see sub-tables for each level of the variables **smoker** and **obesity**. See the illustration below.

Obes ity	Smoker			History of diabetes		
				No	Yes	Total
No	No	Gender	Male	311	22	333
			Female	286	16	302
			Total	597	38	635
	Yes	Gender	Male	69	4	73
			Female	87	5	92
			Total	156	9	165
Yes	No	Gender	Male	76	16	92
			Female	90	9	99
			Total	166	25	191
	Yes	Gender	Male	25	6	31
			Female	20	6	26
			Total	45	12	57

Such multi-layered cross-tabulations are only available through syntax.

Sometimes you may want your contingency tables to follow a set layout (e.g. all having the expected value in each cell, all with the column percentages). In this situation there is the facility in syntax to put multiple combinations of tables within the same syntax command and make them subject to the same set of sub-commands.

Syntax 8:4 Multiple contingency tables using the CROSSTABS command

The syntax will use the data in the SPSS sample dataset stroke_valid.sav.

GET FILE='C:\Program Files\SPSSInc\SPSS16\Samples\stroke_valid.sav'.

CROSSTABS
 /TABLES=gender diabetes BY smoker obesity
 /TABLES=agecat BY result
 /TABLES=rehab BY hospsize
 /FORMAT=DVALUE TABLES
 /CELLS=COUNT EXPECTED COLUMN.

Above you can see three separate TABLES sub-commands. These will create

- four 2 × 2 tables for the **/TABLES=gender diabetes BY smoker obesity** sub-command,
- a separate 4 × 4 table for **/TABLES=agecat BY result** and
- a separate 4 × 3 table for **/TABLES=rehab BY hospize**

but all with the same **FORMATS** and **CELLS** requirements as specified.
 The facility to create multiple separate tables is **only available through syntax** (i.e. it is not available via the drop-down, menu-driven method).

Occasionally you may want only some of the value ranges to be displayed in your contingency tables, and it is possible to specify such ranges via syntax.

Syntax 8:5 Selecting ranges for contingency tables using the CROSSTABS command

The syntax will use the data in the SPSS sample dataset stroke_valid.sav.

GET FILE='C:\Program Files\SPSSInc\SPSS16\Samples\stroke_valid.sav'.

CROSSTABS VARIABLES = result (1,2) agecat (1,3)
 /TABLES=result BY agecat.

Within the **CROSSTABS** command, the addition of **VARIABLES** is followed by a list of variables and ranges to be included. Here **VARIABLES = result (1,2) agecat (1,3)** specifies that the table should only include the two variables listed, and will only include cases with value label ranges of 1–2 for **result** and 1–3 for **agecat**. This will create a 2 × 3 table.
 If you had run a simple command **CROSSTABS /result BY agecat.** requesting a 'standard' cross-tabulation between **result** (a four-category variable) and age category variable **agecat** (a four-category variable) it would produce a 4 × 4 table.
 The facility to create range-specific tables is **only available through syntax**.

ERROR ALERT
If you need to specify a range for *any* variable, then it is a requirement that a range is specified for *all* variables that are included within that **CROSSTABS** syntax command.

Exploring (or Describing) Numerical Data

Descriptive statistics describe or summarise your numerical data. Common ways of presenting descriptives are through the identification of midpoints (mean, median, mode), spread (range, standard deviation, etc.) and distribution (normal or otherwise).

Midpoints and spread can be examined through a number of commands in syntax, which generally reflect the various ways that it can be done using the drop-down, menu-driven methods:

- using the FREQUENCIES command (pasted via ANALYZE → DESCRIPTIVE STATISTICS → FREQUENCIES);
- using the DESCRIPTIVES command (pasted via ANALYZE → DESCRIPTIVE STATISTICS → DESCRIPTIVES); or
- using the EXAMINE command (pasted via ANALYZE → DESCRIPTIVE STATISTICS → EXPLORE).

The next six examples will show these different ways of exploring data. As the different methods produce different outputs, you will need to choose the appropriate one for your requirements.

Syntax from ANALYZE → DESCRIPTIVE STATISTICS → FREQUENCIES

The first example will using the FREQUENCIES command unticking the ☐ Display frequency tables box and then clicking some of the statistical options in the dialogue box obtained via the Statistics... button.

Syntax 8:6 Midpoints and spread using the FREQUENCIES command

The syntax will explore numerical data in the SPSS sample dataset stroke_valid.sav.

GET FILE='C:\Program Files\SPSSInc\SPSS16\Samples\stroke_valid.sav'.

FREQUENCIES VARIABLES=age cost
    /FORMAT=NOTABLE
    /NTILES=4
    /STATISTICS=STDDEV MINIMUM MAXIMUM MEAN MEDIAN SKEWNESS
    /ORDER=ANALYSIS.

The GET FILE command opens the datafile if not already open.

The FREQUENCIES command must be followed by VARIABLES (or VAR) and then an equals sign followed by a list of the variable names to be analysed **FREQUENCIES VARIABLES=age cost.** and as many variable names as you like can be entered; alternatively the word ALL can be used to indicate that all variables should be included VAR=ALL. Analysis would be carried out for numeric variables only.

There are then four sub-commands.

The first sub-command **/FORMAT=NOTABLE** is to stop the production of the default frequency table – it is saying NO TABLE (not that the format is notable).

The second sub-command **/NTILES=4** is to produce quartiles. To change the percentiles displayed, simply change the number after the equals sign, for example inserting a 10 **/NTILES=10** would produce deciles.

The third sub-command specifies which statistics are required, **/STATISTICS= STDDEV MINIMUM MAXIMUM MEAN MEDIAN SKEWNESS**; the list can also include the variance (**VARIANCE**), the standard error of the mean (**SEMEAN**) and so forth (*Command Syntax Reference* guide, see the Resources section, page 30, for a full list of sub-commands and options). Alternatively you can specify ALL or NONE.

The last sub-command **/ORDER=ANALYSIS.** specifies how the output will be displayed and also completes the command with a full stop.

An option that is only available through syntax (i.e. not available via the drop-down, menu-driven method) is **/ORDER=VARIABLES** which displays the outputs in a separate table for each variable, rather than in a combined table.

Syntax from ANALYZE → DESCRIPTIVE STATISTICS → DESCRIPTIVES

When using FREQUENCIES you have to actively select descriptive statistics. However, the DESCRIPTIVES command always provides some descriptive statistics whether you ask for them or not. Syntax 8:7 shows the command pasted from the default settings from the drop-down, menu-driven method.

Syntax 8:7 Midpoints and spread using the DESCRIPTIVES command

The syntax will explore numerical data in the SPSS sample dataset stroke_valid.sav.

GET FILE='C:\Program Files\SPSSInc\SPSS16\Samples\stroke_valid.sav'.

DESCRIPTIVES VARIABLES=age cost
    /STATISTICS=MEAN STDDEV MIN MAX.

The **GET FILE** command opens the datafile if not already open.

The **DESCRIPTIVES** command must be followed by **VARIABLES** (or **VAR**) and then an equals sign followed by a list of the variable names to be analysed **DESCRIPTIVES VARIABLES=age cost**.

The sub-command **STATISTICS** specifies which statistics are required, **/STATISTICS= MEAN STDDEV MIN MAX.**.

OPTIONS

As many variable names as you like can be entered following the **VARIABLES** keyword on the **DESCRIPTIVES** command. Alternatively the word ALL can be used to indicate that all variables should be included VAR=ALL. The analysis would be carried out for numeric variables only.

The **STATISTICS** sub-command can also include the variance (**VARIANCE**), the kurtosis (**KURTOSIS**) and many others. You may also specify **ALL** or **DEFAULT** (mean, stdev, min & max); alternatively you would *still* get the default statistics if you just use the first line (**DESCRIPTIVES VARIABLES=age cost.**).

The *Command Syntax Reference* guide (see Resources section, page 30) has a full list of sub-commands and options. Note that **MEDIAN** and **MODE** are not available in the **DESCRIPTIVES** statistics sub-command.

Z-scores (standardised deviation scores from the mean) can also be used to explore the spread and distribution of data, and creating z-score variables is a very easy process. In the dialogue box obtained from ANALYZE → DESCRIPTIVE STATISTICS → DESCRIPTIVES you just tick the ☑ Save standardized values as variables. In syntax you add the name of the new z-score variable.

Syntax 8:8 Creating z-scores for any or all variables using the DESCRIPTIVES command

The syntax will create z-scores using the SPSS sample dataset stroke_valid.sav.

GET FILE='C:\Program Files\SPSSInc\SPSS16\Samples\stroke_valid.sav'.

COMMENT to create a variable with z-scores for an existing variable, simply type a new z-score variable name in brackets immediately after the existing variable name – note that the default statistics will be provided for the variable listed.
DESCRIPTIVES VARIABLES=age (z_age).
VARIABLE LABELS z_age 'z-scores for the age variable'.

COMMENT if you want to get any descriptives for the z-score variable then you need a further command with the variable name now outside the brackets and it will be treated as any other variable.
DESCRIPTIVES VARIABLES=age z_age
    /STATISTICS=MIN MAX.

COMMENT to create z-scores for all variables simply put the sub-command /SAVE in – note that the default statistics will be provided for the variables listed (here ALL pre-existing ones).
DESCRIPTIVES VARIABLES=ALL
    /SAVE.

Syntax from ANALYZE → DESCRIPTIVE STATISTICS → EXPLORE

The EXAMINE command has the facility to explore data by groups, or factors. There is, though, less flexibility about which statistics are displayed. The default descriptive statistics are the mean, median, 5% trimmed mean, standard error, variance, standard deviation, minimum, maximum, range, interquartile range, skewness, standard error, kurtosis, and kurtosis standard error. Alternatively you can select to have none of the descriptive statistics. As in the drop-down menu-driven method for descriptive statistics of using EXPLORE, using EXAMINE is an 'all or nothing' choice really.

Figure 8.1 shows the command pasted from the default settings from the drop-down, menu-driven method when only Statistics is selected on the front screen of the Explore option.

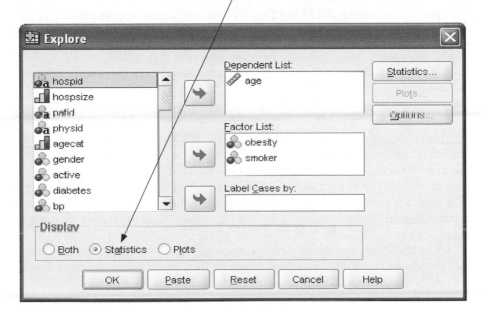

Figure 8.1

Syntax 8:9 Midpoints and spread using the EXAMINE command

The syntax will explore numerical data in the SPSS sample dataset stroke_valid.sav.

GET FILE='C:\Program Files\SPSSInc\SPSS16\Samples\stroke_valid.sav'.

EXAMINE VARIABLES=age BY obesity smoker
    /PLOT NONE
    /STATISTICS DESCRIPTIVES
    /CINTERVAL 95
    /MISSING LISTWISE
    /NOTOTAL.

The GET FILE command opens the datafile if not already open.

The EXAMINE command must be followed by VARIABLES (or VAR) and then an equals sign followed by a list of the variable names to be analysed EXAMINE VARIABLES=age. The command then continues, BY obesity smoker identifying the factors by which the data should be examined.

The first sub-command suppresses the graph defaults /PLOT NONE as only the statistics option was selected in the dialogue box (as shown in Figure 8.1).

The second sub-command /STATISTICS DESCRIPTIVES specifies the default descriptives.

The third sub-command /CINTERVAL 95 specifies the confidence intervals to be presented for the mean.

The fourth sub-command /MISSING LISTWISE specifies that the dependent variable data is not reported for cases with missing values.

The last sub-command /NOTOTAL. is a default command and specifies that the descriptives should not be calculated for the overall group (i.e. by the total sample) but only by the factors listed.

Note that the full-stop is at the very end of the last sub-command.

By going through this process of unpicking the **EXAMINE** command (as pasted from the drop-down menu) I hope you will be able to see how you can start to adapt this in a syntax file. First you should paste the command into the syntax file and then start to amend it to fit your analysis needs better. Initially you may feel a bit wary, so it may not be best to try this just before a deadline; try a time when you can experiment and examine in detail the resulting outputs (and any error and/or warning messages).

EXAMINE has some default settings, some of which cannot be altered through the drop-down, menu-driven method. Syntax 8:10 is an amended version of Syntax 8:9 which shows some additional facilities afforded by the use of syntax.

Syntax 8:10 Additional options for midpoints and spread using the EXAMINE command

The syntax will again explore numerical data in the SPSS sample dataset stroke_valid.sav.

```
GET FILE='C:\Program Files\SPSSInc\SPSS16\Samples\stroke_valid.sav'.

EXAMINE VARIABLES=age BY obesity smoker, obesity BY smoker
    /PLOT BOXPLOT
    /PERCENTILES(25, 50, 75)
    /STATISTICS DESCRIPTIVES EXTREME(10)
    /CINTERVAL 90
    /MISSING INCLUDE
    /TOTAL.
```

The GET FILE command opens the datafile if not already open.

The **EXAMINE** command is followed by the dependent variable to be examined (**age**) as before and then by the identified factors by which the data is to be examined **BY obesity smoker**. Note, though, that there is now a comma and a further instruction **obesity BY smoker** which is specifying examination of the dependent variable by each of the combinations created by the different levels in the factors specified. In this example, this additional 2 × 2 model creates four combinations:

- obesity no & smoking no;
- obesity no & smoking yes;
- obesity yes & smoking no;
- obesity yes & smoking yes.

This option is only available through syntax.

The first sub-command **/PLOT BOXPLOT** requests boxplots.

The second sub-command specifies quartiles **PERCENTILES(25,50,75)** (opting for an alternative to the default percentiles is only available through syntax).

The third sub-command specifies the default descriptives (see page 105) and instead of the default five most extreme cases being presented, an alternative number of extreme cases are specified. Here the 10 most extreme cases will be presented. This option is only available through syntax.
/STATISTICS DESCRIPTIVES EXTREME(10)

The fourth sub-command **/CINTERVAL 90** specifies 90% confidence intervals to be presented for the mean.

The fifth sub-command **/MISSING INCLUDE** specifies that the dependent variable data is reported for each valid level within the factors, including user-assigned missing values, but excluding system-missing values. This particular option is only available through syntax.

The last sub-command **/TOTAL.** is a command that specifies that the descriptives should also be calculated for the overall group (i.e. by the total sample) as well as by the factors listed. This option is only available through syntax as to carry it out using the drop-down, menu-driven method would require two separate analyses (one with the factors specified, and then one with no factor specified).

Note that the only full-stop is at the very end of the last sub-command **/TOTAL.**.

Other sub-commands and options are available and can be found in the *Command Syntax Reference* guide (see Resources section, page 30). Also, if you are in the syntax editor you can place your cursor is in the command line and press the F1 key for help that is specific to the current command.

FREQUENCIES and EXAMINE commands can both produce plots or graphs. These will be covered in Chapter 10.

Statistics to Examine the Distribution of Data

The EXAMINE command can produce normality distribution statistics and graphs, which can also be accessed via ANALYZE → DESCRIPTIVE STATISTICS → EXPLORE. In syntax it requires only the addition of one sub-command /PLOT NPPLOT. This command produces normal and detrended Q–Q plots with the Kolmogorov–Smirnov statistic (and sometimes the Shapiro–Wilk statistic also) test of normality.

Syntax 8:11 Testing for normality using the EXAMINE command

The syntax will explore the distribution of numerical data in the SPSS sample dataset stroke_valid.sav.

GET FILE='C:\Program Files\SPSSInc\SPSS16\Samples\stroke_valid.sav'.

EXAMINE VARIABLES=age BY gender
   /PLOT NPPLOT
   /STATISTICS NONE
   /TOTAL.

The GET FILE command opens the datafile if not already open.

The **EXAMINE** command has the keyword **VARIABLES** followed by the dependent variable to be examined **age** and then identified factor by which the data is to be examined, **gender**.

The first sub-command **/PLOT NPPLOT** creates not only the normality plots but also the normality statistics.

The second sub-command **/STATISTICS NONE** specifies that no descriptive statistics are produced.

The third sub-command **/TOTAL.** specifies that the analysis should also be calculated for the overall group (i.e. by the total sample) as well as by the factor listed. This option is **only available through syntax**. To do it using the drop-down, menu-driven method would require two separate analyses (first one with no factor specified, and then one with the factor specified).

The **/TOTAL.** option is able to be used for any of the EXAMINE sub-commands and will apply to all sub-commands listed in the syntax command within which it is used.

An alternative way to examine distribution statistics is through the non-parametric test command accessed via the drop-down menu method via ANALYZE → NONPARAMETRIC TESTS → 1-SAMPLE K-S.

Syntax 8:12 Testing for normal, Poisson, uniform or exponential distributions using the NPAR TESTS command

The syntax will explore the distribution of numerical data in the SPSS sample dataset stroke_valid.sav.

```
GET FILE='C:\Program Files\SPSSInc\SPSS16\Samples\stroke_valid.sav'.
NPAR TESTS
    /K-S(NORMAL)=age
    /STATISTICS DESCRIPTIVES QUARTILES.
```

The sub-command options available allow you to look at the descriptive statistics of any or all variables listed, as well as test against the normal distribution and also test against three other distributions: Poisson, uniform and exponential. See below for the different syntax sub-commands, any of which you can paste via the drop-down, menu-driven method.

```
NPAR TESTS
    /K-S(NORMAL)=age
    /K-S(UNIFORM)=age
    /K-S(POISSON)=age
    /K-S(EXPONENTIAL)=age.
```

Syntax has the additional facility of allowing you to specify the parameters within the distribution against your wish to compare the variable's cumulative distribution function – these options are only available through syntax. For example, you may wish to specify the mean and standard deviation within the normal distribution, or the minimum and maximum within a uniform distribution; you can refer to the SPSS *Command Syntax Reference* guide (see Resources section, page 30) for specific details.

Summary

If you have an analysis plan drafted, then you can start writing your syntax file as soon as you have set up your datafile with the variable names, formats, etc. You can, of course, use syntax to help make the datafile more usable (see Chapter 3).

Many of the syntax commands for exploring data can be pasted via the drop-down, menu-driven method, but there are additional options that are only available through syntax.

You can always start by changing the options selected in using the drop-down method, and seeing how they look in the Log part of the output file (see page 8) or when pasted into the syntax file (see page 11). You can then save useful combinations of commands. You can also start to use the *Command Syntax Reference* guide (see Resources section, page 30) to look for the full list of sub-commands and options associated with any given command.

Using the *Command Syntax Reference* guide (see Resources section, page 30) will also let you see any options that are available only through the use of syntax, rather than just those choices offered by the drop-down, menu-driven method of accessing SPSS analysis capabilities. If you look at the guide and it all feels too advanced or too scary, just glance through it now and again, but actually leave using these options until your confidence, knowledge and skills have increased sufficiently for you to want to explore further.

Useful Tips

- The keyword VARIABLES can be shorted to VAR in a command.
- Note that all the sub-commands that follow the initial command are presented as indented and start with a forward slash.
- Sub-commands *could* just follow each other on the same line without starting a new indented line, but I use a fresh line for ease of reading.
- You have a full stop only when the overall command is complete, the sub-commands should not be separated by a full stop.
- You can start extending our familiarity with syntax by changing the options selected in using the drop-down method, pasting them, and seeing how they differ.
- If the command only seems to run part of your requested option, check whether you have included any extra full stops by mistake at the end of sub-commands.

9

Syntax to Enable the Use of Only Sub-sections of the Data

All examples in this chapter will use the following SPSS sample dataset stroke_valid.sav.

During your data analysis, you may need to carry out some analysis on a specific subset of the data, for example producing descriptives separately for two groups such as an experimental group and a control group. Likewise, you may want to exclude a group of subjects who may, for example, not have met certain criteria for inclusion in a specific analysis. The syntax to enable you to analyse only certain sections of the data will be covered in this chapter, together with suggestions about best use of these commands.

There will be examples to cover the use of commands to select cases, to split files and to return to full datasets. Examples of how the commands can be used to analyse data more effectively and more efficiently will be outlined.

There are two key ways of sectioning your data:

- Selecting only a certain part of your data to be included in the analysis: for example, include only females under the age of 75.
- Requesting the analysis be split and presented separately for certain groups in your data: for example, for males and for females separately.

Both of these, selecting cases or splitting the data, can be achieved through the drop-down, menu-driven method of using SPSS and a good place to start is through pasting commands via that route. Selecting cases or splitting the data can help when you look through your data to get a feel for it and can also be helpful when carrying out univariate and multivariate inferential statistics.

Good Practice

- Base your analysis on the data analysis plan (see page 96).
- When you select specific sub-sets of your data for exploration, remember to return to the whole dataset as required for further work.
- When you select specific sub-sets of your data for exploration, ensure this is clearly identifiable in the output; to consistently do this, ensure that you have the Log set to print into the output files.

Selecting only a Certain Part of Your Data to Be Included in the Analysis

You can specify that only a section of the data is used for analysis. In the drop-down, menu-driven method of using SPSS this is via the DATA → SELECT CASES and choosing the second option ⊙ If condition is satisfied , moving the relevant variables across and then typing in the criteria you want to select by.

Note that the default selection in the Output box is that the unselected cases are filtered out (generally what you want to happen). An alternative option is to select that the unselected cases are deleted (generally *not* what you want to happen).

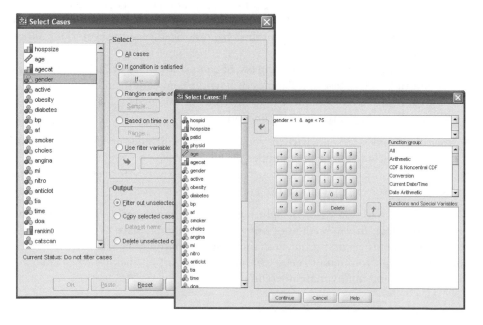

Figure 9.1

The syntax pasted from Figure 9.1 is the source of Syntax 9:1.

Syntax 9:1 Selecting data using the FILTER command (pasted syntax from DATA → SELECT CASES)

The syntax will use the SPSS sample dataset stroke_valid.sav.

GET FILE='C:\Program Files\SPSSInc\SPSS16\Samples\stroke_valid.sav'.

USE ALL.
COMPUTE filter_$=(gender = 1 & age < 75).
VARIABLE LABEL filter_$ 'gender = 1 & age < 75 (FILTER)'.
VALUE LABELS filter_$ 0 'Not Selected' 1 'Selected'.
FORMAT filter_$ (f1.0).
FILTER BY filter_$.
EXECUTE.

The syntax looks quite complicated but, examined line by line, can be shown to be quite straightforward.

The GET FILE command opens the datafile if not already open.

There are then seven separate commands – none are sub-commands and therefore:

- Each starts at the beginning of the line.
- They are not preceded by a forward slash.
- Each command line ends with a full stop.

The first command **USE ALL.** starts the process with a 'clean slate' beginning the process using all the observations in the data.

The second command **COMPUTE filter_$=(gender = 1 & age < 75).** creates a new variable with the default name filter_$ ($ indicates a wildcard).

The third command **VARIABLE LABEL filter_$ 'gender = 1 & age < 75 (FILTER)'.** labels the new variable using the filter criteria as the label, and, for good measure, the label ends with FILTER in capitals.

The fourth command **VALUE LABELS filter_$ 0 'Not Selected' 1 'Selected'.** labels the values within the variable.

The fifth command **FORMAT filter_$ (f1.0).** formats the variable allocating a single-character width.

The sixth command **FILTER BY filter_$.** is the command that finally selects the cases you require. The **FILTER** command will always exclude any cases with a zero or a missing value in the specified variable (hence the automatic value label of **0 'Not Selected'** in the fourth command line**).**

The last command **EXECUTE.** simply executes the commands that precede it.

Reading through the above commands you may start to envisage how you could improve this for your own data. Imagine that you are going to need to run several things several times using a couple of pre-specified subsets of your data. Two examples below illustrate how you can create some variables for future selection, tailoring the names and values for ease of understanding.

COMMENT this syntax works on the stroke_valid dataset and will create a selection variable for women under 75.
USE ALL.
COMPUTE filter_yng_wom=(gender = 1 & age < 75).
VARIABLE LABEL filter_yng_wom 'selects women under 75 years only when used as a filter'.
VALUE LABELS filter_yng_wom 0 'others, not women under 75 years' 1 'women under 75 years'.
FORMAT filter_yng_wom (f1.0).
FILTER BY filter_yng_wom.
EXECUTE.

COMMENT this syntax works on the stroke_valid dataset and will create a selection variable for men over 75.
USE ALL.
COMPUTE filter_old_men=(gender = 0 & age >= 75).
VARIABLE LABEL filter_old_men 'selects men 75 years and older when used as a filter'.
VALUE LABELS filter_old_men 0 'others, men 75 years and older' 1 'men 75 years and older'.
FORMAT filter_old_men (f1.0).
FILTER BY filter_old_men.
EXECUTE.

The creation of named selection variables also means that these filter variables can remain in your datafile rather than being overwritten next time a filter_$ variable is created.

You may have noticed when reading through the line-by-line explanation in Syntax 9:1 that the effects of the command FILTER are not necessarily specific to specially created filter variables. FILTER will work with any numeric variable and will exclude all cases with a zero or missing value in the variable named after the BY keyword.

Syntax 9:2 Selecting data using the FILTER command

The syntax will select specified data in the SPSS sample dataset stroke_valid.sav.

FILTER diabetes.

The single command line will exclude all cases with a zero or missing value in the specified variable which, in this instance, leaves all those with diabetes selected (as the values in this variable in this dataset are 0 for no diabetes and 1 for yes diabetes). The selection will remain until specified otherwise.

Having used the FILTER command, whether with specifically created variables or otherwise, you must remember to return to the full dataset again once you no longer have the need for using just a sub-set of your data.

Syntax 9:3 Returning to the full dataset using FILTER OFF and USE ALL commands

The syntax will work on any data in SPSS. It is pasted from the drop-down, menu-driven method via DATA → SELECT CASES and choosing the first option ⦿ All cases .

FILTER OFF.
USE ALL.
EXECUTE.

The **FILTER OFF.** command turns off the filter and includes all cases in subsequent analysis and procedures.

The **USE ALL.** command includes all observations in the file in subsequent analysis and procedures.

The last command **EXECUTE.** simply executes the preceding commands.

Example of Usefulness

I was carrying out exploratory analysis on a dataset. The research team required the descriptives for the overall sample, and also for two subgroups within the data.

First, I wrote the syntax for the exploratory analysis following my analysis plan (see page 96). This syntax worked on the whole dataset and was saved as a syntax file. For illustrative purposes I will call the syntax file proj_explore_all.sps.

In a new syntax file called proj_explore_spec1.sps I started with a syntax command to specify the subset. This was an individualised version of Syntax 9:1 accompanied by a COMMENT command as per Syntax 2:6. Following on from this I pasted all the syntax from proj_explore_all.sps. I completed the process by returning to the full dataset with Syntax 9:3 and then saved the file.

I then repeated the process again in a further syntax file proj_explore_spec2.sps using a second individualised version of Syntax 9:1, pasting the analysis commands as before and then returning to the full dataset.

Re-running these two extra 'specified' sets of descriptives took just minutes. Additionally, I knew that I had covered all the analysis as per the whole dataset and without having missed anything out.

> **Quick reminder about the usefulness of the LOG (pages 6–8)**
>
> When carrying out analysis on 'not the full dataset' you should avoid having output that is easy to misattribute or misunderstand. Thus the information about which cases your output is referring to needs to be easily accessible. You can of course go onto the output sheet and enter some text explaining what you have done.
>
> A much more consistent system is to ensure that you have the Log set to display on your outputs. Set correctly the Log will automatically record all of your actions onto the output sheets by 'logging' all of the syntax commands for the actions you have undertaken. Once set correctly, it will do this automatically for you.
>
> Without the commands being logged in this way the *n* values may give an indication that it is not the full dataset being analysed, but not always, and it may not be obvious if returning to the outputs after a time when you may be less familiar with the data than you were at the time you carried out the analysis. In datasets where variables may have a considerable number of missing values, you may not always know what value of *n* you are looking for anyway.
>
> With the Log on, you have a reliable record there in the output file of which cases are being analysed and their findings presented.

There is a further way that you can select cases, using the SELECT IF command. Although it is simple to use, this command permanently deletes all of those cases not selected so I avoid use of this command. The SELECT IF command is discussed in the section 'Use of the TEMPORARY and SELECT IF commands' at the end of this chapter. However, I do not recommend the use of the SELECT IF command because of the risk of the non-selected cases being unintentionally and permanently dropped from the dataset.

As mentioned in the introduction to this chapter, there are two main ways of sectioning your data. We have covered selecting only a certain part of your data to be included in the analysis and now will look at splitting the file and enabling the analysis be presented separately for certain groups in your data.

Enabling the Analysis to Be Presented Separately for Certain Groups

You can specify a variable (or variables) to split the data for the purpose of analysis using the drop-down, menu-driven method. You can access the dialogue box via DATA → SPLIT FILE, choose the second option ◉ Compare groups (see Figure 9.2) and then select and move the variable(s) across by which you want the analysis split.

Pasting from here will created a syntax SPLIT FILE command. The SPLIT FILE command (simply put) 'splits the file' by the values in the variable you have specified. It does not remove any of the data, just examines it in separate groups or categories within whichever variable has been selected for 'splitting'. The SPLIT FILE command allows you to carry out the same procedure *x* number of times simultaneously and presented in one of a number of ways. Its usefulness is that it allows you to run your analysis on the overall data, and then simply by use of the SPLIT FILE command and copying and pasting the analysis syntax to follow it, you can ask for the

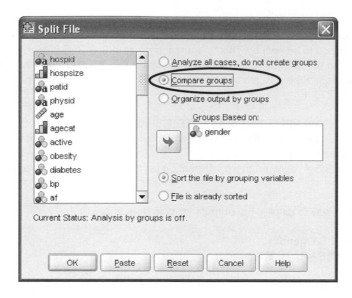

Figure 9.2

analysis to then be repeated but this time with the analysis and outputs split by (for example) the different groups represented in the variable **gender**. Whatever commands are run after the SPLIT FILE command will be carried out separately for each differing value within the variable(s) specified. In this example, using gender, the analysis will be carried out first for the males and then for the females.

The syntax pasted from Figure 9.2 will form the basis of Syntax 9:4 below.

Syntax 9:4 Splitting the file for analysis using the SPLIT FILE command

The syntax will split the data in the SPSS sample dataset stroke_valid.sav on the basis of the GENDER variable.

GET FILE='C:\Program Files\SPSSInc\SPSS16\Samples\stroke_valid.sav'.

SORT CASES BY gender.
SPLIT FILE LAYERED BY gender.

COMMENT you follow with the analysis syntax that you want to be carried out on groups within your split variable (here gender) and in this example we use Syntax 8:6 from the previous chapter.

FREQUENCIES VARIABLES=age cost
    /FORMAT=NOTABLE
    /NTILES=4
    /STATISTICS=STDDEV MINIMUM MAXIMUM MEAN MEDIAN SKEWNESS
    /ORDER=ANALYSIS.

The GET FILE command opens the datafile if not already open.

The command **SORT CASES BY gender.** sorts the datafile by the variable that we want the analysis to be split by. This is a necessary step that SPSS needs to carry out prior to splitting the file. You may not have realised it, but this sorting of the data is carried out automatically every time you use the drop-down, menu-driven method via DATA → SPLIT FILE.

The next command **SPLIT FILE LAYERED BY gender.** specifies that the file should be split by the values within the variable gender and that the outputs should be shown within one *layered* table.

See Syntax 8:6 if you want more information on the **FREQUENCIES** command.

OPTIONS

An alternative way to display the outputs for split data is below.

SORT CASES BY gender.
SPLIT FILE SEPARATE BY gender.

The syntax above is obtained using the drop-down menu-driven method via DATA → SPLIT FILE and choosing the third option ⊙ Organize output by groups and pasting to the syntax file. This command **SPLIT FILE SEPARATE BY gender.** will display the outputs in multiple *separate* tables.

So, you just use the LAYERED BY keywords to obtain the output in a layered table, and use the SEPARATE BY keywords to obtain the output in separate tables. See Figure 9.3 for an illustration of the outputs from the two syntax examples in Syntax 9:4.

Output using SPLIT FILE LAYERED BY gender

Statistics

Gender			Age in years	Total treatment and rehabilitation costs in thousands
Male	N	Valid	529	529
		Missing	0	0
	Mean		62.10	33.5091
	Median		62.00	29.7800
	Std. Deviation		9.088	26.10482
	Skewness		.313	1.510
	Std. Error of Skewness		.106	.106
	Kurtosis		-.654	5.381
	Std. Error of Kurtosis		.212	.212
	Minimum		45	.00
	Maximum		86	200.23
Female	N	Valid	519	519
		Missing	0	0
	Mean		62.83	34.0239
	Median		62.00	27.7800
	Std. Deviation		9.132	28.51408
	Skewness		.291	1.825
	Std. Error of Skewness		.107	.107
	Kurtosis		-.659	5.999
	Std. Error of Kurtosis		.214	.214
	Minimum		45	2.40
	Maximum		85	200.51

Output using SPLIT FILE SEPERATED BY gender

Gender = Male

Statistics[a]

		Age in years	Total treatment and rehabilitation costs in thousands
N	Valid	529	529
	Missing	0	0
Mean		62.10	33.5091
Median		62.00	29.7800
Std. Deviation		9.088	26.10482
Skewness		.313	1.510
Std. Error of Skewness		.106	.106
Kurtosis		-.654	5.381
Std. Error of Kurtosis		.212	.212
Minimum		45	.00
Maximum		86	200.23

a. Gender = Male

Gender = Female

Statistics[a]

		Age in years	Total treatment and rehabilitation costs in thousands
N	Valid	519	519
	Missing	0	0
Mean		62.83	34.0239
Median		62.00	27.7800
Std. Deviation		9.132	28.51408
Skewness		.291	1.825
Std. Error of Skewness		.107	.107
Kurtosis		-.659	5.999
Std. Error of Kurtosis		.214	.214
Minimum		45	2.40
Maximum		85	200.51

a. Gender = Female

Figure 9.3

As with the FILTER command, you need to remember to return to the full dataset again once you have no need for the sectioning of your dataset. Again, the command can be pasted from the drop-down, menu-driven method via DATA →
SPLIT FILE and choosing the first option ⊙ Analyze all cases, do not create groups .

Syntax 9:5 Returning to entire dataset analysis using the SPLIT FILE OFF command

The syntax will work on any data in SPSS.

SPLIT FILE OFF.

The **SPLIT FILE OFF.** command removes the split and uses the dataset in its entirety for subsequent analysis and procedures.

Use of the TEMPORARY and SELECT IF Commands

The TEMPORARY (or TEMP) command is only available through syntax and is not available when using the drop-down menu. The TEMP command permits a command (like SPLIT or SELECT) to take place and be valid for the one command that follows it. You use the TEMP command prior to the command that you would like to be temporarily in force solely for the one command line following it. In all there are three command lines involved.

1.   Line 1 – The TEMP command line.
2.   Line 2 – The command line that you want to be a temporary state in the dataset (e.g. select the data for females only).
3.   Line 3 – The command line that you want the temporary state to apply to (e.g. carrying out a FREQUENCY analysis).

The TEMPORARY command is one that requires you to be even more specific than usual in the way you write your syntax. It is not suitable for actions that require a combination of series of commands. For example, in Syntax 9:4 above, if you use the TEMPORARY command at the *beginning* of this syntax it will not work – mainly because it will not work on the SORT command – but even if it did work on the SORT command it would then temporarily sort the file and be in effect for the next command line, in this case the SPLIT command, but stop before the FREQUENCY command which you require. It will though work if you put the TEMPORARY command after the SORT command, which means it is immediately prior to and therefore applied to the SPLIT command, which will remain in effect for the next command (here the FREQUENCY command).

Syntax 9:6 Using the TEMPORARY command with the SPLIT FILE command

The syntax will work in the SPSS sample dataset stroke_valid.sav applying the split of the data on the basis of the GENDER variable for one command only.

GET FILE='C:\Program Files\SPSSInc\SPSS16\Samples\stroke_valid.sav'.

SORT CASES BY gender.
TEMP.
SPLIT FILE LAYERED BY gender.

FREQUENCIES VARIABLES=obesity diabetes.

FREQUENCIES VARIABLES=smoker.

The GET FILE command opens the datafile if not already open.
The first command **SORT CASES BY gender.** sorts the cases (see Syntax 9:4 for details).
The second command **TEMP.** specifies that the next command line will come into effect and apply to only the single command line that follows after that.
The third command **SPLIT FILE LAYERED BY gender.** specifies that the file should be split by gender(see Syntax 9:4 for details). This will remain in effect for one further command line.
The next command **FREQUENCIES VARIABLES= obesity diabetes.** explores the numerical data *split by gender*.
The last command **FREQUENCIES VARIABLES=smoker.** will give the frequencies for smokers across the entire dataset, *not* split by gender as the temporary effect of the split command has expired.

Personally I think it is just as easy to write a SPLIT FILE OFF command line after the event (see below), as it is to write a TEMP command line before the event.

SORT CASES BY gender.
SPLIT FILE LAYERED BY gender.

FREQUENCIES VARIABLES= obesity diabetes.

SPLIT FILE OFF.
FREQUENCIES VARIABLES=smoker.

If you browse or look through the *Command Syntax Reference* guide (SPSS, 2007a) you may come across the SELECT IF command. This is a command I do not use because it must be used with absolute caution, as it permanently deletes all of those cases not selected. If you precede the command with the TEMPORARY command then the unselected cases are not deleted. However, if SELECT IF is used without the TEMP command line preceding it, then the data that is not selected will be lost to the datafile, that is *the unselected data will be deleted*.

The drop-down, menu-driven method makes the consequences of the action explicit in a way that the SELECT IF command does not. To paste the SELECT IF syntax from the drop-down, menu-driven method, go to DATA → SELECT CASES, selecting the last option ⊙ Delete unselected cases in the output box (see Figure 9.4).

Figure 9.4

The pasted syntax from Figure 9.4 will form the basis of Syntax 9:7 below.

Syntax 9:7 Selecting data using the SELECT IF command (pasted syntax from DATA → SELECT CASES)

The syntax will use the SPSS sample dataset stroke_valid.sav.

GET FILE='C:\Program Files\SPSSInc\SPSS16\Samples\stroke_valid.sav'.

FILTER OFF.
USE ALL.
SELECT IF(gender = 1).
EXECUTE.

The **GET FILE** command opens the datafile if not already open.

The first two command lines **FILTER OFF.** and **USE ALL.** clear previous filters etc. (see Syntax 9:3) starting the following commands with the whole dataset.

The next command **SELECT IF(gender = 1).** is the command that selects the cases you require.

WARNING it also permanently deletes all the unselected cases.

The last command **EXECUTE.** actions the commands that precede it.

As selection criteria are usually required for more than one thing I recommend that, to select data, you use the syntax commands illustrated in Syntax 9:1 and Syntax 9:2. I question whether the value of the SELECT IF command is worth the risks of using it, especially for the newcomer to syntax. Better to spend a little time creating a filter variable to match your needs (see text between Syntax 9:1 and Syntax 9:2) and use that, than to risk unintentionally deleting data.

Summary

Selecting or splitting your datafile is as easy in syntax as it is through the drop-down, menu-driven method of using SPSS. Just do not be tempted to use the SELECT IF command.

It is worth creating filter variables to select your specific subset of data (cases). When labelled meaningfully they can be easy for others to use also, or for you to return to the data at a later date. Setting the Log to show on the Output sheets is a valuable way of clearly indicating which data has been selected and used for the analysis. This is so handy when discussing your data with others, such a supervisor or research team.

Syntax can be very efficient if you need to carry out analysis not only on your full dataset, but also on selected sections of your data (e.g. include only females under the age of 75) or presented separately for certain groups (e.g. for males and for females separately). The syntax for selecting or splitting the file can be written, then the syntax for the analysis on the full dataset can be copied after this. What a brilliant time-saver! Just remember to return to the full dataset later.

Useful Tips

- Take time to create, label and save any filter variables that you will need.
- Remember, every FILTER command needs a FILTER OFF command.
- Remember, every SPLIT FILE command needs a SPLIT FILE OFF command.
- Do not use the SELECT IF command.
- If your syntax does not work as expected check the full stops are in the correct places, and that EXECUTE has been run if required. These account for a large number of syntax hiccups.
- Read the Log when reading the Output files if you have been selecting subsets of your data so that you correctly understand which cases used in the analysis.

10

Syntax for Graphs

*Examples in this chapter will use the SPSS sample dataset
stroke_valid.sav*

The syntax for graphs creation should be routinely stored alongside the exploratory analysis syntax. In SPSS the different ways of creating graphs using the drop-down, menu-driven method each produce syntax commands that look quite different even when the resulting graphs remain similar.

Use of syntax can make creating graphs more efficient, but this is not always the case. The main purpose of this chapter is to explain why those differences in syntax arise, so that you are not puzzled by the differing commands when they appear in the Log and Journal. There are many different types of graphs but only common graph commands will be outlined in this chapter, such as bar charts, scatterplots, boxplots and pie charts.

This chapter will explain the syntax commands that enable the user to create graphs and, where possible, add features such as axis titles, scale changes or inserting a line of best fit. It will also promote the value of templates for more efficient formatting to improve the appearance of your graphs.

Overview of Creating Graphs in SPSS

There are three main ways of creating graphs via the drop-down, menu-driven method of using SPSS:

1. The oldest method requires you to select the graph type via a drop-down list, now categorised under LEGACY DIALOGS.
2. Then came the INTERACTIVE chart options, also accessed via LEGACY DIALOGS.
3. The most recent method uses CHART BUILDER.

If you access the graphs via the two methods that use the LEGACY DIALOGS route then you will choose the graph type from a list on the drop-down menu as shown in Figure 10.1. If you access the graphs via CHART BUILDER then the choice of graph type is a part of the dialogue box.

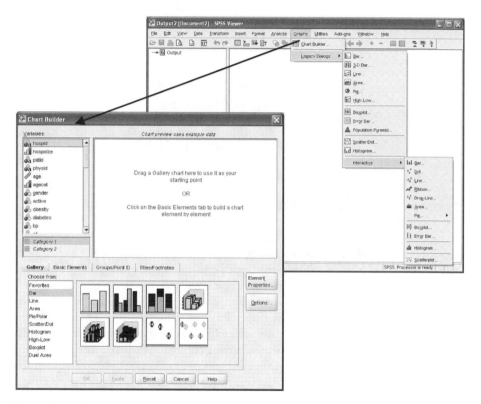

Figure 10.1   **How to access graphs via the drop-down menus**

The syntax produced from each of the methods is each different. It is beyond the scope of this chapter to cover all of the issues that this creates, but in short:

- Graphs created using LEGACY DIALOGS via the individual graph options have simple syntax commands with limited options for amending the resultant graph.
  Graphs created using LEGACY DIALOGS via the INTERACTIVE option for graph types have syntax commands with wide-ranging options for amendment and formatting of the graph.
- Graphs created using CHART BUILDER do not use just SPSS syntax, but instead require a language called Graphics Production Language (GPL).

It is also possible to access graphs and plots via some of the DESCRIPTIVE options in ANALYZE, as mentioned in Chapter 8 and these are covered at the end of this chapter.

Good Practice

- Save your graph syntax alongside your other exploratory analysis syntax.
- Use chart templates to improve the consistency and appearance of your graphs.
- Where possible use syntax to label elements such as your axes, pie slices and so forth to enable others to understand the graphs.

Templates

We should start with a quick section on templates. All three main methods of creating graphs have the facility to use a chart template to alter the appearance of created graphs. If you do not already use templates then it may be useful to have a little 'play' with a few graphs.

Go to the Graph menu, create a pie chart using any of the methods you are familiar with (CHART BUILDER, LEGACY DIALOG or INTERACTIVE). Once you have been through all of your selections for the chart options, click OK and create the graph. Have a look at the graph created. Now we are going to add a template. Go back to the Chart option and this time finish off by selecting the Template option in the dialogue box and clicking the button to find or add your template file.

Table 10.1

In LEGACY DIALOGS, templates are accessed via the Template section at the bottom of the chart dialogue box	
In INTERACTIVE, templates are accessed via the Options tab and the Chart templates part of that dialogue box	
In CHART BUILDER, templates are accessed via the Options button on the right of the dialogue box	

If, on clicking the button, you are not immediately taken to a folder containing the templates then you can browse your SPSS program folder and there should be a folder called Looks, which is where you should find the templates. Alternatively search your computer for files which end with a .sgt suffix (e.g. Dante.sgt).

Whichever method you use, you should be presented with the opportunity to select a template file, from a list ending with the .sgt suffix as in Figure 10.2.

Once done, go back to creating the chart, and return to the dialogue box for the chart that you created previously. In the Chart Template dialogue box select the Dante template. Click OK and look at the differences in font, colour of text, colours in the chart, etc., compared to the standard chart. Go back and select GrayScale.sgt and look again.

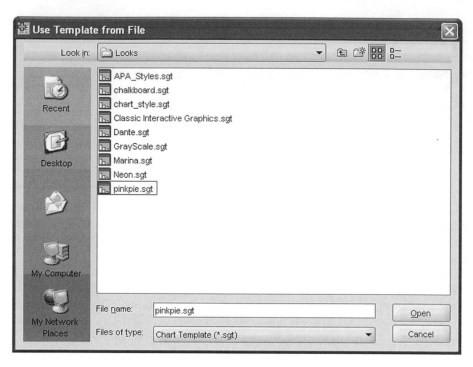

Figure 10.2   **List of chart templates**

If you do not like the automatically generated SPSS chart colours and font then find a template you prefer, or alternatively design one yourself. You can create your own templates by opening any chart in Chart Editor (double-click on a chart from the output file), make all your preferred changes to colour, font, etc., and (still in Chart Editor) click on FILE and select SAVE AS CHART TEMPLATE. (In Figure 10.2 you will see a template called pinkpie.sgt – this is my own self-created template which can be found only on my computer.)

The resulting looks vary within the templates ready supplied with SPSS, even for different graph types using the same template. For example, a scatterplot or error bar chart created with the Dante template is really *very* bright and vibrant whereas a pie chart with the same Dante template is really quite restrained (give it a try). A template to remember is GrayScale.sgt, which is handy for those with only black and white printers.

Once you have pasted the syntax for a graph, which includes a template, then to change the template that the graph is created with (and get an instant transformation in its appearance) you only have to change the name of the template in the appropriate sub-command.

For newcomers to syntax wanting to work more efficiently, the most useful of the three main methods is the syntax from graphs created using the INTERACTIVE option. Thus this will be the method that this chapter covers in the main. I will include a concise overview of the other two methods, but these sections will be brief; LEGACY DIALOGS individual graph options are available through pasting commands from the dialogue box with limited extra syntax facilities; and CHART BUILDER options require a further new computer programming language to be learned.

Graphs Created from Legacy Dialogs via the Interactive Option

Many graph types are available via the interactive method of creating graphs: bar charts, boxplots, scatter graphs, pie charts and so forth; and the syntax commands generated through this method all begin with the syntax command IGRAPH.

Within each graph type the dialogue boxes found in the interactive method of producing graphs are laid out in the form of tabs, and clicking on each tab moves you to a specific dialogue box (and also turns that tab yellow to indicate that it is currently the active dialogue box). Only one tab's dialogue box is viewed at any one time, although in Figure 10.3 they are placed one on top of another to illustrate the options.

Each graph has slightly different tabs and options. The different graph types can be accessed via the drop-down method and here the scatterplot is accessed via GRAPH → LEGACY DIALOGS → INTERACTIVE → SCATTERPLOT.

As can be seen in Figure 10.3 the different dialogue boxes give rise to different selections and options. In common with analyses and other SPSS procedures that have these multiple options, the syntax is usually lengthened as more options are selected. In this example titles have been added, scales amended, a best fit line added and so forth. These all impact on the syntax, but also mean that changes to these elements can be quickly introduced into the syntax once it is pasted.

Figure 10.3   **Dialogue boxes for a scatterplot via the Interactive drop-down menu**

The options and selections are made to create a simple scatterplot with age by cost, with points identified by gender. A regression line is fitted, titles and subtitles are added, and the scales for the X- and Y-axes are specified. The command is pasted in Syntax 10:1.

Syntax 10:1 Scatterplot created using the IGRAPH command and SCATTERPLOT sub-command

The syntax is pasted from the drop-down, menu-driven method of creating a simple scatterplot from data in the SPSS sample dataset stroke_valid.sav.

GET FILE='C:\Program Files\SPSSInc\SPSS16\Samples\stroke_valid.sav'.

```
IGRAPH
    /VIEWNAME='Scatterplot'
    /X1=VAR(age) TYPE=SCALE
    /Y=VAR(cost) TYPE=SCALE
    /COLOR=VAR(gender) TYPE=CATEGORICAL
    /COORDINATE=VERTICAL
    /FITLINE METHOD=REGRESSION LINEAR LINE=TOTAL SPIKE=OFF
    /TITLE='Scatterplot created via Interactive'
    /SUBTITLE='Age by cost'
    /CAPTION='Regression line selected'
    /YLENGTH=5.2
    /X1LENGTH=6.5
    /CHARTLOOK='NONE'
    /SCALERANGE=VAR(age) MIN=40.0 MAX=90.0
    /SCALERANGE=VAR(cost) MIN=0.0 MAX=200.0
    /CATORDER VAR(gender) (ASCENDING VALUES OMITEMPTY)
    /SCATTER COINCIDENT=NONE.
```

The data is opened with the GET FILE command (only required if the dataset is not already open).

The IGRAPH command line starts the interactive graph procedure and is followed by *16* sub-commands.

The first sub-command /VIEWNAME='Scatterplot' states how the chart will be noted in the viewer pane of the output file.

The next two sub-commands /X1=VAR(age) TYPE=SCALE /Y=VAR(cost) TYPE=SCALE identify the variables on the (first and only) X-axis **X1** and the Y-axis **Y**. On each of these sub-commands the variable type (**SCALE**) is identified automatically from the variable definition.

The fourth sub-command /COLOR=VAR(gender) TYPE=CATEGORICAL identifies the variable used to colour-code the dots on the scatter graph by a variable value, here **gender**. Again the variable type (**CATEGORICAL**) is identified automatically from the variable definition.

The fifth sub-command /COORDINATE=VERTICAL is automatically generated and specifies that the Y-axis is the vertical one (=**HORIZONTAL** would put the Y-axis on the horizontal).

The sixth sub-command **/FITLINE METHOD=REGRESSION LINEAR LINE=TOTAL SPIKE=OFF** requires a linear regression line of best fit for the whole sample to be added, as I selected. The option to have spikes from the reference line to each individual data point is on the default setting, **OFF**.

The next three sub-commands **/TITLE='Scatterplot created via Interactive' /SUBTITLE='Age by cost' /CAPTION='Regression line selected'** specify the text to be added to the graph, as typed into the dialogue box before pasting. Note the inverted commas enclosing each length of text.

The next two sub-commands **/YLENGTH=5.2 /X1LENGTH=6.5** are automatically generated and define the length of each of the axes in inches. If you want, for example, a taller graph just try changing the Y-axis length to 9.2 and see how that looks.

The 12th sub-command **/CHARTLOOK='NONE'** specifies that no template is to be used. If a template were to be used, its filename and location would be specified **/CHARTLOOK=['C:\Program Files\SPSSInc\SPSS16\Looks\APA_Styles.sgt'].** Note the use of the square brackets and inverted commas.

The next two sub-commands **/SCALERANGE=VAR(age) MIN=40.0 MAX=90.0 /SCALERANGE=VAR(cost) MIN=0.0 MAX=200.0** have been generated because I specified the ranges of the **age** and **cost** scales.

The 15th sub-command **/CATORDER VAR(gender) (ASCENDING VALUES OMITEMPTY)** specifies the order of displaying the values within a category, here **gender** is **ascending**, and also specifies that the graph should **omit** displaying values for a category that is **empty** of cases **OMITEMPTY**.

The final sub-command **/SCATTER COINCIDENT=NONE.** specifies the type of chart, a **Scatterplot**, to be created and has the default option that when dots coincide (are in the same place as another dot) no action is taken, they are just 'placed on top' of one another. As this is the last sub-command it is followed by the full stop to complete the command.

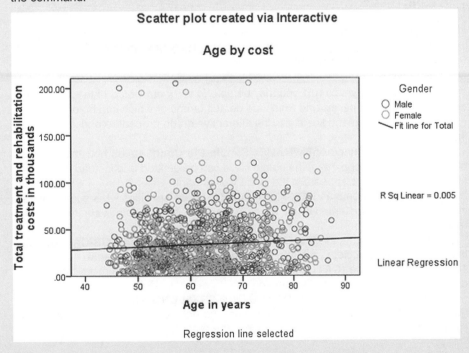

There are many sub-commands available for use with the IGRAPH syntax command. The number of sub-commands simply reflects the options that can be altered, and that are available to you. Some of the sub-commands are automatic, some of which are defaults and as such the actions may still occur even if the sub-command is not present. Others are not defaults per se but removing them has no major impact. Still, SPSS records them routinely, which I think is useful, as it identifies what may be able to be changed. However, they can make the syntax look more off-putting than is necessary. To illustrate this the following syntax is a simple pie chart created via GRAPH → LEGACY DIALOGS → INTERACTIVE → PIE → SIMPLE. On the front dialogue box [Assign Variables] the age category **agecat** variable has been moved into the 'slice by' option and that is all – no selections made, no options used. The subsequent syntax is pasted below.

Syntax 10:2 Pie chart created using the IGRAPH command and PIE sub-command

The syntax is pasted from the drop-down, menu-driven method of creating a simple pie chart from data in the SPSS sample dataset stroke_valid.sav.

```
IGRAPH
    /VIEWNAME='Simple Pie Chart'
    /SUMMARYVAR=$count
    /COLOR=VAR(agecat) TYPE=CATEGORICAL
    /YLENGTH=5.2
    /X1LENGTH=6.5
    /CHARTLOOK='NONE'
    /CATORDER VAR(agecat) (ASCENDING VALUES OMITEMPTY)
    /PIE KEY=ON START 90 CW.
```

If you look back at Syntax 10:1 you may be able to work out which of the syntax sub-command lines are specific and which are default (some of which can be omitted).

The IGRAPH command line starts the interactive graph procedure and is absolutely imperative.

The first sub-command /VIEWNAME='Simple Pie Chart' states how the chart will be noted in the viewer pane of the output file; it can be omitted and instead the generic term 'Interactive chart' appears in the in the viewer pane.

The second sub-command /SUMMARYVAR=$count specifies what summary data in the variable is represented by the slices in the pie. It is not a default command and is required.

The third sub-command /COLOR=VAR(agecat) TYPE=CATEGORICAL identifies the variable used to colour code the slices in the pie chart, here **agecat**. As in Syntax 10:1 the variable type (**CATEGORICAL**) is identified automatically from the variable definition. This sub-command is needed.

The next two sub-commands /YLENGTH=5.2 /X1LENGTH=6.5 are automatically generated as noted in Syntax 10:1. These are the default dimensions and these sub-commands can be omitted with no change in the output.

The sixth sub-command **/CHARTLOOK='NONE'** specifies no template is to be used. Again as a default sub-command it can be omitted with no change in the output.

The seventh sub-command **/CATORDER VAR(gender) (ASCENDING VALUES OMITEMPTY)** specifies the order of displaying the values within a category, here **gender** is **ascending**, and also specifies that the graph should **omit** displaying values for a category that is **empty** of cases **OMITEMPTY**. This is a default command and can be omitted.

The last sub-command **/PIE KEY=ON START 90 CW.** specifies the type of chart, a **PIE** chart, to be created, and is followed by three keywords. **KEY** is the keyword that indicates whether the key is displayed in the chart (**ON** is the default). However, the two keywords that follow can be omitted. **START 90** indicates where around the circle the first slice should start, and **CW** indicates the slices should go around in a ClockWise direction. **Pie must be followed by at least one keyword.**

As this is the last sub-command it is followed by the full stop to complete the command.

COMMENT you could therefore slim down this syntax to the following shorter syntax with little loss.

IGRAPH
    /SUMMARYVAR=$count
    /COLOR=VAR(agecat) TYPE=CATEGORICAL
    /PIE CW.

COMMENT however, if you are pasting the commands, not writing them out yourself, you might as well include the default sub-commands in your syntax file as it is much easier, and can also remind you of the options available.

Some sub-commands are specific to one or more of the graph types available via the interactive options. Likewise there can be a different effect for a generic sub-command when used in different types of graphs. It is not the place to go through them all in this chapter, but I suggest that you begin to read and interpret the meaning of the commands and sub-commands as you paste and use the syntax via the drop-down, menu-driven method.

It is useful if you make your usual chart choice, options and selections, and then paste the syntax, saving it alongside your other exploratory analysis in the syntax file. You may return to it and add sub-commands to improve the appearance of the graph later when you are perhaps preparing reports. You can also set up graph syntax files with your preferred options and selections, storing them in your syntax library for use at a later date and applying to future data analyses. As with the use of templates this can assist you in gaining consistency in your graphs, for example through a report or thesis.

Graphs Created from Legacy Dialogs via Individual Graph Type Options

Most of the graphs created using the individual graph types accessed via the Legacy Dialog options use the syntax command GRAPH. However, one or two graphs such as boxplots, although created via the same drop-down, menu-driven route, have their syntax origin in syntax from a different command (e.g. EXAMINE). Graphs created with the GRAPH command have the option to add titles, subtitles, etc., and to use a chart template. Those created with others, such as the EXAMINE command for boxplots, do not have these options.

First, we will create a simple scatterplot created through the drop-down, menu-driven method GRAPH → LEGACY DIALOGS → SCATTER/DOT. The variable for **age** has been selected for the X-axis, the **cost** variable for the Y-axis, and the marker has been set by the **gender** variable (this indicates cases by colour coding dots by their variable value). No options have been selected. This creates a basic version of the same graph created by Syntax 10:1.

Syntax 10:3 Scatterplot created using the GRAPH command and SCATTERPLOT sub-command.

The syntax is pasted from the drop-down, menu-driven method of creating a simple scatterplot from data in the SPSS sample dataset stroke_valid.sav.

```
GRAPH
    /SCATTERPLOT(BIVAR)=age WITH cost BY gender
    /MISSING=LISTWISE.
```

The **GRAPH** command line starts the graph procedure and is followed by two sub-commands.

The first sub-command **/SCATTERPLOT(BIVAR)=age WITH cost BY gender** states the type of chart, a bivariate scatterplot, to be created. The dependent variable **age** is plotted against the variable **cost** which follows the **WITH** keyword and markers are set by the variable **gender** which follows the **BY** keyword.

The second sub-command **/MISSING= LISTWISE.** states that cases with missing values for any dependent variables are excluded. As this is the last sub-command it is followed by the full stop to complete the command.

The limited options available reflect those found in the drop-down, menu-driven method. Titles, subtitles, footnotes and templates can be added. Unfortunately elements of the graph such as the scales on the axes, a line of best fit, the colour of the dots, etc., cannot be added/amended using the GRAPH sub-command, instead you need to add them the 'long' way via the Chart Editor facility available from the output file.

The next example, an error bar graph, has a few of the options selected and then pasted via the drop-down, menu-driven route GRAPH → LEGACY DIALOGS → ERROR BAR.

Syntax 10:4 Error bar chart created using the GRAPH command and ERRORBAR sub-command

The syntax is pasted from the drop-down, menu-driven method of creating a chart from data in the SPSS sample dataset stroke_valid.sav.

GRAPH
  /ERRORBAR(STDDEV 2)=age BY result
  /TEMPLATE='C:\Program Files\SPSSInc\SPSS16\Looks\GrayScale.sgt'
  /TITLE='Error chart with 2 SD'
  /SUBTITLE='Created using the GrayScale template'
  /MISSING=REPORT.

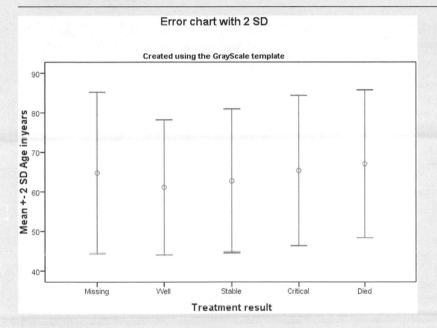

The **GRAPH** command line starts the graph procedure and is followed by five sub-commands.

The first sub-command **/ERRORBAR(STDDEV 2)=age BY result** states the type of chart to be created (error bar) and in brackets is the unit to be displayed (I selected 2 standard deviations in the main dialogue box). The dependent variable is **age** and is displayed by groups within the variable **result**.

The second sub-command is present because I opted to select a template suitable for a book printed in black and white. The sub-command includes the file location **/TEMPLATE='C:\Program Files\SPSSInc\SPSS16\Looks\GrayScale.sgt'**. Note the inverted commas enclosing the file location.

The third sub-command **/TITLE='Error chart with 2 SD'** reflects the title that was typed into the Titles dialogue box and the fourth sub-command **/SUBTITLE='Created using the GrayScale template'** reflects the subtitle that I added. Again, note the inverted commas.

The fifth sub-command **/MISSING=REPORT.** states that the error bar should be reported for the age of those whose **result** status is a missing value. **NOREPORT** is the default whereby missing values are not reported.

As this is the last sub-command it is followed by the full stop to complete the command.

You can also create boxplots through the GRAPH → LEGACY DIALOGS → BOXPLOT. The syntax that is created does not use the GRAPH commands, instead you will see the EXAMINE command. In Syntax 8:10 I noted the creation of box-plots is possible via this process with the addition of a sub-command /PLOT BOXPLOT.

You can see via the drop-down, menu-driven options that the GRAPH → LEGACY DIALOGS → BOXPLOT route allows access to a slightly different range of sub-commands to those available via ANALYZE → DESCRIPTIVE STATISTICS → EXPLORE. Figure 10.4 illustrates a facility to select categorical variables to create clustered boxplots.

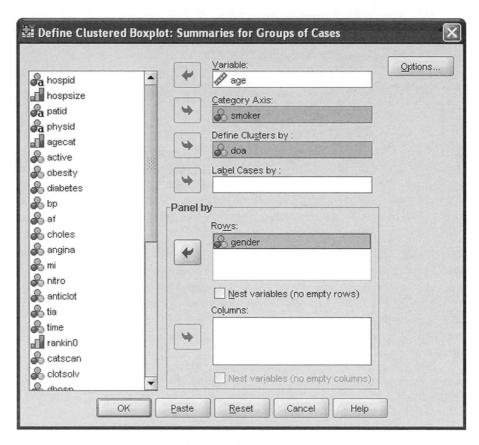

Figure 10.4   **The Legacy Dialogs Boxplot dialogue box**

Syntax 10:5 Creating a boxplot using the EXAMINE command

The syntax is pasted from Figure 10.4 using data in the SPSS sample dataset stroke_valid.sav.

EXAMINE VARIABLES=age BY smoker BY doa
  /PLOT=BOXPLOT
  /STATISTICS=NONE
  /NOTOTAL
  /PANEL ROWVAR=gender ROWOP=CROSS.

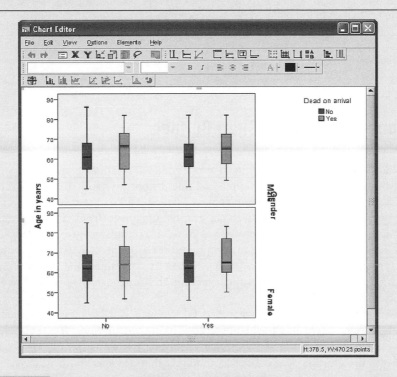

The **EXAMINE** command is followed by the **VARIABLES** keyword, an equals sign and then the dependent variable to be examined **VARIABLES=age**. The two grouping variables follow the BY keyword **BY smoker BY doa**. The order of the variables identifies how the data will be grouped.

The first sub-command **/PLOT=BOXPLOT** states that boxplots are to be created.

The second sub-command **/STATISTICS=NONE** states that no statistics are to be displayed. The EXAMINE command has default descriptive statistics (see page 105) so this command is required to suppress the production of these.

The third sub-command **/NOTOTAL** is a default command and specifies that the box plot should not be created for the overall group (i.e. for the total sample) but only by the factors listed. Try omitting this command from your syntax and you will see that as well as the graph produced as below you will get additional boxplots for all cases (still panelled).

The fourth sub-command **/PANEL ROWVAR=gender ROWOP=CROSS.** is a result of the gender variable being moved into the panel option in the dialogue box and creates the panelled effect (see below). As this is the last sub-command it is followed by the full stop to complete the command.

While the graph produced is a box plot similar to those created through a command issued via the ANALYZE → DESCRIPTIVES → EXAMINE there is additional clustering (allowed by the **BY** keyword and the variable specified after it) and also creation of panels (allowed by the **/PANEL ROWVAR=gender ROWOP=CROSS** sub-command).

Additional sub-commands specific to the **GRAPH** command are not available, so there is no access to template or title sub-commands.

Graphs Created from Chart Builder

Regarding the use of Chart Builder I must admit a personal bias, as I find using Chart Builder is not always as simple as I might hope and so I still tend to use the older methods. However, for completeness I will still go over a brief explanation of the syntax generated when you create graphs and paste from the Chart Builder options. The good news is, like always, you can continue to use the drop-down, menu-driven method of creating the graph and then just press PASTE to record it in your syntax file. The not-so-good news is that to start amending and altering the syntax requires knowledge of a further computer language over and above SPSS syntax.

Chart Builder uses a language called GPL which is a language specifically for creating graphs. According to the SPSS (2007b) documentation: 'It is a concise and flexible language based on the grammar described in *The Grammar of Graphics*. Rather than requiring you to learn commands that are specific to different graph types, GPL provides a basic grammar with which you can build any graph.' Thus it seems to be ideal for those who are already proficient in programming, perhaps with SAS or STATA, who now need to program in SPSS also. This is probably less useful, however, for those new to syntax who are (for the first time) getting to grips with any sort of programming.

I myself have just begun to look at GPL and cannot provide an experienced view on how to use it. I will, though, use a couple of pasted examples just to illustrate it and will show how colours can be altered 'relatively' easily in response to the pasted commands.

Accessing Chart Builder via the drop-down, menu-driven method of using SPSS is via GRAPH → CHART BUILDER and you are then presented with the dialogue box in Figure 10.5.

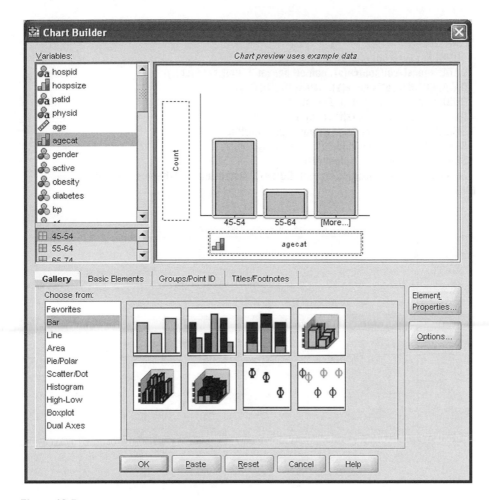

Figure 10.5

Make your selections (here it is a simple bar chart) and then paste the command.

Syntax 10:6 Simple bar chart created using the GGRAPH command and GPL computing language

The syntax is pasted from Figure 10.5 using data in the SPSS sample dataset stroke_valid.sav.

```
GGRAPH
  /GRAPHDATASET NAME="graphdataset" VARIABLES=agecat
    COUNT()[name="COUNT"] MISSING=LISTWISE
    REPORTMISSING=NO
  /GRAPHSPEC SOURCE=INLINE.
```

```
BEGIN GPL
  SOURCE: s=userSource(id("graphdataset"))
  DATA: agecat=col(source(s), name("agecat"), unit.category())
  DATA: COUNT=col(source(s), name("COUNT"))
  GUIDE: axis(dim(1), label("Age bands"))
  GUIDE: axis(dim(2), label("Count"))
  GUIDE: text.title(label("Age category bar chart"))
  SCALE: cat(dim(1), include("1", "2", "3"))
  SCALE: linear(dim(2), include(0))
  ELEMENT: interval(position(agecat*COUNT), shape.interior(shape.square))
END GPL.
```

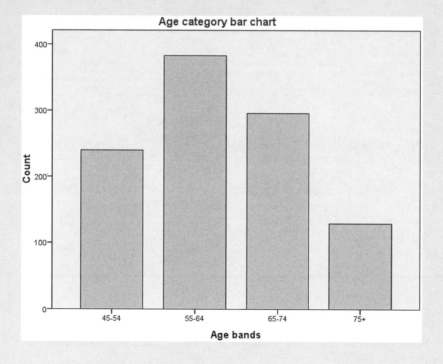

You will see that from BEGIN GPL onwards it looks quite different to the usual syntax commands and sub-commands. The initial GGRAPH command and sub-commands are SPSS syntax commands but between BEGIN GPL and END GPL, the commands are different in both their structure and language. This is because they are not written in SPSS syntax but in GPL. It is beyond the scope of this book (and my expertise) to go into this additional language. However, for those interested in learning more about this, you should first look at the *SPSS 16.0 Command Syntax Reference* guide (SPSS, 2007a) guide and study the elements required from the GGRAPH command because without correct GGRAPH commands GPL will not run. Then you will need to look at the *SPSS 16.0 GPL Reference* guide (SPSS, 2007b)

to learn about the new language. Both of these can be found in electronic form on the SPSS website.

While I do not use GPL myself, I have been able to identify that changing the colour can be relatively simple. By reading through the GPL reference guide I realised that you can add **color** sub-commands for different elements of a graph. The range of colours available is huge, and according to the GPL guide, all you need is an RGB value or a HEX value and you can create that colour. I did not really know what RGB or HEX values were so did a quick search of the Internet and quickly found several webpages (e.g. http://cloford.com/resources/colours/500col.htm) that provide 'lists' of colours and their RGB and HEX values. I am sure there are many websites that do this. GPL will also let you just write in the name of a basic colour (e.g. blue).

In this black and white text examples are limited, but in Syntax 10:7 I have repeated the commands from Syntax 10:6 and added **color** sub-commands to change the text and outer edge of the bars to basic 'grey' and to change the bars to a specified grey (HEX value **ADADAD**) with a black outline to them.

Syntax 10:7 Simple bar chart created using the GGRAPH command and GPL computing language, with the addition of GPL color sub-commands

The syntax is pasted from the drop-down, menu-driven method of creating a chart from data in the SPSS sample dataset stroke_valid.sav.

```
GGRAPH
  /GRAPHDATASET NAME="graphdataset" VARIABLES=agecat
    COUNT()[name="COUNT"] MISSING=LISTWISE REPORTMISSING=NO
  /GRAPHSPEC SOURCE=INLINE.
BEGIN GPL
  SOURCE: s-userSource(id("graphdataset"))
  DATA: agecat=col(source(s), name("agecat"), unit.category())
  DATA: COUNT=col(source(s), name("COUNT"))
  GUIDE: axis(dim(1), label("Age bands"),color (color.grey))
  GUIDE: axis(dim(2), label("Count"), color (color.grey))
  GUIDE: text.title(label("Age category bar chart"))
  SCALE: cat(dim(1), include("1", "2", "3"))
  SCALE: linear(dim(2), include(0))
  ELEMENT:  interval(position(agecat*COUNT),  shape.interior(shape.square),  color
    (color. "ADADAD"), color.exterior (color.black))
END GPL.
```

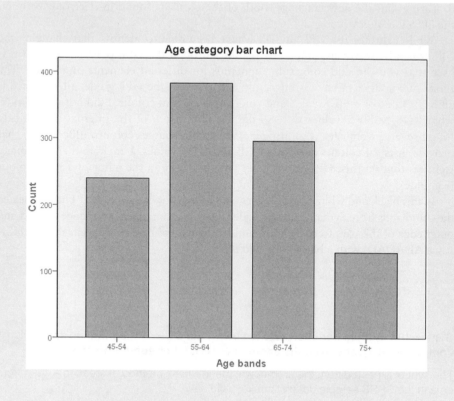

Alternatively, as with the other methods of creating a graph you could just select a template file. In Chart Builder the facility to add a chart template is via the Options button on the bottom right of the main Chart Builder dialogue box.

Syntax 10:8 Simple bar chart created using the GGRAPH command and GPL computing language, with use of a template file

The syntax is pasted from the drop-down, menu-driven method of creating a chart from data in the SPSS sample dataset stroke_valid.sav.

```
GGRAPH
    /GRAPHDATASET NAME="graphdataset" VARIABLES=agecat
        COUNT()[name="COUNT"] MISSING=LISTWISE REPORTMISSING=NO
    /GRAPHSPEC SOURCE=INLINE
    TEMPLATE=["C:\Program Files\SPSSInc\SPSS16\Looks\GrayScale.sgt"].
BEGIN GPL
    SOURCE: s=userSource(id("graphdataset"))
    DATA: agecat=col(source(s), name("agecat"), unit.category())
```

```
  DATA: COUNT=col(source(s), name("COUNT"))
  GUIDE: axis(dim(1), label("Age bands"))
  GUIDE: axis(dim(2), label("Count"))
  GUIDE: text.title(label("Age category bar chart"))
  SCALE: cat(dim(1), include("1", "2", "3"))
  SCALE: linear(dim(2), include(0))
  ELEMENT: interval(position(agecat*COUNT), shape.interior(shape.square))
END GPL.
```

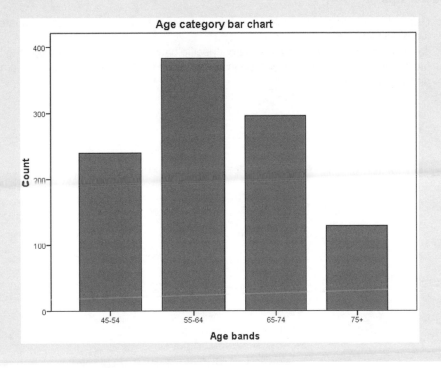

Apart from these small tips about changing the colour of the graph elements and text I shall not be explaining further about GPL – it is a second computer language, with a completely different type of syntax (in linguistic) terms. As noted earlier in this section, the keen, curious or adventurous can access a pdf version of the *SPSS 16.0 GPL Reference Guide* (SPSS, 2007b). This can be found in the Manuals folder on the SPSS installation discs and also online at http://www.spss.com.

Summary

The syntax file you create for your data exploration and analysis is a record of what you have carried out. This should also include the syntax used for your graphs. There are three main ways to create graphs in SPSS and each has a different pattern of syntax. Pasting the commands from the drop-down, menu-driven method of using SPSS is often the most useful way to start using the syntax, but for some graphs this may be as far as you can go – either because the syntax is itself limited, or because of the GPL language. Use of the Interactive method of graph production is likely to be the most helpful syntax in which to develop expertise. Whether using syntax or the drop-down, menu-driven method, using a chart template can quickly transform the appearance of the graph.

Useful Tips

- Get to know how graphs look when they are generated from the chart templates supplied by SPSS.
- Take some time to work on a couple of specific chart templates, one for working in black and white and one for working in colour. Save them as graph templates in an appropriate folder.

11

Syntax for Univariate Analysis

Examples in this chapter will use the following SPSS sample datasets
recidivism.sav
New drug.sav
dietstudy.sav
stroke_valid.sav

This chapter will explain the syntax commands that enable you to carry out univariate data analysis for categorical, ordinal and interval data. Tests that analyse the differences between groups will be covered as well as those examining associations between variables, using parametric and distribution free (non-parametric) tests as appropriate.

Creating a syntax file which has your univariate analysis commands is very useful. As mentioned in previous chapters, you may need to carry out the analysis on more than one occasion. This can be because you want to carry out analysis on not only your full dataset, but also on selected sections of your data (e.g. include only males under the age of 75). Syntax is helpful because you can write the syntax for the univariate analysis on the full dataset, save and run the file. Then you can open a new syntax file, write the appropriate syntax for selecting or splitting the file (see Chapter 9), then just copy and paste the syntax for the full dataset analysis after this. You then save and just re-run. It can be so efficient and this is when you can really start to see why it is worth learning SPSS syntax.

This chapter will not go into the selection of the 'correct' statistics for your data. As stated in Chapter 8 (and repeated here for those who have jumped straight to this chapter) this book is not intended to teach you about statistics; it is written for newcomers to syntax, not newcomers to statistics or SPSS. Thus, assumptions are made (1) that readers are already experienced and familiar with statistics and (2) that readers are also experienced and familiar with the drop-down, menu-driven methods of using SPSS.

Good Practice

- Check the type of data that you have before carrying out the tests.
- Carry out exploratory analysis first.
- Follow the analysis plan.
- Save the syntax files with meaningful names.

Categorical Data

An infrequently used but quite useful test is the goodness-of-fit chi-square test for a single categorical variable. This test examines the distribution of the values within a categorical variable, for example how many respondents (in proportional terms) fall

Syntax 11:1 Single-sample goodness-of-fit chi-square using the NPAR TESTS command and the CHISQUARE sub-command

The syntax will analyse categorical data in the SPSS sample dataset recidivism.sav.

GET FILE='C:\Program Files\SPSSInc\SPSS16\Samples\recidivism.sav'.

NPAR TEST
  /CHISQUARE=agecat ed
  /EXPECTED=EQUAL
  /MISSING ANALYSIS.

The **GET FILE** command opens the datafile if not already open.

The command line **NPAR TEST** specifies that a non-parametric test is to be performed and is followed by three sub-commands.

The first sub-command **/CHISQUARE=agecat ed** specifies the test to be carried out, then has an equals sign followed by the variables to be tested. As many variables as you wish can be listed and they will be examined separately.

The second sub-command **/EXPECTED=EQUAL** specifies the distribution you are expecting. This default is that the equal frequencies are expected in each category, and as a default you could miss out the command line and SPSS would still work to this default.

The third sub-command **/MISSING ANALYSIS.** specifies that those cases with missing values are excluded only on a test-by-test basis. Again, as a default you could miss out the command line and SPSS would work to this default.

As this is the last sub-command it is followed by the full stop to complete the command.

OPTIONS
On the **/CHISQUARE** sub-command it is possible to select ranges for the categorical variables – see Syntax 8:5.

For the **/ EXPECTED** sub-command you can specify the distribution you would expect to find. After the equals sign list the number of cases you expect to find for each category, in the order of the values of the categories. In recidivism.sav there are 1000 cases, so your expected values must total 1000. All four categories must be expected to have cases, so a value of 0 is not permitted. Try running the syntax again, but this time with **/EXPECTED=400 300 200 100**.

For the **/MISSING** sub-command alternative options, **/MISSING LISTWISE** means cases would be excluded if there is data missing for any of the variables listed on any sub-command (here after the chi-square sub-command) and **/MISSING INCLUDE** means user-specified missing values are included as valid values.

within each of the possible options. In the example below, the categorical data on education (**ed**) and on age (**agecat**) will be analysed.

More commonly a chi-square test is used to see if there are associations between groups across two or more categorical variables. This is accessed through the drop-down, menu-driven method via ANALYZE → DESCRIPTIVE STATISTICS → CROSSTABS then clicking on the STATISTICS button and selecting the chi-square tick-box in the top right. The command has been pasted below, following selection of my favourite cell layout – inclusion of the expected values and the row percentages. When the chi-square statistic is significant this layout helps me to interpret the direction of the association.

Syntax 11:2 Chi-square test to examine associations between two categorical variables using CROSSTABS command and the STATISTICS sub-command

The syntax will analyse categorical data in the SPSS sample dataset recidivism.sav.

GET FILE='C:\Program Files\SPSSInc\SPSS16\Samples\recidivism.sav'.

CROSSTABS
   /TABLES=social BY employ
   /FORMAT=AVALUE TABLES
   /STATISTICS=CHISQ
   /CELLS=COUNT EXPECTED ROW
   /COUNT ROUND CELL.

The **GET FILE** command opens the datafile if not already open.

Apart from the sub-command line **/STATISTICS=CHISQ** the syntax is the same as for simple cross-tabulations and contingency tables as covered in Chapter 8. For a detailed explanation of the command and sub-command lines above see Syntax 8:2.

The one new line we have introduced into the crosstabs **/STATISTICS=CHISQ** is the one that produces the statistical analysis.

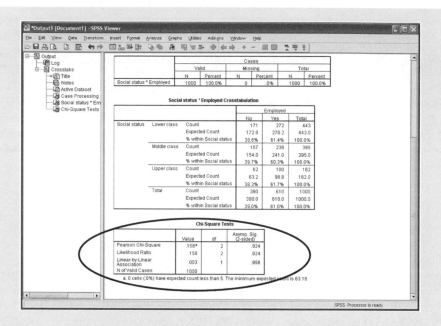

If you are not interested in the information detailed in the tables above (expected values, row percentages, etc.) then you can simplify the syntax to get a basic table and the statistical information only.

CROSSTABS
  /TABLES=social BY employ
  /STATISTICS=CHISQ.

Again on the **/ CROSSTABS** command you can select ranges for the categorical variables – see Syntax 8:5.

For 2 × 2 tables created using syntax such as that in Syntax 11:2 (but with two variables with two categories each) Fisher's exact test will automatically be displayed. Other tests that can be carried out on 2 × 2 categorical variables include the McNemar test to examine changes in dichotomous data that has been collected on two occasions. This is accessed through the drop-down, menu-driven method by going ANALYZE → DESCRIPTIVE STATISTICS → CROSSTABS then clicking on the STATISTICS button and selecting the McNemar tick-box on the lower right-hand side.

In a 2 × 2 table you can also run statistics for Risk. On 2 × 2 (or 3 × 3, 4 × 4, 5 × 5, etc.) tables you can also run a Kappa statistic, often used to analyse rater agreement.

The syntax for these three tests is very simple and requires only the changing of the test name following the /STATISTICS sub-command line (see below).

Syntax 11:3 Additional tests (McNemar, Kappa, Risk) for 2×2 categorical variables using CROSSTABS command and the STATISTICS sub-command

The syntax will analyse categorical data in the SPSS sample dataset recidivism.sav.

GET FILE='C:\Program Files\SPSSInc\SPSS16\Samples\recidivism.sav'.

COMMENT The short version syntax below will carry out the McNemar test on the type of crime committed by individuals on two occasions.
```
CROSSTABS
    /TABLES=violent1 BY violent2
    /STATISTICS=MCNEMAR.
```

COMMENT The syntax below will carry out the Risk analysis for each of the variables listed before the BY keyword against all variables listed after, here employment status and gender analysed for risk of a conviction for a second offence.
```
CROSSTABS
    /TABLES=employ gender BY convict2
    /FORMAT=AVALUE TABLES
    /STATISTICS=RISK
    /CELLS=COUNT EXPECTED ROW
    /COUNT ROUND CELL.
```

Running the Kappa statistic is equally simple. On the **/TABLES** sub-command after the equals sign list the variable name for your first rater and then, after the **BY** keyword, list the variable name for the second rater. I cannot find an SPSS sample dataset with suitable data, but I hope that it is fairly clear from the example below what you need to do.

```
CROSSTABS
    /TABLES= rater_a BY rater_b
    /STATISTICS=KAPPA.
```

Ordinal Data – Differences

This section will cover the tests for ordinal data (and for non-normally distributed interval data), first for two unrelated groups and for two related groups, then tests for more than two unrelated groups, and for more than two related groups.

Two Unrelated Groups

The Mann–Whitney test is used to examine ordinal data for differences between two independent groups. This is accessed through the drop-down, menu-driven method via ANALYZE → NONPARAMETRIC TESTS → 2 INDEPENDENT SAMPLES.

In the sample dataset recidivism.sav the variables **crime1** and **crime2** are both ordinal. The lowest level of crime listed in the dataset (based on the US legal system) is misdemeanour B which scores 1 and the highest listed, felony A, scores 5. Put **crime1** into the 'Test Variable List' box, and move gender across as the 'Grouping Variable' and define the groups as 0 and 1 via the button below the Grouping Variable. The Mann–Whitney tick-box should already be ticked as the default. Click on the PASTE button to create the syntax below.

Syntax 11:4 Mann–Whitney U test using the NPAR TESTS command and the M-W sub-command

The syntax will analyse data in the SPSS sample dataset recidivism.sav.

GET FILE='C:\Program Files\SPSSInc\SPSS16\Samples\recidivism.sav'.

NPAR TESTS
    /M-W= crime1 BY gender(0 1)
    /MISSING ANALYSIS.

The **GET FILE** command opens the datafile if not already open.
    The first command **NPAR TESTS** is followed by two sub-command lines.
    The first sub-command line **/M-W= crime1 BY gender(0 1)** identifies the nonparametric test to be used (**M-W** is just short for Mann–Whitney) followed by an equals sign and the dependent variable to be analysed. The group variable for the analysis follows after the **BY** keyword and in brackets the two values to be used to identify the two groups within the group variable.
    The second sub-command **/MISSING ANALYSIS.** specifies that those cases with missing values are excluded only on a test-by-test basis. Again, as a default you could miss out the command line and SPSS would work to this default. As this is the last sub-command it is followed by the full stop to complete the command.

OPTIONS
On the **/M-W=** sub-command line as many dependent variables as you wish can be listed here providing they all need to be analysed by the same groups within the same grouping variable. The two values for the grouping variable can be typed in any order and do not need to be concurrent.

    /M-W= crime1 crime2 BY gender(1 0)

For the **/MISSING** sub-command alternative options see Syntax 11:1.
    Alongside the test here is also an option to produce descriptive statistics and quartiles for the overall sample using the sub-command **/STATISTICS=DESCRIPTIVES QUARTILES**.

Other two independent sample tests that can be run instead of the Mann–Whitney test are the Moses test (to test the range of an ordinal variable is the same within groups) and the Wald–Wolfowitz and the Kolmogorov–Smirnov tests (both tests examine whether the distribution is the same in groups). Just replace the **/M-W=** sub-command in Syntax 11:4 with the appropriate line.

  /MOSES= age cost BY gender(0 1)
  /W-W= age cost BY gender(0 1)
  /K-S= age cost BY gender(0 1)

Two Related Groups

Next we will look at analyses for paired ordinal variables, the most common of which is the Wilcoxon. The syntax is similar to Syntax 11:4 and to change the test you need to change the statistics test sub-command. In the analysis of related variables you also need to replace the BY keyword with the WITH keyword, and then add (PAIRED) to the end.

The Wilcoxon test is accessed through the drop-down, menu-driven method via ANALYZE → NONPARAMETRIC TESTS → 2 INDEPENDENT SAMPLES.

Syntax 11:5 Wilcoxon test using the NPAR TESTS command and the WILCOXON sub-command

The syntax will analyse data in the SPSS sample dataset recidivism.sav.

GET FILE='C:\Program Files\SPSSInc\SPSS16\Samples\recidivism.sav'.

NPAR TEST
  /WILOOXON=crime1 WITH crime2 (PAIRED)
  /MISSING ANALYSIS.

The **GET FILE** command opens the datafile if not already open.

The first command **NPAR TESTS** is followed by two sub-command lines.

The first sub-command line **/WILCOXON = crime1 WITH crime2 (PAIRED)** identifies the nonparametric test to be used followed by an equals sign and two dependent variables to be analysed, separated by the **WITH** keyword. The command line is completed with the **(PAIRED)** keyword.

The second sub-command **/MISSING ANALYSIS.** specifies that those cases with missing values are excluded only on a test-by-test basis (as per Syntax 11:4).

The last sub-command is followed by the full stop to complete the command.

OPTIONS

The **/WILCOXON** sub-command line can have many pairs of dependent variables to analyse.

For paired variables, the first of each pair is listed before a single WITH keyword, with the second of each pair of variables *listed in the same order* as the first pair and the command completed with the (PAIRED) keyword. There isn't a sample dataset to illustrate this, but in the example below three Wilcoxon analyses would be run on imaginary pairA, pairB and pairC.

  /WILCOXON=pairA_1 pairB_1 pairC_1 WITH pairA_2 pairB_2 pairC_2 (PAIRED).

Using syntax you can also specify that each variable is to be paired with every other variable in the list. This is done by simply omitting the WITH keyword – this is only available through syntax. There is not a sample dataset to illustrate this, but in the example below six Wilcoxon analyses would be run – on all combination pairs of four (imaginary) variables v1 & v2   v1 & v3   v1 & v4   v2 & v3   v2 & v4   v3 & v4

  /WILCOXON=v1 v2 v3 v4 (PAIRED).

A further option only available through syntax is for each variable before the **WITH** keyword to be paired with each variable after the **WITH** keyword; simply omit the **(PAIRED)** keyword. There is not a sample dataset to illustrate this, but in the example below four Wilcoxon analyses would be run – each of the (imaginary) variables before WITH paired with each of the two after b1 & a1 b1 & a2 b2 & a1 b2 & a2
   /WILCOXON=b1 b2 WITH a1 a2

Other tests for two related (or paired) variables that can be run instead of the Wilcoxon test are the Sign test (to examine whether the distribution of two paired variables in a two-related-samples test is the same), the McNemar test (to examine whether combinations of values between two dichotomous variables are equally likely) and the marginal homogeneity test (to examine whether combinations of values between two paired ordinal variables are equally likely). Just replace the /WILCOXON = sub-command in Syntax 11:5 with the appropriate test sub-command **SIGN, MCNEMAR** or **M-H**. All options listed at the end of Syntax 11:5 for the use of WITH and (PAIRED) are available.

More than Two Unrelated Ordinal Variables

Next we will look at analyses for more than two unrelated ordinal variables, the most common of which is the Kruskal–Wallis. The syntax is very similar to Syntax 11:4, you just need to change the statistics test keyword and increase the number of group values specified. To paste the command from the drop-down, menu-driven method you go via ANALYZE → NONPARAMETRIC TESTS → K INDEPENDENT SAMPLES.

Syntax 11:6 Kruskal–Wallis test using the NPAR TESTS command and the K-W sub-command

The syntax will analyse data in the SPSS sample dataset recidivism.sav.

GET FILE='C:\Program Files\SPSSInc\SPSS16\Samples\recidivism.sav'.

NPAR TESTS
   /K-W=crime1 BY social(1 3)
   /MISSING ANALYSIS.

The **GET FILE** command opens the datafile if not already open.
   On the **/K-W=** sub-command line as many dependent variables as you wish can be listed here providing they all need to be analysed by the same groups within the same

grouping variable: **(1 3)** means that groups represented by those values and all values in between them will be included **/M-W= crime1 crime2 BY social(1 3)** – so in this example 1, 2 and 3 will be used.

The second sub-command **/MISSING ANALYSIS.** specifies that those cases with missing values are excluded only on a test-by-test basis (as per Syntax 11:4), for alternative missing value options see Syntax 11:1.

The last sub-command it is followed by the full stop to complete the command.

ERROR ALERT

On the **/K-W=** sub-command line where two values are entered for the grouping variable **(1 3)** it is important to note that for all values between the two stated values to be included as groups in the analysis, then the numbers need to be in ascending order. If **(3 1)** had been specified then only groups represented by 3 and 1 would have been included.

More than Two Related Ordinal Variables

Next we will look at analyses for more than two related ordinal variables, the most common of which is the Friedman test. To paste the command from the drop-down, menu-driven method you go via ANALYZE → NONPARAMETRIC TESTS → K RELATED SAMPLES.

Syntax 11:7 Friedman test using the NPAR TESTS command and the FRIEDMAN sub-command

The syntax will analyse data in the SPSS sample dataset New drug.sav.

GET FILE='C:\Program Files\SPSSInc\SPSS16\Samples\New drug.sav'.

NPAR TESTS
   /FRIEDMAN=resp1 resp2 resp3
   /MISSING LISTWISE.

The data is opened with the **GET FILE** command (only required if the dataset is not already open).

The first command **NPAR TESTS** is followed by two sub-command lines.

The first command line **/FRIEDMAN = resp1 resp2 resp3** identifies the non-parametric test to be used followed by an equals sign and the list of related variables to be analysed.

The second sub-command **/MISSING ANALYSIS.** specifies that those cases with missing values are excluded only on a test-by-test basis (as per Syntax 11:4); for alternative missing value options see Syntax 11:1.

The last sub-command is followed by the full stop to complete the command.

Other tests for more than two related variables that can be run instead of the Friedman test are Kendall's W test (to examine agreement among judges or raters, where each case is one person's rating of several items) and Cochran's Q test (to examine whether the distribution of values is the same for more than two related dichotomous variables). Just replace the **FRIEDMAN** sub-command in Syntax 11:7 with the appropriate test sub-command **KENDALL** or **COCHRAN**.

Interval Data – Differences

This section will cover the tests for normally distributed interval data, first for two unrelated groups and for two related groups, then the tests for more than two unrelated groups and for more than two related groups.

Two Unrelated Groups

To examine interval data for differences between two unrelated, or independent, groups we use the t-test. This is accessed through the drop-down, menu-driven method via ANALYZE → COMPARE MEANS → INDEPENDENT-SAMPLES T TEST. In this example we examine the syntax commands pasted from the drop-down, menu-driven method to compare two baseline variables, weights **wgt0** and triglycerides **tg0**, by **gender** in the dietstudy.sav sample dataset.

Syntax 11:8 Independent samples t-test test using the T-TEST GROUPS command

The syntax will analyse data in the SPSS sample dataset dietstudy.sav.

GET FILE='C:\Program Files\SPSSInc\SPSS16\Samples\dietstudy.sav'.

T-TEST GROUPS=gender(0 1)
    /MISSING=ANALYSIS
    /VARIABLES=wgt0 tg0
    /CRITERIA=CI(.95).

The **GET FILE** command opens the datafile if not already open.

The first command **T-TEST GROUPS=gender(0 1)** has the **T-TEST** command followed by the **GROUPS** keyword. This is followed by an equals sign and the variable used to group cases for the t-test. In brackets are the two values belonging to the groups to be included in the analysis.

The first sub-command /**MISSING ANALYSIS** specifies that those cases with missing values are excluded only on a test-by-test basis (as per Syntax 11:4); for alternative missing value options see Syntax 11:1.

The second sub-command line /**VARIABLES=wgt0 tg0** identifies the variables to be analysed. As many dependent variables as you wish can be listed here providing they all need to be analysed by the same groups within the same grouping variable.

The third sub-command line /**CRITERIA=CI(.95).** identifies the value of the confidence interval, with a default of 0.95. As this is the last sub-command it is followed by the full stop to complete the command.

Two Related Groups

To examine interval data for differences between two related groups we use the paired t-test. This is accessed through the drop-down, menu-driven method via ANALYZE → COMPARE MEANS → PAIRED-SAMPLES T TEST. In this example we compare the baseline weights and final weights in the dietstudy.sav sample dataset.

Syntax 11:9 Paired-samples t-test test using the T-TEST PAIRS command

The syntax will analyse data in the SPSS sample dataset dietstudy.sav.

GET FILE='C:\Program Files\SPSSInc\SPSS16\Samples\dietstudy.sav'.

T-TEST PAIRS=wgt0 WITH wgt4 (PAIRED)
  /CRITERIA=CI(.9500)
  /MISSING=ANALYSIS.

The **GET FILE** command opens the datafile if not already open.

The first command **T-TEST PAIRS=wgt0 WITH wgt4 (PAIRED)** has the T-TEST command followed by the PAIRS keyword. This is followed by an equals sign and two dependent variables to be analysed, separated by the WITH keyword. The command line is completed with the (PAIRED) keyword.

The first sub-command line **/CRITERIA=CI(.9500)** identifies the value of the confidence interval, with a default of 0.95.

The second sub-command **/MISSING ANALYSIS.** specifies that those cases with missing values are excluded only on a test-by-test basis (as per Syntax 11:4); for alternative missing value options see Syntax 11:1. As this is the last sub-command it is followed by the full stop to complete the command

---

OPTIONS

The **T-TEST** command line can have many pairs of dependent variables to analyse. Use of the **WITH** and **(PAIRED)** keywords is consistent with their use in the **WILCOXON** command and allow:

- many specified pairs on the same command;
- each variable to be paired with every other variable in the list;
- each variable before the WITH keyword to be paired with each variable after the WITH keyword.

(See the OPTIONS section at the end of Syntax 11:5.)

More than Two Unrelated Interval Variables

Next we will look at analyses for interval variables analysed by more than two unrelated groups, the most straightforward of which is the one-way analysis of variance (ANOVA). To paste the command from the drop-down, menu-driven method you go via ANALYZE → COMPARE MEANS → ONE-WAY ANOVA where there are many choices to be made in the analysis. As you can see in Figure 11.1 each of the three buttons on the right opens up a new dialogue box and decisions and selections need to be made.

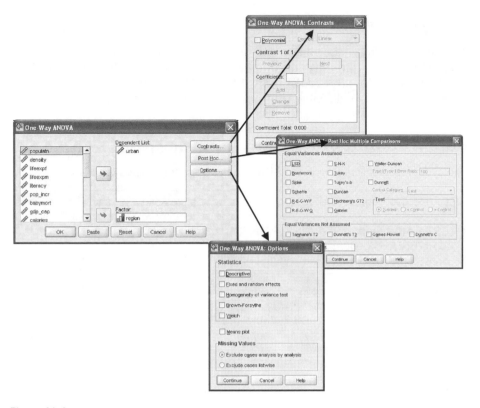

Figure 11.1

Not surprisingly, the syntax for the one-way ANOVA has the facility to address the many decisions and selections that are available via the drop-down, menu-driven method, which can make it look a bit scary. Try not to get put off by all the choices, they are pretty much the ones you make using the drop-down, menu-driven method anyway. So, as you start using syntax, use the drop-down, menu-driven method as you would do normally, then use the paste function to create the syntax. Alternatively, you could carry out the analysis as normal with the drop-down, menu-driven method and clicking on OK, then later go back through the Log entries on the Output file, copying and pasting to create your syntax file. The syntax generated from selecting no options (as per Figure 11.1) can be seen in Syntax 11:10.

In syntax if you have a favoured option for your one-way ANOVA decisions and selections, then you can set up a syntax file in your syntax library called something like anova_1way_default.sps with all your preferences specified. This can then be used each and every time you want to run a one-way ANOVA for any of your projects just requiring you to change the variable names.

Syntax 11:10 One-way ANOVA test using the ONEWAY command

The syntax will analyse data in the SPSS sample dataset World95.sav.

GET FILE='C:\Program Files\SPSSInc\SPSS16\Samples\World95.sav'.

ONEWAY urban BY region
  /MISSING ANALYSIS.

The **GET FILE** command opens the datafile if not already open.

The first command **ONEWAY urban BY region** identifies the test to be used **ONEWAY** followed by the dependent variable to be analysed – as many dependent variables as you wish can be listed here providing they all need to be analysed by the same groups within the same grouping variable. The group variable for the analysis follows after the **BY** keyword. Note: all values in the grouping variable are used in the analysis, so if you do not want them all to be included in the analysis you must first select a sub-set of the data as per Syntax 9:1.

The sub-command **/MISSING ANALYSIS.** specifies that those cases with missing values are excluded only on a test-by-test basis (details as per Syntax 11:4); for alternative missing value options see Syntax 11:1. As this is the last sub-command it is followed by the full stop to complete the command.

OPTIONS

There are many options within the ONEWAY command. However, this is a syntax *beginner's* text and so I do not want to overwhelm or put off readers by listing every one of the many sub-commands available. I will outline the more commonly used ones, and for the rest I suggest you look up **ONEWAY** in the *Command Syntax Reference* guide, (SPSS, 2007a), available in searchable pdf format via the SPSS HELP drop-down menu (see Resources section, page 30). Alternatively for command-specific information press the F1 button when you are in the syntax editor and while your cursor is in the **ONEWAY** command line.

You can begin by going through your normal selections in the drop-down, menu-driven method and pasting the commands from there.

If you usually select alternatives from the [Options...] box in the ┌Statistics─ section (see Figure 11.1) then in syntax you will need to run the **STATISTICS** sub-command followed by the keywords you wish to apply, for example **/STATISTICS DESCRIPTIVES EFFECTS HOMOGENEITY.**. Here three boxes have been ticked (and the syntax pasted) providing statistics for descriptives (mean, 95%CIs, min, max, SD, SE) and for random and fixed effects models, and also running a homogeneity of variance test.

If you get a significant result on your one-way ANOVA and need to run a post-hoc analysis to carry out comparisons of pairs of group means, you re-run the one-way ANOVA, this time selecting your preferred alternative, for example Least Significant Difference (LSD) from the [Post Hoc...] box (see Figure 11.1), and inserting the significance level (there is a 0.05 default) **/POSTHOC=BTUKEY LSD BONFERRONI ALPHA(0.05).**. Note: you can use only one **POSTHOC** sub-command line per **ONEWAY** command but, as you can put multiple keywords on the single sub-command line, this should not be problematic.

If you usually select alternatives from the [Contrasts...] box (see Figure 11.1) and want guidance on the syntax for those, refer to the *Command Syntax Reference* guide.

Univariate multifactorial ANOVAs for unrelated groups are more complex than one-way ANOVAs. This analysis is accessed via ANALYZE → GENERAL LINEAR MODEL → UNIVARIATE. Again, as with one-way ANOVAs, using the drop-down, menu-driven method still offers many choices within the analysis. As you can see in Figure 11.2 each of the buttons on the right opens up a new dialogue box (though only one at a time thankfully) and decisions and selections need to be made.

If you do not understand what to select from the drop-down, menu-driven dialogue boxes then I recommend you read a good SPSS-based statistical textbook such *Discovering Statistics Using SPSS* by Andy Field (2009), or *SPSS for Psychologists* by Brace et al. (2006) before you progress with the analysis.

Just as with the one-way ANOVA, the syntax for the univariate ANOVAs has the facility to address all of the decisions and selections within the drop-down, menu-driven dialogue boxes, and again this can make the syntax look quite scary. As mentioned on page 154, try not to get put off by all the alternatives, they are the same as those found using the drop-down, menu-driven method.

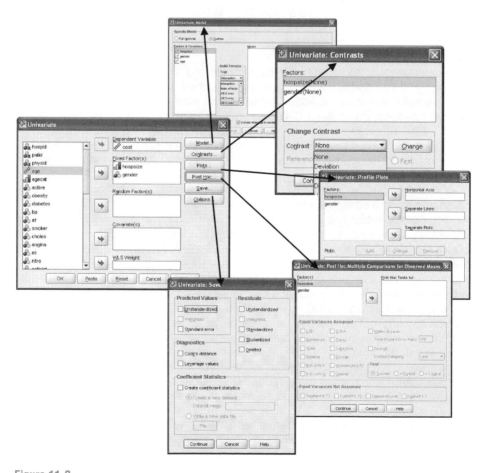

Figure 11.2

Syntax 11:11 has been pasted from the screens above, with no options selected in any of the secondary dialogue boxes for plots, contrasts, etc.

Syntax 11:11 Univariate two-way ANOVA test using the UNIANOVA command

The syntax will analyse data in the SPSS sample dataset stroke_valid.sav.

GET FILE='C:\Program Files\SPSSInc\SPSS16\Samples\stroke_valid.sav'.

UNIANOVA cost BY hospsize gender
   /METHOD=SSTYPE(3)
   /INTERCEPT=INCLUDE
   /CRITERIA=ALPHA(0.05)
   /DESIGN=hospsize gender hospsize*gender.

The **GET FILE** command opens the datafile if not already open.

The first command **UNIANOVA cost BY hospsize gender** identifies the test to be used **UNIANOVA** followed by the dependent variable to be analysed. As many dependent variables as you wish can be listed here providing they all need to be analysed by the same groups within the same grouping variable. The group variables for the analysis follow after the **BY** keyword. As in the **ONEWAY** command (Syntax 11:10) all values in the grouping variables are used in the analysis, so if you do not want them all to be included in the analysis you must first select a subset of the data as per Syntax 9:1.

The command line is followed by four sub-commands; note that they are indented and each is preceded by a forward slash.

The first sub-command **/METHOD=SSTYPE(3)** specifies the computational aspects of the **UNIANOVA** analysis. The Type III sum-of-squares method is the default – **SSTYPE(1)**, **SSTYPE(2)** and **SSTYPE(4)** are the alternatives.

The second sub-command **/INTERCEPT=INCLUDE** specifies whether the intercept is included in the model. **INCLUDE** is the default (**EXCLUDE** is the alternative).

The third sub-command **/CRITERIA=ALPHA(0.05)** specifies the alpha level used to build the model; 0.05 is the default but can be altered as required.

The fourth sub-command **/DESIGN=hospsize gender hospsize*gender.** builds the model. Listed is the 'full model' (the default), in this case two main effects (**hospsize gender**) and one interaction (**hospsize*gender**). As this is the last sub-command it is followed by the full stop to complete the command

---

Without the default sub-commands (which can be omitted as they are the default), Syntax 11:11 can look as streamlined as
UNIANOVA cost BY hospsize gender
   /DESIGN=hospsize gender hospsize*gender.

OPTIONS
Again, I do not want to overwhelm or put off readers by listing every one of the many sub-commands available so I will just outline a couple of useful ones.

To see what else syntax can offer beyond the choices available via the [Paste] button you can look up **UNIANOVA** in the *Command Syntax Reference* guide, available in searchable pdf format via the SPSS HELP drop-down menu (more details in Resources section, page 30). Alternatively for command-specific information press the F1 button when you are in the syntax editor and while your cursor is on the **UNIANOVA** command line.

If you need to carry out an analysis of covariance (ANCOVA) command then covariates need to be listed on the **UNIANOVA** sub-command, after the factors, and following the WITH keyword, that is **UNIANOVA cost BY hospsize WITH age**.

For those needing to analyse data using complex models, syntax has more flexibility than the drop-down, menu-driven method in the models that you can build. It is possible to have models with nested effects, or even multiple nested effects, only available through syntax and through the use of keywords and brackets on the **/DESIGN=** sub-command (see **UNIANOVA** in the pdf *Command Syntax Reference* guide – more details of how to access this are in Resources section, page 30).

These univariate ANOVAs and ANCOVAs accessed via the Univariate GLM option on the drop-down, menu-driven method again have decisions and selections which can be made via each of the dialogue boxes accessed via the buttons on the right (as shown in Figure 11.2). Each of these buttons leads to options which can also be accessed using syntax sub-commands. The syntax can be complex, and therefore you should begin by going through your normal selections in the drop-down, menu-driven method and pasting the commands from there. Using this method, without having to write a single command line yourself, you can create a syntax file for analysis of the project data. This can be saved and stored alongside the data and the outputs in case you need to revisit the analysis, re-run it, add cases, discuss with your supervisor, and so on.

Once you understand the sub-commands and recognise your preferred selections you may decide then that you want set up a new syntax file with your univariate ANOVA 'default model'. This can go in your syntax library called something like anova_univar_default.sps with all your preferences specified as a template for future projects.

More than Two Related Interval Variables

Next we will look at analyses for interval variables analysed by more than two related groups, the repeated measures analysis of variance (ANOVA). To paste the command from the drop-down, menu-driven method you go via ANALYZE → GENERAL LINEAR MODEL → REPEATED MEASURES. As with all general linear models, there are many choices available in the dialogue boxes accessible via the buttons in the top right side.

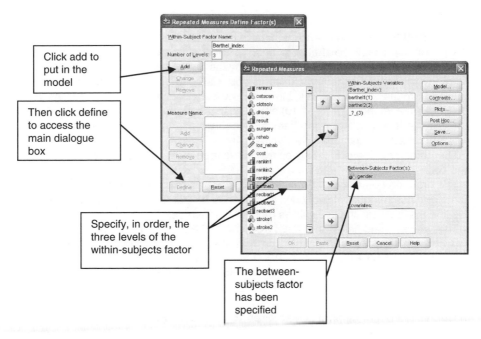

Figure 11.3

Data from the stroke_valid.sav SPSS sample dataset will be used to demonstrate the syntax. An assessment score, Barthel index, is our within-subjects factor. It is repeated three times (**barthel1, barthel2, barthel3**) so has three levels. We will also examine the effects of a between-subjects factor, gender. Syntax 11:12 is pasted from the analysis being carried out via the drop-down, menu-driven process and is pasted as if from Figure 11.3.

Syntax 11:12 Repeated ANOVA using the GLM command

The syntax will analyse data in the SPSS sample dataset stroke_valid.sav.

GET FILE='C:\Program Files\SPSSInc\SPSS16\Samples\stroke_valid.sav'.

```
GLM barthel1 barthel2 barthel3 BY agecat
    /WSFACTOR=Barthel_index 3 Polynomial
    /METHOD=SSTYPE(3)
    /CRITERIA=ALPHA(.05)
    /WSDESIGN=Barthel_index
    /DESIGN=agecat.
```

The **GET FILE** command opens the datafile if not already open.

The command **GLM barthel1 barthel2 barthel3 BY agecat** identifies the test to be used **GLM** (General Linear Model) followed by the dependent variables to be analysed. As many related dependent variables as you wish can be listed here. As we have a between-groups analysis as well, this group variable follows the **BY** keyword. As in the **ONEWAY** command (Syntax 11:10) all values in the grouping variables are used in the analysis, so if you do not want them all to be included in the analysis you must first select a subset of the data as per Syntax 9:1.

The command line is followed by five sub-commands; note that they are indented and each is preceded by a forward slash.

The first sub-command **/WSFACTOR=Barthel_index 3 Polynomial** specifies the name and number of levels added in the dialogue box for the within-subjects factor. It is this line that 'sets up' the analysis as repeated measures.

The second sub-command **/METHOD=SSTYPE(3)** specifies the computational aspects of the **UNIANOVA** analysis. The Type III sum-of-squares method is the default – **SSTYPE(1)**, **SSTYPE(2)** and **SSTYPE(4)** are the alternatives.

The third sub-command **/CRITERIA=ALPHA(0.05)** specifies the alpha level used to build the model; 0.05 is the default but can be altered as required.

The fourth sub-command **/WSDESIGN=Barthel_index** builds the within-subjects model. Listed is the name that was given to the **W**ithin-**S**ubjects factor on the initial screen (see Figure 11.3) and added in the dialogue box.

The fifth sub-command **/DESIGN=agecat.** builds the unrelated, or between-subjects, part of the model. As this is the last sub-command it is followed by the full stop to complete the command.

ON REFLECTION …

Looking at the syntax above, start to view it in the context of previous syntax that we have looked at.

The command **GLM barthel1 barthel2 barthel3 BY agecat** has the same layout as many earlier commands. First a command that specifies the statistical test, then a list of dependent variables, then use of **BY** to analyse by groups.

The first sub-command **/WSFACTOR=Barthel_index 3 Polynomial** is new. WSFACTOR just means **W**ithin-**S**ubjects **factor**, which may help clarify. This factor and number of levels was set up in the ⊞ Repeated Measures Define Factor(s) initial dialogue box seen in Figure 11.3.

The second sub-command **/METHOD=SSTYPE(3)** is the same as in the univariate ANOVA.

The third sub-command **/CRITERIA=ALPHA(0.05)** is the same as in the univariate ANOVA.

The fourth sub-command **/WSDESIGN=Barthel_index** is similar to the /DESIGN sub-command in the univariate ANOVA, but has an additional element (WS) for repeated measures. WSDESIGN just means **W**ithin-**S**ubjects **design**.

The fifth sub-command **/DESIGN=agecat.** builds the unrelated, or between-subjects, part of the model, just as in the univariate ANOVA.

And everything always has to end with a full stop.

OPTIONS

A repeated measures ANOVA accessed via the Univariate GLM option on the drop-down, menu-driven method ANALYZE → GENERAL LINEAR MODEL → REPEATED MEASURES has decisions and selections which can be made via each of the buttons on the right of the dialogue box. These choices can require sophisticated understanding of the analysis required. By going through your normal selections in the drop-down, menu-driven method, and pasting the commands from there, you can access the syntax sub-commands associated with your specified analysis.

To see what else syntax can offer beyond the choices available via the [Paste] button you can look up GLM in the *Command Syntax Reference* guide. Alternatively, for command-specific information press the F1 button when you are in the syntax editor and while your cursor is on the GLM command line.

To complete this chapter on univariate analysis we will return to more everyday analyses. Correlations are widely used statistical tests. This section will cover both Spearman's and Pearson's correlations, as well as partial correlations.

Correlations

To obtain correlations using the drop-down, menu-driven method, use ANALYZE → CORRELATIONS and then select the appropriate option.

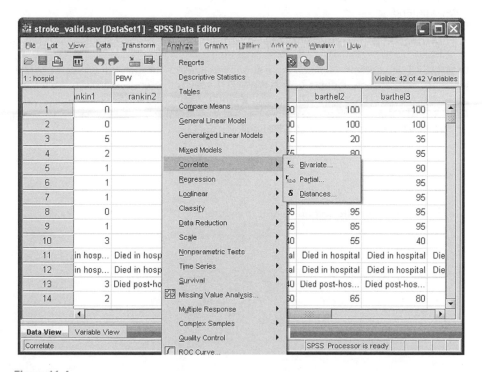

Figure 11.4

For all three correlations discussed below there is the facility to create more specific, streamlined tables by use of the WITH keyword in the syntax command line. This facility is ▐only available through syntax▐.

The examples below use the sample dataset stroke_valid.sav and explore how the age of patients correlates with the length of stay in hospital or the cost of their treatment.

Pearson's correlations are the default through the ANALYZE→CORRELATIONS → BIVARIATE option.

Syntax 11:13 Pearson's correlations using the CORRELATIONS command

The syntax will analyse data in the SPSS sample dataset stroke_valid.sav.

GET
FILE='C:\Program Files\SPSSInc\SPSS16\Samples\stroke_valid.sav'.
COMMENT the syntax is pasted from the drop-down, menu-driven method creating the following syntax.
CORRELATIONS
    /VARIABLES=los_rehab cost age
    /PRINT=TWOTAIL NOSIG
    /MISSING=PAIRWISE.

COMMENT it can be streamlined as below – you just lose the flagging of significant results specified in the previous syntax through the NOSIG part of the /PRINT= sub-command.
CORRELATIONS
    /VARIABLES=los_rehab cost age.

COMMENT you can create much more streamlined tables through the use of the **WITH** keyword, where each variable before the **WITH** keyword is correlated with each variable after the **WITH** keyword – this is ▐only available through syntax▐.
CORRELATIONS
    /VARIABLES=los_rehab cost **WITH** age.

The output from the second option in Syntax 11:13 can be seen below.

Correlations

		Length of stay for rehabilitation	Total treatment and rehabilitation costs in thousands	Age in years
Length of stay for rehabilitation	Pearson Correlation	1.000	.491	.140
	Sig. (2-tailed)		.000	.000
	N	787	787	787
Total treatment and rehabilitation costs in thousands	Pearson Correlation	.491	1.000	.073
	Sig. (2-tailed)	.000		.017
	N	787	1048	1048
Age in years	Pearson Correlation	.140	.073	1.000
	Sig. (2-tailed)	.000	.017	
	N	787	1048	1048

With a little syntax knowledge as shown in the third option in Syntax 11:13 you can create a specific output as below.

Correlations

		Age in years
Length of stay for rehabilitation	Pearson Correlation	.140**
	Sig. (2-tailed)	.000
	N	787
Total treatment and rehabilitation costs in thousands	Pearson Correlation	.073*
	Sig. (2-tailed)	.017
	N	1048

Spearman's correlations are available by ticking the Spearman option ☑ Spearman in the dialogue box obtained via the ANALYZE → CORRELATIONS → BIVARIATE option. The use of the WITH command has the same effect as in Syntax 11:13.

Syntax 11:14 Spearman's correlations using the NONPAR CORR command

The syntax will analyse data in the SPSS sample dataset stroke_valid.sav.

GET FILE='C:\Program Files\SPSSInc\SPSS16\Samples\stroke_valid.sav'.

COMMENT the syntax pasted from the drop-down, menu-driven method creates the following syntax.
NONPAR CORR
   /VARIABLES=age cost
   /PRINT=SPEARMAN TWOTAIL NOSIG
   /MISSING=PAIRWISE.

COMMENT it can be streamlined as below – you just lose the flagging of significant results specified in the previous syntax through the NOSIG part of the /**PRINT**= sub-command.
NONPAR CORR
   /VARIABLES=age cost.

COMMENT you can create much more streamlined tables through the use of the **WITH** keyword, where each variable before the **WITH** keyword is correlated with each variable after the **WITH** keyword – this is only available through syntax.
NONPAR CORR
    /VARIABLES=age **WITH** los_rehab cost.

Partial correlations are accessed via the ANALYZE → CORRELATIONS → PARTIAL option. The use of the WITH command has the same effect as in Syntax 11:13.

Syntax 11:15 Partial correlations using the PARTIAL CORR command

The syntax will analyse data in the SPSS sample dataset stroke_valid.sav.

GET FILE='C:\Program Files\SPSSInc\SPSS16\Samples\stroke_valid.sav'.

COMMENT the syntax pasted from the drop-down, menu-driven method creates the following syntax.
PARTIAL CORR
 /VARIABLES=cost age BY los_rehab
 /SIGNIFICANCE=TWOTAIL
 /MISSING=LISTWISE.

COMMENT it can be streamlined as below with no loss in output.
PARTIAL CORR
 /VARIABLES=cost age BY los_rehab.

COMMENT you can create much more specific tables through the use of the **WITH** keyword, where each variable before the WITH keyword is correlated with each variable after the **WITH** keyword – this must precede the **BY** keyword – note: only available through syntax.
PARTIAL CORR
    /VARIABLES=cost age **WITH barthel1** BY los_rehab.

Summary

The complexity of the syntax often reflects the level of complexity in the analysis that you are carrying out. By reading it line by line, either in your Log in the output files, or via pasted syntax commands, you start to familiarise yourself with the way syntax is written. Creating syntax files to encapsulate your analysis is worthwhile should you ever need to re-run the analysis (due to new cases, recoding, etc.) or perhaps to discuss the analysis with a supervisor.

In early stages of gaining syntax experience, knowledge and skills it is probably best to use your existing expertise in using SPSS via the drop-down, menu-driven method to arrive at the analysis you want, then press the PASTE button to create the syntax. I anticipate that for those of you reading this book the vast majority of your analysis can be accessed via this method, therefore there may be no need to physically type any of the syntax commands or sub-commands yourself. Considering, for example, the range of options and selections available via the drop-down, menu-driven method for ANOVAs, I believe that it will be a small minority who have to create their own syntax rather than pasting it. That said, once you are comfortable with the pasted version, you may feel happy working with that pasted syntax to adapt it quickly to your analysis.

Useful Tips

- Use the drop-down, menu-driven method as you would do normally to set up the statistics test you need, then use the paste function to create the syntax you require.
- You could just do the analysis as normal with the drop-down, menu-driven method and then go back through the Log text on the output file, copying and pasting to create your syntax file.
- If you do not understand which boxes to select for different options using the drop-down, menu-driven method (e.g. for the ANOVAs), then get to understand them using that method first *before* trying to work with the syntax for those options.
- Name syntax files in a way that links them to the dataset.
- It can be helpful to create several syntax files, each covering a different aspect of the analysis (e.g. projectx_explore.sps and projectx_univar.sps).

12

Syntax for Linear and Logistic Regression Analysis

Examples in this chapter will use the SPSS sample dataset stroke_valid.sav

This chapter on regression analysis is the last chapter that will address data management and analysis. It discusses analysis with syntax that is more complex than in previous chapters. However, now that you have got to this stage in the book, and have hopefully understood the preceding chapters, I anticipate that it will not feel too much more complicated or complex to understand.

The purpose of this book, as outlined in Chapter 1 and returned to in later chapters, is about learning to use syntax alongside the drop-down, menu-driven methods. Its goal is not to turn you into a computer programmer, rather to take the best of each way of working to help you to be more robust and efficient in your data handling. If you have skipped the other chapters and dived straight into this chapter it may be helpful to take some time to read the introduction and summary sections for the earlier chapters. As before, we will not go into the selection of the 'correct' statistics for your data.

In this chapter I will be going through the syntax for linear and logistic regression and de-mystifying the syntax that supports these analyses and moving on to some of the facilities that syntax supports, such as better management of manual stepwise analysis, which I find very handy when there are variables with missing values and where it is not appropriate to use imputed values.

Good Practice
- Understand the statistics that you are carrying out.
- Annotate the syntax files using COMMENT to explain what you have done and why.
- Link the syntax file to the dataset by use of names that 'connect' them meaningfully.

Linear Regression

First we will look at linear regression analysis. In linear regression analysis there can be multiple independent variables (dichotomous, ordinal or continuous) that are hypothesised to predict or explain a continuous dependent outcome variable. The results report:

- the strength of the relationship between each predictor and the outcome (the β value);
- the strength of the correlation between the observed values and the predicted values (the R value);
- the proportion of the variance of the outcome variable that is explained by the predictor variables (the adjusted R^2 value).

To paste the command from the drop-down, menu-driven method go via ANALYZE → REGRESSION → LINEAR. As with other general linear model analyses, there are many choices to be made in the analysis.

If you do not understand what to select from the drop-down, menu-driven methods then, before you progress with the analysis, I recommend you read a good SPSS-based statistical text book such *Discovering Statistics Using SPSS* by Andy Field (2009), or *SPSS for Psychologists* by Brace et al. (2006).

You must select the method you want to use to assess which predictors to have in the model. You can choose to have all of the predictors entered into the model in one go and left in (ENTER); you can have all of the predictors entered into the model in one go and then removed one at a time (weakest predictor first) if they fail to meet specified criteria (BACKWARD); or you can start with a blank sheet and have them added one at a time (strongest predictor first) as they manage to meet specified criteria (FORWARD). You can also choose STEPWISE which adds (or removes) one predictor at a time, but then re-tests all existing variables in the model to see if they still 'fit'.

You should also look at the diagnostics available for the model and also check your assumptions (collinearity, outliers, residuals, influential cases, leverage, etc.).

Data from the stroke_valid.sav SPSS sample dataset will be used to demonstrate the syntax. The cost of the treatment is our dependent (outcome) variable. The explanatory variables that we will put into the model are age (continuous), smoking status (yes/no), diabetes present (yes/no), obesity (yes/no), and the baseline Rankin score (ordinal): **age smoker diabetes obesity los_rehab rankin0**.

Syntax 12:1 is pasted from the analysis carried out via the drop-down, menu-driven process shown in Figure 12.1, with the options as selected. Just as for the one-way ANOVA and univariate ANOVA in Chapter 11, linear regression syntax sub-commands are linked to the many selections made via the drop-down, menu-driven process, which make it look rather scary. Try not to get put off by all the sub-commands, they are just representations of the tick-boxes etc. selected via the dialogue boxes from the drop-down, menu-driven method.

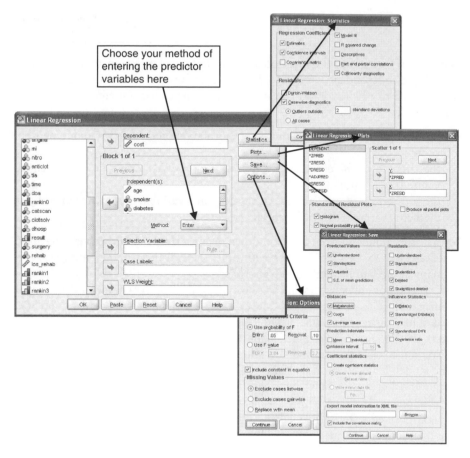

Figure 12.1

Syntax 12:1 Linear regression using the REGRESSION command

The syntax will analyse data in the SPSS sample dataset stroke_valid.sav.

GET FILE='C:\Program Files\SPSSInc\SPSS16\Samples\stroke_valid.sav'.

```
REGRESSION
    /MISSING LISTWISE
    /STATISTICS COEFF OUTS CI R ANOVA COLLIN TOL
    /CRITERIA=PIN(.05) POUT(.10)
    /NOORIGIN
    /DEPENDENT cost
    /METHOD=ENTER age smoker diabetes obesity rankin0
    /SCATTERPLOT=(*ZPRED, *ZRESID)
    /RESIDUALS HIST(ZRESID) NORM(ZRESID)
    /CASEWISE PLOT(ZRESID) OUTLIERS(2)
    /SAVE  PRED ZPRED ADJPRED MAHAL COOK LEVER ZRESID DRESID
        SDRESID SDBETA SDFIT.
```

The **GET FILE** command opens the datafile if not already open.

The command line **REGRESSION** specifies that a linear regression is to be performed and is followed by 10 sub-commands, which reflect the fact that quite a few tick-box options have been selected via the drop-down menu.

The first sub-command **/MISSING LISTWISE** specifies that only those cases with valid values for all named variables are included; this sub-command line is a default.

The second sub-command **/STATISTICS COEFF OUTS CI R ANOVA COLLIN TOL** specifies the statistics to be presented.

The default statistics are:

- **COEFF** to display the regression coefficients, and their significance, for those variables in the model;
- **OUTS** limited regression coefficients for those not in the model – not needed if the ENTER method is used;
- **ANOVA** statistics and probability;
- **R** displays R, R^2, adjusted R^2, and standard error of the estimates.

I selected additional statistics:

- **CI** to give the confidence intervals for the β values;
- **COLLIN** to give the collinearity statistics, including the variance-inflation factor (VIF) for each variable in the model;
- **TOL** to give the tolerance statistic for each predictor variable being considered.

The third sub-command **/CRITERIA=PIN(.05) POUT(.10)** specifies the statistical criteria used to build a model (**PIN** is the **p**robability required for a variable to go **in**to the model, **POUT** is the **p**robability required for a variable to be taken **out** of the model). The criteria here are both the defaults. This sub-command line is one of those where order matters. It must be *before* the **/DEPENDENT** and the **/METHOD** sub-commands.

The fourth sub-command **/NOORIGIN** specifies the inclusion of the constant in the model. This sub-command line is a default.

The fifth sub-command **/DEPENDENT cost** specifies the dependent variable.

The sixth sub-command **/METHOD=ENTER age smoker diabetes obesity rankin0** specifies the method by which the listed predictor variables are put in the model and specifies the predictor variables to go into the model. Here all five variables are entered at once.

The seventh sub-command **/SCATTERPLOT=(*ZPRED, *ZRESID)** has been generated because the variables were selected in the Plot dialogue box, and will create a scatterplot of the standardised predicted dependent variable and the standardised residuals.

The eighth sub-command **/RESIDUALS HIST(ZRESID) NORM(ZRESID)** has been generated because I ticked the corresponding boxes in the Plot dialogue box. A histogram and a normal P–P plot are created for the standardised residuals.

The ninth sub-command **/CASEWISE PLOT(ZRESID) OUTLIERS(2)** has been generated by selecting the casewise option in the residuals section of the Statistics dialogue box. The default is to list the outliers with standardised residuals which have absolute values greater than 3 (in an ordinary sample expect about 0.3% of cases). I have changed this to 2 (expect approx. 5%).

The 10th sub-command **/SAVE PRED ZPRED ADJPRED MAHAL COOK LEVER ZRESID DRESID SDRESID SDBETA SDFIT.** has been generated from the Save dialogue box selections. The predicted values etc. are saved to allow you to use these created variables to carry out further diagnostic and casewise checks.

The last sub-command is followed by the full stop to complete the command.

Three of the lines above are default sub-commands (**/MISSING, /CRITIERIA, /NOORIGIN**) and so could be omitted without any change to the output, making the syntax marginally more streamlined.

OPTIONS

The command line **REGRESSION** has the option to specify a selected group on which to carry out the analysis by use of the sub-command **SELECT**. For example, you could request the above analysis on females only **REGRESSION SELECT gender EQ 1**. While the regression coefficients are produced only for those selected, the residuals etc. are displayed for those selected (here females) and separately also for those not selected (males). This 'selection' is a temporary state only for the duration of the REGRESSION command in which it is embedded.

In the first sub-command **/MISSING LISTWISE** you can replace missing values with the variable mean **/MISSING MEANSUBSTITUTION**. Beware, though, that if **INCLUDE** is also specified, user-missing values are treated as valid and are included in the computation of the means. For other alternative missing value options see Syntax 11:1.

The fourth sub-command /NOORIGIN alternative is **/ORIGIN** which suppresses the use of the constant and the regression is forced to go through the origin (zero). Only really used when it is known that absolutely all of the dependent variables are present in the model. That is, when you know that taking away the contribution of those combined variables would be expected to result in an outcome value of 0.

The fifth sub-command **/DEPENDENT cost** specifies the dependent variable. Using the drop-down, menu-driven method you can specify only a single outcome variable for a model. Using syntax you can list more than one outcome variable providing you want them to be tested with exactly the same predictor variables, specified options, etc. **/DEPENDENT cost los_rehab** would result in two separate linear regression analyses, one with cost as the outcome, one with los_rehab (length of stay in rehab). This is **only available through syntax**.

The sixth sub-command **/METHOD=ENTER** has several alternatives: BACKWARD, FORWARD, STEPWISE, REMOVE and TEST. There can be more than one METHOD sub-command line, so (for example) you can have some predictor variables following the ENTER keyword, and others following BACKWARD and so forth. The order of these sub-commands makes a difference.

The syntax below will enter age and smoker in every step of the backward model.

REGRESSION
    /DEPENDENT cost
    /METHOD=BACKWARD rankin0 hospsize obesity diabetes
    /METHOD=ENTER age smoker.

The sixth sub-command **/SCATTERPLOT=(*ZPRED, *ZRESID)** can have numerous pairs for the scatterplot (see Plot dialogue box); just put each pair, separated by a comma, in brackets.

I have outlined a couple of useful options in the listed sub-commands. There are further possible sub-commands that have not been listed. To see what else syntax can offer you can look up REGRESSION in the *Command Syntax Reference* guide, also available in searchable pdf format via the SPSS HELP drop-down menu (see Resources section, page 30). Alternatively for command-specific information press the F1 button when you are in the syntax editor and while your cursor is on the REGRESSION command line.

Logistic Regression

Next we will look at logistic regression analysis. In logistic regression analysis there can be multiple independent variables (dichotomous, categorical, ordinal or continuous) which are hypothesised to predict or explain the value reported for a dichotomous dependent outcome variable. The results report:

- the proportion of the variance of the outcome variable that is explained by the model (the Cox and Snell R^2 value and the Nagelkerke R^2 value);
- how well the model assigns outcome values to the correct group (the classification table);
- the strength of the relationship between each predictor and the outcome (the β value);
- the significance of the β values (the Wald statistic and its p value);
- the change in the odds with every unit change in the predictor variable (the exp β).

To paste the command from the drop-down, menu-driven method you go via ANALYZE → REGRESSION → BINARY LOGISTIC. The initial dialogue box has buttons on the top right-hand side to open other supplementary dialogue boxes. As with other statistical tests you need to understand your selections in these dialogue boxes, so if you are unsure then take time to look through a good SPSS-based statistics text.

Move the dependent variable across, and then the independent variables. Select the method of entry, and then click through the supplementary dialogue boxes. Syntax 12:2 is pasted from the analysis being carried out via the drop-down, menu-driven process in Figure 12.2, with the options as selected. As for Syntax 12:1 and several syntax examples in Chapter 11, the selection of options increases the syntax sub-commands and for some may initiate feelings of dread. However, working through them is hopefully now becoming a familiar process so with any luck I can be brief.

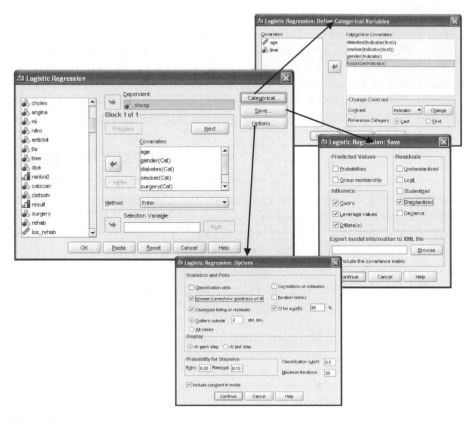

Figure 12.2

Syntax 12:2 Logistic regression using the LOGISTIC REGRESSION command

The syntax will analyse data in the SPSS sample dataset stroke_valid.sav.

GET FILE='C:\Program Files\SPSSInc\SPSS16\Samples\stroke_valid.sav'.

```
LOGISTIC REGRESSION VARIABLES dhosp
  /METHOD=ENTER age gender diabetes smoker time hospsize
  /CONTRAST (diabetes)=Indicator(1)
  /CONTRAST (smoker)=Indicator(1)
  /CONTRAST (gender)=Indicator
  /CONTRAST (hospsize)=Indicator
  /SAVE=COOK LEVER DFBETA ZRESID
  /CASEWISE OUTLIER(2)
  /PRINT=GOODFIT CI(95)
  /CRITERIA=PIN(0.05) POUT(0.10) ITERATE(20) CUT(0.5).
```

The **GET FILE** command opens the datafile if not already open.

The command line **LOGISTIC REGRESSION VARIABLES dhosp** specifies that a logistic regression is to be performed and that the outcome variable is **dhosp**. This is followed by nine sub-commands, which reflect the fact that quite a few tick-box options have been selected via the drop-down menu.

The first sub-command **/METHOD=ENTER age gender diabetes smoker time hospsize** specifies the method by which the listed predictor variables are put in the model. Here all are entered at once.

The next four sub-commands are **/CONTRAST** sub-commands. Each categorical predictor has its own **/CONTRAST** sub-command and a value against which all others are contrasted; the value is either the first (indicated by a one in brackets after the word Indicator) or last value.

The sixth sub-command **/SAVE=COOK LEVER DFBETA ZRESID** has been generated from the Save dialogue box selections. The statistics are saved to allow you to use these created variables to carry out further diagnostic and casewise checks.

The seventh sub-command **/CASEWISE OUTLIER(2)** has been generated by selecting the casewise option in the Statistics and Plots section of the Options dialogue box. Here two is the default (unlike three in linear regression).

The eighth sub-command **/PRINT=GOODFIT CI(95)** has been generated by the selection of the Hosmer–Lemeshow goodness-of-fit option in the Statistics and Plots section of the Options dialogue box.

The last sub-command **/CRITERIA=PIN(0.05) POUT(0.10) ITERATE(20) CUT(0.5).** has the default statistical criteria used to build a model.

The last sub-command is followed by the full stop to complete the command.

OPTIONS

The command line **LOGISTIC REGRESSION VARIABLES dhosp** can be written in a slightly different way to enable interactions between variables to be used as predictors, for example smoking and gender. This is only available through syntax. To use this facility not only does the dependent variable need to be noted here but following the keyword **WITH** you need to list *all* of the predictor variables (separated by commas). The interaction term can then be added at the end of this list with the two 'interacting' variables separated by the keyword **BY**.

LOGISTIC REGRESSION VARIABLES dhosp WITH age, gender, diabetes, smoker, time, hospsize, gender BY smoker

Remember to include the interaction term on the **/METHOD** sub-command or it will not be entered into the model as a predictor.

On the **/CONTRAST** there are multiple ways of making this contrast as indicated by the drop-down selection in the Categorical Variable dialogue box and in the *Command Syntax Reference* guide.

Usefulness of Syntax

You may have noticed that I have selected ENTER as my method of choice for both linear and logistic regression. There are a couple of reasons for this, but the main one is that although I do like to carry out backward conditional regression analyses, I usually do this 'by hand'. In part this is to be able to see and make the decisions rather than have the computer do it (gives a better feel for what is happening), but it is really useful for the types of messy data that I have to deal with. It is a rare dataset for me that has complete data for all of the variables in an analysis. This is a common situation in datasets where people are the participants, in those generated by service providers, in longitudinal data, national cohort data, and so forth. You may recollect from statistics classes that for a case to be entered into a regression analysis you can impute data for the missing variables and be able to include the case in the model, or you can accept that a case has missing values and accept it cannot be in the model. In many cases imputing values is not appropriate. In situations where imputing data is not appropriate using the automated FORWARD, BACKWARD or STEPWISE methods runs the risk of carrying out analyses on less cases than are actually available. Manually running a backward regression analysis is relatively easy using syntax, and also allows you to annotate the decision-making process, especially useful when taking data to supervisors for discussion. Manually you carry out the process using the ENTER method, reviewing the output, deciding which variable (if any) should be removed, re-run the regression with that variable removed, reviewing the output, etc., until you have your final model. You can then run diagnostics fully on that model. The syntax that results can be quite long to print out for you to review, and so I have a streamlined version of a real analysis I carried out.

Example of Usefulness

The data had been retrieved and compiled by others from several sources. It was data that had been recorded by healthcare staff as part of the normal assessment of 1780 children attending hospitals with signs of an infectious illness. The retrospective analysis was to explore whether it was possible to predict (from these baseline, early assessments) which of the children were going to develop a serious illness. Not all children had every investigation or assessment carried out. One assessment in particular was carried out for a minority of cases, but was felt by the research team to be a possibly useful predictor. The data was very 'messy', it was not what you would choose to start with, but it was potentially going to answer an important clinical question. Accordingly what I did was start with an exploratory model. It contained the dichotomous outcome variable and nine possible predictors identified by the clinical team members (listed as var1 to var9 below for simple and concise syntax), four of which were categorical. Var5 had the least case data.

You can see in Syntax 12:3 that when all 9 predictors were in the model of the possible 1780 cases, only 220 were entered in the initial model: removing var8 (as least significant) made no change; removing var4 increased the cases to 242; removing var1 increased the cases to 265; removing var5 increased the cases (hugely) to 1534. As var5 was not significant but removing it made such a difference to the numbers entered it was worth beginning again with a new 'initial' model, this time excluding var5. This second initial model, with eight predictors, had 1364 cases, thus allowing a more robust examination of the predictors in this much larger sample with *6 times* as many cases.

Syntax 12:3 Logistic regression 'example of usefulness' for messy data with many missing values

Note: this will not work on any of the sample datasets.
LOGISTIC REGRESSION outcome_var
    /METHOD = ENTER var1 var2 var3 var4 var5 var6 var7 var8 var9
    /CONTRAST (var6)=Indicator /CONTRAST (var8)=Indicator /CONTRAST (var9)=Indicator
    /CRITERIA = PIN(.05) POUT(.10) ITERATE(20) CUT(.5).
COMMENT output reviewed n=220. var8 least significant (p=0.996) so remove.

LOGISTIC REGRESSION outcome_var
    /METHOD = ENTER var1 var2 var3 var4 var5 var6 var7 var9
    /CONTRAST (var6)=Indicator /CONTRAST (var9)=Indicator
    /CRITERIA = PIN(.05) POUT(.10) ITERATE(20) CUT(.5).
COMMENT output reviewed n=220. var4 least significant (p=0.913) so remove.

LOGISTIC REGRESSION outcome_var
    /METHOD = ENTER var1 var2 var3 var5 var6 var7 var9
    /CONTRAST (var6)=Indicator /CONTRAST (var9)=Indicator
    /CRITERIA = PIN(.05) POUT(.10) ITERATE(20) CUT(.5).
COMMENT output reviewed n=242 var1 least significant (p=0.761) so remove.

LOGISTIC REGRESSION outcome_var
    /METHOD = ENTER var2 var3 var5 var6 var7 var9
    /CONTRAST (var6)=Indicator /CONTRAST (var9)=Indicator
    /CRITERIA = PIN(.05) POUT(.10) ITERATE(20) CUT(.5).
COMMENT output reviewed n=265 var5 least significant (p=0.406) so remove.

LOGISTIC REGRESSION outcome_var
    /METHOD = ENTER var2 var3 var6 var7 var9
    /CONTRAST (var6)=Indicator /CONTRAST (var9)=Indicator
    /CRITERIA = PIN(.05) POUT(.10) ITERATE(20) CUT(.5).
COMMENT output reviewed n=1534 So as var5 would not be sig in final model but hugely reduces numbers, begin again with it removed.

LOGISTIC REGRESSION outcome_var
    /METHOD = ENTER var1 var2 var3 var4 var6 var7 var8 var9
    /CONTRAST (var6)=Indicator /CONTRAST (var8)=Indicator /CONTRAST (var9)=Indicator
    /CRITERIA = PIN(.05) POUT(.10) ITERATE(20) CUT(.5).
COMMENT output reviewed n=1361 var7 least significant (p=0.923) so remove.

LOGISTIC REGRESSION outcome_var
    /METHOD = ENTER var1 var2 var3 var4 var6 var8 var9
    /CONTRAST (var6)=Indicator /CONTRAST (var8)=Indicator /CONTRAST (var9)=Indicator
    /CRITERIA = PIN(.05) POUT(.10) ITERATE(20) CUT(.5).
COMMENT output reviewed n=1564. var1 least significant (p=0.284) so remove.

```
LOGISTIC REGRESSION outcome_var
    /METHOD = ENTER var2 var3 var4 var6 var8 var9
    /CONTRAST (var6)=Indicator /CONTRAST (var8)=Indicator /CONTRAST
    (var9)=Indicator
    /CRITERIA = PIN(.05) POUT(.10) ITERATE(20) CUT(.5).
COMMENT output reviewed n=1780. var4 least significant (p=0.213) so remove.

LOGISTIC REGRESSION outcome_var
    /METHOD = ENTER var2 var3 var6 var8 var9
    /CONTRAST (var6)=Indicator /CONTRAST (var8)=Indicator /CONTRAST
    (var9)=Indicator
    /CRITERIA = PIN(.05) POUT(.10) ITERATE(20) CUT(.5).
COMMENT output reviewed n=1780, var3 now the only ns variable.

LOGISTIC REGRESSION outcome_var
    /METHOD = ENTER var2 var6 var8 var9
    /CONTRAST (var6)=Indicator /CONTRAST (var8)=Indicator /CONTRAST
    (var9)=Indicator
    /PRINT = CI(95)
    /CRITERIA = PIN(.05) POUT(.10) ITERATE(20) CUT(.5).
COMMENT output reviewed var3 removed, n=1780, predictors are var2, var6,
var8 and var9.
```

Carrying out regression analyses in this way is so much better using syntax rather than the drop-down, menu-driven method. You run the initial model obtaining the syntax from the paste function, review the output, make a comment on the syntax file about what you find, then copy and paste the previous model, delete the predictor to be removed, re-run it, examine the output, make a comment in the syntax, and so on. Using the drop-down, menu-driven method you would have had to click through to the dialogue box, remove the variable each time (including clicking through to the categorical variable dialogue box to remove the variable there if required), but not too arduous. However, if a new 'initial' model had to be written you would have to find the variables again, move across, re-check the categorical variable dialogue box, and so forth. Furthermore, you need to record somewhere what you do, and why, so that you have a clear record to discuss with others, or to return to at a later date.

Communicating the process to a wider team or to a supervisor is made much easier with the syntax as a clear auditable record of what has been done, including the decision-making process.

Summary

Linear and logistic regression analyses have been chosen as the final two tests covered in this book simply because during my research and supervision they are the two multivariate statistical tests that I most commonly use. For others the selection would have been different. SPSS has syntax commands for all of its analyses (factor analysis, survival analysis, cluster analysis, generalised estimating equations, and so on) and these can be accessed using the PASTE button or the Log. However, to keep the book as an introductory text means keeping it simple, and also keeping the book focused on the basics, the principles, of using syntax commands.

If you carry out complex analysis and can understand it and have read this book and can understand it, I am confident that you will be able to carry forward (into your analyses) the principles of SPSS syntax use. With judicious use of pasting the commands created via the drop-down, menu-driven analysis and then exploring the sub-command options via use of the *SPSS 16.0 Command Syntax Reference* guide (SPSS, 2007a), I believe that you can go on to create the correct syntax for all of your analytical requirements.

Many statistical tests accessed via the drop-down, menu-driven method have decisions and selections which can be made via various buttons on the initial dialogue box which lead to supplementary dialogue boxes with a range of choices. All of these can also be accessed using syntax sub-commands. The syntax can be complex, and therefore it makes sense to begin by going through your normal selections in the drop-down, menu-driven method and pasting the commands from there. Using this method, without having to write a single command line yourself, you can create a syntax file for analysis of the project data. This can be saved and stored alongside the data and the outputs in case you need to revisit the analysis, re-run it, add cases, discuss with your supervisor, and so on.

Once you understand the sub-commands and recognise your preferred selections you may decide then that you want set up a new syntax file with your linear regression and logistic regression 'default models'. These can go in your syntax library and be called something like lin_reg_default.sps and log_reg_default.sps with all your preferences specified as a template for future projects.

The key messages of this book are that you can use syntax alongside the drop-down, menu-driven method of using SPSS, and that you can learn syntax in a stepwise progression. You can stop at any of the following stages, it is up to you:

1. Look at the Log to see the commands for your procedures.
2. Start with pasting commands to make a syntax file.
3. Develop syntax files alongside all your datafiles and outputs.
4. Learn to amend and adapt them as you understand more.
5. Develop syntax file templates appropriate for complex data analysis.
6. Build a syntax library.

Useful Tips

- Use the drop-down, menu-driven method (as you would do normally) to set up the statistics test you need, then use the paste function to create the syntax you require.
- If you do not understand which boxes to select for different options using the drop-down, menu-driven method then you need to understand them using that method first *before* trying to work with the syntax for those options.
- Name syntax files in ways that link them to the dataset.
- It can be helpful to create several syntax files, each covering a different aspect of the analysis (e.g. projectx_lin_reg.sps and projectx_log_reg.sps).
- Find out about extra facilities which are available only via syntax, by looking through *SPSS 16.0 Command Syntax Reference* guide (SPSS, 2007a).

13

Understanding Error Messages and Warnings

Examples in this chapter will use the following SPSS sample datasets
stroke_valid.sav
ceramics.sav
World95.sav
GSS93 subset.sav

This is the last chapter of the book. The subject matter, error messages and warnings could have been covered earlier in the book, as you will most likely have started encountering error messages and warnings a while back. However, I decided that putting it nearer the beginning might be of less use. Why 'of less use'? Well, this book is about syntax, and the error messages and warnings that will primarily be addressed in this chapter are error messages and warnings that are 'syntax related'. To understand the error messages that are associated with syntax (as opposed to messages generated through the drop-down, menu-driven method) you usually need to understand the syntax that you have created and run. Thus, putting this chapter at the beginning would be 'of less use' because the explanations of the errors and the remedies would generally involve readers needing a greater understanding of the syntax than is likely for those just beginning this book.

Please do not get discouraged if once you begin to use syntax the number of error messages and warnings increases. Instead, learn how to interpret the error messages and warnings, and to use their content, which can become a key part of working with syntax. If there is a mistake in the syntax, SPSS will supply a message in the Output window. In my experience, many users of SPSS cannot make sense of these messages, or tend to ignore them. This is not usually the most efficient thing to do as the error messages and warnings contain useful information to help you remedy whatever it is that is not working as you expected.

The reasons that people have given to me for paying little attention to the content of the error messages and warnings broadly fall into two camps: (1) often they feel thwarted because the program is not doing what it is supposed to and so are irritated and too frustrated to pay much heed; and (2) because the content of the error messages generated by the program is not always immediately understood (and if they are frustrated in the first place, this does not help).

On first viewing, the messages do not always look user-friendly, especially to the uninitiated (or unwilling) user. However, the messages usually contain all the information you need to rectify the mistake, if only it could be understood. This chapter will attempt to de-mystify the way that errors and warnings are presented and will do this by using specific error messages to illustrate some general principles.

Good Practice

- Whether error messages and warnings are generated via the drop-down, menu-driven method or from syntax, you should try to read them all, understand them and rectify the problem.
- Reduce the number of syntax errors by starting with the pasting of commands from the drop-down, menu-driven method of using SPSS and using this as a 'template' for creating your own syntax.
- Read the error messages carefully; do not allow frustration to stop you working things through.
- Read the warning messages carefully and do not ignore them just because they may seem to have had little effect.

Some error messages and warnings give you a 'column' number. These can be very useful to help you identify where things are not as they should be. The column number relates to the position of the character on the command or sub-command line in question. Each 'letter', 'number', 'space' or 'punctuation' is allocated one column space on a syntax line, and SPSS 'counts' along the line to find the position of the piece of text in the syntax that is a problem. Sometimes this column information may seem a little superfluous as the text identified may appear only once anyway and therefore easy to find; but sometimes text (like a space or full stop) may be repeated many times and so a column number is very helpful. Each error message and warning refers to the command or sub-command that is printed (in the Output view) most immediately prior to the warning. However, while the error message or warning will often direct you to the position in the syntax where a *problem* has been found, that position is not always the place where you will find the syntax *error* that has caused the problem. Sounds confusing I know. An analogy may be helpful. Imagine you are driving a car along a winding country lane. There should be a sign warning you of a junction ahead in 100 metres, but unfortunately the sign has gone missing. When you get to the unexpected junction you fail to stop in time and end up in a ditch. The place where the problem occurred (the junction) is not the same as the place as the error that caused the problem (the missing sign). OK, so that may not have helped everyone but I hope that this apparent 'disconnection' (between where the problem seems to occur and where the syntax error actually is) will make more sense after reading a few syntax examples below.

Differences between ERROR and WARNING Messages

As a general rule of thumb WARNING messages are less severe than ERROR messages, and often the syntax will still work despite a WARNING message, while generally the syntax will not work if an ERROR message is given. As such you *have* to pay attention to the ERROR messages as the commands just will not be carried out. However, while you could possibly ignore WARNING messages, this is not advisable as they carry important information potentially telling you that the syntax has not been carried out in exactly the way it was written and inaccuracies can be introduced into your datafile or analysis. An example provided on page 41 of the *SPSS 16.0 Command Syntax Reference* guide (SPSS, 2007a) shows how the Journal file will record actions and warnings and gives the example below:

```
>Warning # 1102
>An invalid numeric field has been found. The result has been set to the
>system-missing value.
```

This warning tells you a piece of data was not in the correct format and so a system-missing value has been included in the dataset instead of the intended data value. However, the rest of the command has been executed. The danger here is that you could just carry on regardless, with incomplete data, if you do not read and pay attention to the WARNING. Thus, you need to get into the habit of reading all of your error and warning messages, understanding them and then sorting out whatever caused the error or warning and then rectifying the problem.

The chapter will present a few specific error messages to help you to understand the way in which the error messages and warnings are written, and how careful reading of the messages can be of use. As there are numerous messages that can be generated in SPSS, the intention is for you to use the examples below to begin to understand some general principles rather than as specific messages to learn and commit to memory.

The first example given in Syntax 13:1 is an error message generated from a single MISSING VALUES command line which has been created in order to identify a range of values, 99 and above, as missing values. You can find an explanation of how this syntax should work in Syntax 3:5, example 3:5:4.

Syntax 13:1 ERROR MESSAGE # 4815 caused by putting values in the wrong order within a MISSING VALUES command

A simple syntax command is intended to allocate missing value status to all values in the variable age which are listed as above 99, perhaps because you have 996, 997, 998 and 999 all representing different reasons for a missing age.

The syntax will create an error message from the SPSS sample dataset stroke_valid. sav.

The syntax used
MISSING VALUES age (HIGHEST THRU 99).

The output shown
MISSING VALUES age (HIGHEST THRU 99).

>Error # 4815 in column 34. Text: 99
>The values specified with the THRU keyword on the MISSING VALUES
>command must be in the order of low THRU high.
>This command not executed.

What the message means
Reading the message through tells you the error is found in column 34 and is the part of the syntax written as **99 >Error # 4815 in column 34. Text: 99**.

This may not seem to help if you do not think that 99 should be a problem.

By reading further you will see that the warning tells you that the problem is the way that values (here 99) relate to the keyword THRU, **>The values specified with the THRU keyword on the MISSING VALUES** explaining that on MISSING VALUES commands the values either side of the THRU keyword need to be put in a specified order, **>command must be in the order of low THRU high.** with the lower value *before* THRU and the higher value *after*.

The message then informs you that because of this fundamental syntax error SPSS couldn't carry out the command.
>This command not executed.

Thus reading the error message through, you should be able to see that, as it is written above, the command line MISSING VALUES age (HIGHEST THRU 99). has the values the wrong way round: the higher value (HIGHEST) is before the keyword, and the lower value 99 is after it.

The remedy
Correct the syntax by swapping round the order of the values relative to the THRU keyword, so that the lower value (99) is before the keyword, and the higher value (HIGHEST) is after it.

MISSING VALUES age (99 THRU HIGHEST) .

Hopefully you can see, from reading Syntax 13:1 above, that the content within an error message can sometimes be fairly self-explanatory.

The next example given in Syntax 13:2 is a warning generated from a RECODE command line to convert a string variable into a numeric variable and then a VARIABLE LABELS command to label the new variable appropriately. You can find an explanation of how syntax like this should work, in Syntax 5:3.

Syntax 13.2 WARNING # 4461 caused by a missing full stop in the VARIABLE LABELS command

The following syntax commands are intended to convert the string variable **physid** into a numeric variable **new_physid** and then to label the new variable appropriately.

The syntax will create a warning message from the SPSS sample dataset stroke_valid.sav.

The syntax used
RECODE physid (CONVERT) INTO new_physid .
VARIABLE LABELS new physid 'physid converted from string to numeric'
EXECUTE .

The output shown
RECODE physid (CONVERT) INTO new_physid .
VARIABLE LABELS new_physid 'physid converted from string to numeric' EXECUTE.

>Warning # 4461 in column 1. Text: EXECUTE
>An unknown variable name was specified on the VAR LABELS command.
>The name and the label will be ignored.

What the message means
One of the keys to understanding this error message is to realise that the **RECODE** command line has been carried out with no problems, and that the warning is concerned with the command that follows. Note that the message does not mention the **RECODE** command. Furthermore, checking the Data View and Variable View of the datafile will show you that the variable **new_physid** has been created, and labelled, but with no data entered yet.

Reading the message through tells you the error is found in column 1 so at the beginning of a line and is concerned with text **EXECUTE >Warning # 4461 in column 1. Text: EXECUTE**. As only one **EXECUTE** is on the syntax that is fairly easy to identify. You may be confused, knowing that an **EXECUTE** command is required, yet seeing it identified as the 'problem' text.

By reading further you will see that this warning tells you that the problem is related to variable name on the **VAR LABELS** command (short for **VARIABLE LABELS**) **>An unknown variable name was specified on the VAR LABELS command.**

The warning has told you that the problem text is **EXECUTE** and also identified the problem is with an 'unknown variable name' on the **VARIABLE LABELS** command. Indeed, the warning is telling that the **VARIABLE LABELS** command is mistakenly trying to use the word **EXECUTE** as a variable name.

Now go back to the syntax used and see if you can see how the **VARIABLE LABELS** command can possibly be trying to use the word **EXECUTE** as a variable name. By careful examination of the syntax hopefully you can see that the full stop is missing from the end of the **VARIABLE LABELS** command line – thus SPSS has continued with the command and assumed that **EXECUTE** is a variable name which it cannot recognise. To that end the 'unknown' variable name is ignored and so is any associated label >**The name and the label will be ignored**.

A further consequence of this mistake in the syntax is that the **EXECUTE** command has not been recognised as a command because SPSS was misled into treating it as a variable name instead. Since an **EXECUTE** command was not run, the **RECODE** command has not been completed, hence the missing data in the currently unpopulated new variable.

The remedy
Correct the syntax by adding the missing full stop at the end of the **VARIABLE LABELS** command.

RECODE physid (CONVERT) INTO new_physid .
VARIABLE LABELS new_physid 'physid converted from string to numeric'.
EXECUTE .

The problems arising from the missing full stop in Syntax 13:2 are fairly simple but can be very frustrating if you do not take the time to understand the warning message. If you ignore the warning message you may have run the syntax, gone straight to the Data View and wondered where the data values are, trying to work out what is wrong with the RECODE command – after all, the VARIABLE LABELS command appears to have worked fine as the variable is labelled as requested. You may then spend some time looking at how you have written the RECODE command instead of looking at the VARIABLE LABELS command and spotting the missing full stop.

In my experience, students and researchers seem to encounter problems with syntax which are commonly caused by their use of the full stop – sometimes because it is missing, sometimes because an extra one has been put in too early, perhaps at the end of an early sub-command rather than after the *last* sub-command. Unfortunately, the error or warning messages that result from a full stop mistake can vary tremendously, as a misplaced full stop affects the syntax in different ways, from command to command and misplacement to misplacement. In Syntax 13:3 below, another missing full stop is used to illustrate this point further and is an erroneous version of Syntax 5:8 which (if written correctly) should extract an element of a string variable.

Syntax 13:3 WARNING # 4080 Another error caused by a MISSING FULL STOP

This is based on Syntax 5:8. The following commands are intended to create a new string variable **lab_code** and then place the first character from the variable **labrunid** into the new variable.

The following syntax uses the SPSS sample dataset ceramics.sav.

The syntax used
STRING lab_code (A2)
COMPUTE lab_code=(SUBSTR(labrunid,1,1)).
EXECUTE.

The output shown
STRING lab_code (A2)
COMPUTE lab_code=(SUBSTR(labrunid,1,1)).

>Error # 4080 in column 17. Text: =
>On the STRING command, the list of variables being defined was not
>followed by the formats for those variables.
>This command not executed.
EXECUTE.

What the warning means
Note: just on reading through you can see that the message mentions the **STRING** command. Furthermore, checking the Data View and Variable View of the datafile will show you that the new variable **lab_code** has not been created.

Reading the message through tells you the error is found in column 17 and is the part of the syntax which is an equals sign
>Error # 4080 in column 17. Text: =

This does not seem to help much. 'Why is the equals sign a problem?' you may think.

But read on, and the warning tells you that the problem is in the STRING command.
>On the STRING command, the list of variables being defined was not
>followed by the formats for those variables.
The warning message is stating that the problem is related to a variable name which is not followed by a format.

The warning has now told you that the problem text is = and also identified the problem is with a variable format in the **STRING** command.

Instead of feeling frustrated about this 'bizarre' message (after all, there is no equals sign in the **STRING** command, it is in the **COMPUTE** command) look once more at the syntax used as written above. You may recall that in a **STRING** command you are permitted to create more than one new variable and you can list as many new variable names as you like as long as they are followed by an acceptable format (individually or in groups). So you could have STRING var1 (a2) var2 var3 (A4).

Look again at the syntax used above and see if you can identify why the equals sign is being considered as part of the **STRING** command.

The warning identifies that the equals sign in the **STRING** command is not an accepted format for the preceding variables, simply because there is no full stop at

the end of the **STRING** command line. Because of this, SPSS has continued with the command onto the next line and assumes that the equals sign is within the **STRING** command still. As this cannot be a variable name, SPSS checks if it can be a format instead for the previous 'variable names' (**COMPUTE** and the repetition of **lab_code**), then it recognises that this is not possible. This renders the command invalid, the error message is created and the command cannot be executed
>This command not executed.

The remedy
Correct the syntax by adding the missing full stop at the end of the STRING command.
STRING lab_code (A2) .
COMPUTE lab_code=(SUBSTR(labrunid,1,1)).
EXECUTE .

As you can see, the result of the mistake depends on where the full stop was missing from. In Syntax 13:2 the new variable was created and labelled but not populated with the data, in Syntax 13:3 the variable was not even created. In both circumstances, though, the warning or error message can be deciphered in order to be able to understand where to look for any problem with the syntax.

The next example is based upon the syntax used in Syntax 4:2, but a 'mistake' has been introduced. The syntax is intended to merge two datafiles together, each containing data on the same participants, each with a unique identifier that can be used to match the cases.

Syntax 13:4 Multiple warnings and an error message caused by omitting an inverted comma on the MATCH FILES command

This syntax is intended to open GSS 93 for Missing Values.sav and then add the variables from GSS93 subset.sav.

The syntax used
GET
  FILE='C:\Program Files\SPSSInc\SPSS16\Samples\GSS 93 for Missing Values.sav'.

MATCH FILES
    /FILE=*
    /FILE=C:\Program Files\SPSSInc\SPSS16\Samples\GSS93 subset.sav'
    /BY ID.
EXECUTE.

SAVE OUTFILE
    'C:\Documents and Settings\User\My Documents\GSS93_merge2.sav'.

The output shown
GET
  FILE='C:\Program Files\SPSSInc\SPSS16\Samples\GSS 93 for Missing Values.sav'.
MATCH FILES

```
/FILE=*
/FILE=C:\Program Files\SPSSInc\SPSS16\Samples\GSS93 subset.sav'

>Warning # 206 in column 10. Text: \
>An invalid character has been found on a command.

>Warning # 206 in column 24. Text: \
>An invalid character has been found on a command.

>Warning # 206 in column 32. Text: \
>An invalid character has been found on a command.

>Warning # 206 in column 39. Text: \
>An invalid character has been found on a command.

>Warning # 206 in column 47. Text: \
>An invalid character has been found on a command.

>Warning # 208 in column 64. Text:
>A text string is not correctly enclosed in quotation marks on the command
>line. Literals may not be continued across command lines without the use of
>the continuation symbol '+'.
 /BY ID.

>Error # 5102 in column 9. Text: :
>Invalid symbol for this command. Check for spelling errors or special
>symbols. Syntax checking begins with the next slash.
> This command not executed.

>Note # 5145
>The working file has been restored, and subsequent commands may access the
>working file.
EXECUTE.
SAVE OUTFILE
 'C:\Documents and Settings\User\My Documents\GSS93_merge2.sav'.
```

What the message means

This type of error message and warning can look very scary, and very complicated, mainly because there are six warnings and an error and a fair bit of accompanying text. However, the key is to remain calm, not to get too cross with SPSS and simply read everything through. Each error message and warning refers to the command or sub-command that is found most immediately prior to the warning (though of course that may not be where the error is).

Reading the message through tells you that problems are detected in columns 10, 24, 32, 39, 47, 64, 46 and then on column 10. Take these one at a time.

The first problem is a back slash found at column 10 that is not considered valid
**>Warning # 206 in column 10. Text: **
>An invalid character has been found on a command.

Look through the preceding subcommand and you will see that there is a back slash at the 10th position after G: (there are two spaces at the beginning of the subcommand).
MATCH FILES /FILE=*
/FILE=C:\Program Files\SPSSInc\SPSS16\Samples\GSS93 subset.sav'

The next four warnings tell us four more back slashes that are also deemed invalid.
   You may think that these back slashes must be 'valid' as they are needed to identify the file pathway of the file that SPSS needs to locate.
   After my last two examples you may be looking for a full stop error but read on first.

The next warning can seem a little unfair >Warning # 208 in column 64. Text: as it doesn't identify which text is the problem at column 64. However, if you count the characters to position 64 on the subcommand
   /FILE=C:\Program Files\SPSSInc\SPSS16\Samples\GSS93 subset.sav'
line then you will find it is the inverted comma at the end. Thankfully the message that accompanies this warning is quite helpful and tells you that the problem lies with the way that text is placed in quotation marks.
>A text string is not correctly enclosed in quotation marks on the
>command line. Literals may not be continued across command lines >without the use of the continuation symbol '+'.
Reviewing your syntax at this stage would hopefully show you where the quotation mark problem lies – the file pathway needs to be enclosed, beginning and ending with an inverted comma at each end.

The rest of the message is all related to this non-enclosure of the file pathway. For example, error message #5102 is given because a colon (intended to be enclosed as part of the file pathway C:\) cannot be used in the MATCH FILES command
>Error # 5102 in column 9. Text: :
>Invalid symbol for this command. Check for spelling errors or >special symbols. Syntax checking begins with the next slash.

The message then informs you that because of this fundamental syntax error SPSS could not carry out the command.
>This command not executed.

The note that follows tells you that the datafile that you had already opened has been left untouched and available for further use. The next command (SAVE OUTFILE) will be run, in effect renaming the opened file.
>Note # 5145
>The working file has been restored, and subsequent commands may access the
>working file.
EXECUTE.
SAVE OUTFILE 'G:\spss_sample_datasets\GSS93_music_age.sav' .

The remedy
Add the missing inverted comma and re-run.
GET
  FILE='G:\spss_sample_datasets\GSS93_age.sav'.
MATCH FILES
/FILE=*

```
    /FILE='G:\spss_sample_datasets\GSS93_age.sav'
    /BY id.
EXECUTE.
SAVE OUTFILE 'G:\spss_sample_datasets\GSS93_music_age.sav'.
```

If you do not pay attention to the error message the 'creation' of the new datafile (GSS93_merge2.sav) can be confusing. The 'new' datafile has appeared, but on inspection still only contains the variables from the original 'old' datafile (GSS 93 for Missing Values.sav). Luckily the old datafile is in a different location; the new datafile has been created in addition to the old one, rather than overwriting it.

Sometimes using syntax can be problematic because you do not realise, or forget, about a command that SPSS runs automatically when the drop-down, menu-driven method is used. In Syntax 13:5 below, syntax is written to create a new variable with text taken from an existing string variable and altered so that it is all in uppercase. See Syntax 5:6 if you wish to read how this syntax should work.

Syntax 13:5 Error message on the COMPUTE command caused by omitting a preceding command to create a new string variable

The following syntax is adapted from Syntax 5:6 and is intended to change the case of the text found in the variable **country** in the SPSS sample dataset World95.sav.

The syntax used
```
COMPUTE country_case=UPCASE(country).
EXECUTE.
```

The output shown
```
COMPUTE country_case=UPCASE(country).

>Error # 4309 in column 1024. Text: (End of Command)
>Invalid combination of data types in an assignment. Character strings may
>only be assigned to string variables. Numeric and logical quantities may
>only be assigned to numeric variables. Consider using the STRING or NUMBER
>function.
>This command not executed.
EXECUTE.
```

What the message means
The error can seem a little confusing as it identifies the problem at column place 1024 >Error # 4309 in column 1024. Text: (End of Command) and the problem is with the 'end of the command'. This may not seem very helpful, so read on.

The error message continues by telling you that you have an invalid combination of data types
>Invalid combination of data types in an assignment. Character strings may
>only be assigned to string variables. Numeric and logical quantities may
>only be assigned to numeric variables. Consider using the STRING or NUMBER
>function.
Again you may be confused with this as you are only asking SPSS to change the case (a string function) in a string variable **country**. It also tells you that you can only assign numeric quantities to numeric variables – and this is your clue. To spot this you need to ask yourself 'To which numeric variable does it refer?'

Look back at the command **COMPUTE country_case=UPCASE(country).** You know you are asking it to carry out a function on a pre-existing string variable **country**, therefore the numeric variable being referred to can only really be the new variable **country_case.** You have forgotten (or failed to realise) that unlike numeric variables you must always first create a string variable before you can put any data into it. And then just to help you with your thought processes, SPSS gives you a very big hint. Consider using the STRING or NUMBER function.

The message then informs you that because of this fundamental syntax error SPSS could not carry out the command.
>**This command not executed.**

The remedy
Create the required string variable first and then run.

STRING country_case (A12).
COMPUTE country_case=UPCASE(country).
EXECUTE .

Occasionally you may find that you try to do something that SPSS just will not permit you to do, even though it seems like what you are trying to do is reasonable. For example, you may decide to re-run some syntax that has worked perfectly well on a previous occasion, but on re-running the syntax you are faced with an error message or warning. In the example below, Syntax 5:6 is being run for a second time. Re-running a command can commonly be required if you have set up a data-file, created all the derived variables required and then later added some additional cases which then need the derived variables creating for them. If you plan to run this syntax for yourself to create the error, you will first need to run Syntax 5:6 (or the remedied version of 13:5) and then run it for a second time.

Syntax 13:6 An error message due to re-running syntax and inadvertently trying to create a variable that is already in existence

The following syntax is adapted from Syntax 5:6 and is intended to change the case of the text found in the variable **country** in the SPSS sample dataset World95.sav.

The syntax used
STRING country_case (A12).
COMPUTE country_case=UPCASE(country).
EXECUTE .

The output shown
STRING country_case (A12).

>Error # 4822 in column 8. Text: country_case
>A variable with this name is already defined.
>This command not executed.
COMPUTE country_case=UPCASE(country).
EXECUTE.

What the message means
It can be frustrating when syntax that has worked previously then creates an error message or warning at a later date. However, if you read through the error message you should be fine.

The message identifies the problem at column place 8 and it is with the variable name **country_case >Error # 4822 in column 8. Text: country_case** but as you know that this is the 'correct' variable name this may not seem very helpful, so read on.

The next part of the message **>A variable with this name is already defined.** provides you with the explanation of what the problem is. You are trying to create a variable with a name already allocated to a variable.

OK, so you know that you are happy for the syntax to 'recreate' the variable and then populate it with the data once more, but SPSS syntax cannot assume that. As the variable is in existence it is basically saying that you cannot create another variable of the same name. In effect there is no fault with the syntax used; it is just that the syntax is trying to create a variable with the same name as one which is already in existence and SPSS can't permit that.

The message then informs you that because of this fundamental syntax error SPSS couldn't carry out the command.
>This command not executed.

The next command **COMPUTE country_case=UPCASE(country).** will be run, in effect carrying out the procedure that you require anyway.

The remedy
You could just ignore the error message as when you look in the dataset you will see that the derived variable has been re-run as you hoped. Alternatively, you could remember to run only the last two command lines (the **COMPUTE** and the **EXECUTE** ones), missing out the **STRING** command.

Alternatively, you can rewrite your 'derived variable syntax file' (see page 85 if you are not sure what this might be) so that it deletes previous versions of derived variables (see Syntax 7:1). Then you are free to re-run the derived variable syntax commands as many times as you may need (as you add new batches of cases) without getting the annoying error messages cluttering up the Output view or Journal.

DELETE VARIABLES country_case.
STRING country_case (A12).
COMPUTE country_case=UPCASE(country).
EXECUTE .

Summary

Error messages and warnings are useful tools that are worth getting to grips with. Like most elements of this book the key message is to look at what is produced by SPSS and take the time to understand it. The error messages and warnings that you encounter will usually contain useful information presented in a meaningful way – at least to those who are knowledgeable about the language that is SPSS syntax. The key is to remain calm, not to get too irritated with SPSS and simply to read everything through. Each error message and warning refers to a problem encountered when trying to carry out the command or sub-command that is found most immediately prior to the warning, but remember that of course that may not be where the error is.

If you have journeyed through this book, whether in a straight line, by wandering aimlessly, by targeted reading, or by bumping along as and when you needed to, I hope that SPSS syntax seems less alien and more useful than when you started. Understanding the error messages and warnings gets easier with experience and as your expertise in the use of syntax increases.

Useful tips

- The message usually refers to the command or sub-command printed immediately prior to the warning.
- While each error message and warning usually refers to the command or sub-command line that is found most immediately prior to the warning, you need to remember that this may not be where the error is to be found, it may be earlier in the syntax commands and sub-commands.
- Error messages and warnings have > signs at the beginning of each line. The first line is usually an identification of the message's status (error or warning) plus an indication of where on the line the problem is encountered. The subsequent lines provide details about what the error might be.

- If the column numbers are large (or you cannot be bothered to count along the line), just paste the command line into a Word document. In Word 2007, right click on the status bar (bottom left where word count is found) and select 'column to be displayed'; and as you move the cursor along the command line the column number can be seen on the bottom.

- If you really cannot work out what an error message or warning means try running the syntax one command at a time (if there are multiple commands) and see at which point the message appears.

Glossary

Active dataset
: The dataset which is open and the most recently used; 'using' a dataset includes opening a file, running analysis etc. or clicking on the Data Editor View.

Categorical data
: Data is said to be categorical if the values or observations belonging to it can be sorted according to non-overlapping categories.

Command
: An instruction that you give the program to initiate an action.

Command Syntax Reference guide
: The SPSS manual that provides detailed information about each command in the syntax command language – see the reference list for details.

csv files
: A comma separated values (csv) file is a computer datafile in table form, each line corresponds to a row in the table and within a line, fields are separated by commas, each field belonging to one table column, identified by a .csv suffix.

Data Editor View
: The main view in SPSS where you see (and edit) the data and variable information.

Datafile
: A file containing data, and which in SPSS is identified by a sav suffix.

Default sub-command
: A sub-command option that will run as part of the command even when the sub-command is omitted.

Derived variables
: Variables created after the original data was entered or imported into the SPSS datafile. These may be created through calculations using numeric variables (e.g. age calculated from date of birth and date of completion of the survey), or through coding of categorical variables (e.g. a variable for geographic region obtained from a variable holding countries).

Derived variable syntax file
: A file with all the commands used to carry out the creation of all derived variables for a datafile and that, when run, will recreate all the derived variables.

Free text
: Text that is unstructured and not in assigned categories or limited to specific choices.

GIF or graphical interface
: The drop-down, menu-driven method of accessing commands and functions.

Journal	An auto-generated file containing a record of all commands run during a session, identified by a .jnl suffix.
Keyword	Words used to identify commands, sub-commands, functions, operators, and other specifications.
Log	The record of commands displayed on the SPSS Viewer as they are run; and immediately preceding any output which may result from such commands.
Output file	Files generated from the output displayed in the SPSS Viewer, identified by a .csv suffix (note that they used to be identified by an .spo suffix in older versions).
Repeat analysis syntax file	A syntax file with all the commands used to carry out an analysis plan and that, when run, will repeat the analysis as previously undertaken.
SPSS syntax	The command language used for accessing commands and functions.
String variables	String (alphanumeric) variables containing numbers, letters or characters, including special characters and embedded blanks. Numbers entered as values for string variables cannot be used in calculations unless you convert them to numeric format.
Sub-command	An additional specification or option available within a command.
Syntax file	A text file that contains syntax commands, identified by an .sps suffix.
Variable length	The allocated number of characters for a piece of data within a field in a datafile.
Variable type	There are two basic variable types: string (text) and numeric. The format decides how the data is presented (including date and time).

References

Brace, N., Kemp, R. and Selgar, R. (2006) *SPSS for Psychologists: A Guide to Data Analysis Using SPSS for Windows*, 3rd edn. Basingstoke: Palgrave Macmillan.

Cohen, S. and Williamson, G.M. (1988) Perceived stress in a probability sample of the United States, in S. Spacapan and S. Oskamp (eds) *The Social Psychology of Health*. London: Sage Publication. pp. 31–67.

Cohen, S., Kamarck, T. and Mermelstein, R. (1983) A global measure of perceived stress. *Journal of Health and Social Behaviour* 24: 385–96.

Field, A. (2009) *Discovering Statistics Using SPSS*, 3rd edn. London: Sage Publications.

Hinton, P.R., Brownlow, C., McMurray, I. and Cozens, B. (2004) *SPSS Explained*. Hove: Routledge.

Levesque, R. (2003) *SPSS Programming and Data Management: A Guide for SPSS and SAS® Users*, 4th edn. Chicago, IL: SPSS Inc.

SPSS Inc. (2007a) *SPSS 16.0 Command Syntax Reference*. Chicago, IL: SPSS Inc.

SPSS Inc. (2007b) *SPSS 16.0 GPL Reference Guide*. Chicago, IL: SPSS Inc.

SPSS Inc. (2007c) *SPSS for Windows Documentation*. http://support.spss.com/ProductsExt/SPSS/Documentation/SPSSforWindows/index.html

Index

Index of Commands and Keywords

Supporting researchers for more than forty years

Research methods have always been at the core of SAGE's publishing. Sara Miller McCune founded SAGE in 1965 and soon after she published SAGE's first methods book, *Public Policy Evaluation*. A few years later, she launched the Quantitative Applications in the Social Sciences series – affectionately known as the 'little green books'.

Always at the forefront of developing and supporting new approaches in methods, SAGE published early groundbreaking texts and journals in the fields of qualitative methods and evaluation.

Today, more than forty years and two million little green books later, SAGE continues to push the boundaries with a growing list of more than 1,200 research methods books, journals, and reference works across the social, behavioural, and health sciences.

From qualitative, quantitative and mixed methods to evaluation, SAGE is the essential resource for academics and practitioners looking for the latest in methods by leading scholars.

www.sagepublications.com